Design Patterns using JavaScript

First Edition

By Hemant Jain

Design Patterns using JavaScript

Hemant Jain

ACKNOWLEDGMENT

The author is very grateful to GOD ALMIGHTY for his grace and blessing.

I would like to express profound gratitude to my family and friends for their invaluable encouragement, supervision and useful suggestions throughout this book writing work. Their support and continuous guidance enable me to complete my work successfully.

Hemant Jain

Table of Contents

Introduction to Design Patterns

What are Design Patterns?

Software development is a complex and challenging process that requires a great deal of skill and expertise. As software projects become larger and more complex, it becomes increasingly difficult to manage them effectively. One way to address this challenge is by using design patterns.

Design patterns are reusable solutions to common software development problems that software engineers and designers encounter while developing software. A design pattern is not a complete solution that can be directly copied and pasted into a program, but rather a general solution that can be applied to a particular class of problems in various contexts.

Design patterns provide a language and structure for discussing and documenting software designs, making it easier for developers to communicate and collaborate on software development projects. They help ensure that software designs are modular, maintainable, and extensible.

The Importance of Design Patterns

Design patterns are important in software development for several reasons:

1. **Reusability**: Design patterns provide reusable solutions to common software development problems. By using design patterns, developers can save time and effort by leveraging proven solutions to common problems instead of reinventing the wheel each time a similar problem arises.

2. **Maintainability**: Software projects can become large and complex over time, making them difficult to maintain. Design patterns help ensure that software designs are modular and maintainable by separating different concerns and promoting loose coupling between components.

3. **Extensibility**: As software projects evolve, new requirements may arise that require the software to be extended or modified. Design patterns promote extensibility by making it easier to add new functionality to existing software designs without affecting other parts of the system.

4. **Communication**: Design patterns provide a common language and structure for discussing and documenting software designs. This makes it easier for developers to communicate and collaborate on software

development projects, especially when working on large teams or with developers from different backgrounds.

5. **Quality**: Using design patterns can lead to higher-quality software designs by promoting best practices and proven solutions to common problems. This can result in software that is more robust, reliable, and scalable.

Elements of Design Patterns

The three important elements of a design pattern are:

1. **Problem**: Design patterns are developed to address specific recurring problems in software design. A pattern describes a problem that occurs repeatedly in a particular context and then describes the core of the solution to that problem.

2. **Solution**: A design pattern provides a general reusable solution to a commonly occurring problem in software design. It provides a template for solving a problem that can be adapted to different contexts.

3. **Consequence**: A design pattern also describes the consequences and trade-offs of using the pattern. The consequences can be both positive and negative, and they should be carefully considered before applying the pattern to a particular problem.

Categories of Design Patterns

There are five main categories of design patterns:

1. **Creational Patterns**: Creational patterns deal with object creation mechanisms, trying to create objects in a manner that is suitable for a particular situation. These patterns provide a way to create objects while hiding the creation logic and allowing the flexibility to choose which objects are created or how they are created.

   Examples of Creational patterns include the Singleton pattern, Factory Method pattern, Abstract Factory pattern, Builder pattern, and Prototype pattern.

2. **Structural Patterns**: Structural patterns deal with object composition and simplify the structure of a system by identifying relationships between

objects. They focus on the composition of classes and objects to form larger structures.

Examples of structural patterns include the Adapter pattern, Bridge pattern, Composite pattern, Decorator pattern, and Facade pattern.

3. **Behavioural Patterns**: behavioural patterns deal with communication between objects and the delegation of responsibilities between objects. They define how objects interact with each other and how they operate to accomplish a task.

   Examples of behavioural patterns include the Command pattern, Iterator pattern, Observer pattern, State pattern, and Strategy pattern.

4. **Architectural Patterns**: Architectural patterns deal with the overall structure of a software system and the relationships between components. They define the basic structure of a system and provide a framework for developing and organising large-scale software systems.

   Examples of architectural patterns include the Model-View-Controller (MVC) pattern, the Model-View-Presenter (MVP) pattern, the Model-View-ViewModel (MVVM) pattern and the Layered pattern.

Design Principles

Design principles serve as guidelines for creating well-designed and maintainable software. They provide high-level concepts and best practices that can be applied during the design phase. In this section, you will explore the fundamental design principles and specifically focus on the SOLID principles.

Fundamental Design Principles:

1. **Encapsulation**: The principle of encapsulation emphasises the bundling of data and methods into a single unit, known as a class. It promotes data hiding and provides a clear interface for interacting with objects.

2. **Abstraction**: Abstraction involves identifying the essential features and behaviours of a system while hiding unnecessary details. It simplifies the complexity of a system and allows for easier comprehension and maintenance.

3. **Modularity**: Modularity promotes dividing a system into smaller, self-contained modules. Each module should have a well-defined responsibility and interact with other modules through well-defined interfaces.

4. **High Cohesion**: High cohesion refers to the degree to which the elements within a module are related and contribute to a single, well-defined purpose. It ensures that each module has a clear and focused responsibility.

5. **Low Coupling**: Low coupling signifies the degree of dependency between modules. It aims to minimise dependencies and promote loose coupling, allowing modules to be modified independently without affecting others.

SOLID Principles

The SOLID principles are a set of five principles that guide object-oriented design and promote software that is easy to understand, maintain, and extend.

The acronym SOLID stands for:

1. S - Single Responsibility Principle

2. O - Open-Closed Principle

3. L - Liskov Substitution Principle

4. I - Interface Segregation Principle

5. D - Dependency Inversion Principle

Here's a brief overview of each principle:

1. **Single Responsibility Principle (SRP)**: A class should have only one reason to change, meaning it should only have one responsibility or job. This principle aims to ensure that each class is focused on a specific task and doesn't have too many responsibilities, which can lead to complexity and maintenance issues.

2. **Open-Closed Principle (OCP)**: Software entities (classes, modules, functions, etc.) should be open for extension but closed for modification. This principle suggests that you should be able to add new functionality to a system without modifying its existing code, reducing the risk of introducing bugs.

3. **Liskov Substitution Principle (LSP)**: Subtypes must be substitutable for their base types. This principle ensures that objects of a subclass can be used in place of objects of the superclass without affecting the correctness of the program.

4. **Interface Segregation Principle (ISP)**: Clients should not be forced to depend on interfaces they don't use. This principle suggests that you should separate the interfaces of a system into smaller and more focused interfaces, which can help reduce coupling between different parts of the system.

5. **Dependency Inversion Principle (DIP)**: Depends on abstractions, not concretions. This principle recommends that you should depend on interfaces or abstract classes, rather than concrete implementations, which can help to make a system more flexible and easier to maintain.

The Single Responsibility Principle (SRP)

The **Single Responsibility Principle (SRP)** is a design principle that suggests that a class should have only one reason to change, meaning it should have only one responsibility or job. This principle aims to ensure that each class is focused on a specific task and doesn't have too many responsibilities, which can lead to complexity and maintenance issues.

The idea behind SRP is that a class should have a clear and well-defined responsibility or job, and should only be responsible for one thing. This makes the class easier to understand, test, and maintain, because each method or property in the class is focused on a specific task.

For example, consider a class that is responsible for both handling file input/output and performing calculations on the data in the file. This class violates the SRP because it has two responsibilities: file input/output and data manipulation. To follow the SRP, you could split this class into two separate classes, one responsible for file input/output and the other for data manipulation.

Overall, following the SRP can lead to code that is easier to understand, maintain, and extend, because each class has a clear and focused purpose

Here's an example of how the SRP is used :

```
class Animal {
    constructor(name) {
        this.name = name;
    }

    eat() {
        console.log(this.name + " is eating.");
    }
}
```

```javascript
    sleep() {
        console.log(this.name + " is sleeping.");
    }

    makeSound() {
        console.log(this.name + " is making a sound.");
    }
}

class Mammal extends Animal {
    constructor(name) {
        super(name);
    }

    giveBirth() {
        console.log(this.name + " is giving birth to live
young.");
    }
}

class Reptile extends Animal {
    constructor(name) {
        super(name);
    }

    layEggs() {
        console.log(this.name + " is laying eggs.");
    }
}

class Bird extends Animal {
    constructor(name) {
        super(name);
    }

    fly() {
        console.log(this.name + " is flying.");
    }

    layEggs() {
        console.log(this.name + " is laying eggs.");
    }
}
```

```
// Client code.
const animal1 = new Mammal("Cat");
animal1.giveBirth();
animal1.makeSound();

const animal2 = new Reptile("Snake");
animal2.layEggs();
animal2.eat();

const animal3 = new Bird("Eagle");
animal3.layEggs();
animal3.fly();
```

Explanation:

1. In the code above, each class has a single responsibility:

   - The **Animal** class is responsible for defining basic behaviours common to all animals, such as eating, sleeping, and making sounds.

   - The **Mammal** class is responsible for defining behaviours that are specific to mammals, such as giving birth to live young.

   - The **Reptile** class is responsible for defining behaviours that are specific to reptiles, such as laying eggs.

   - The **Bird** class is responsible for defining behaviours that are specific to birds, such as flying and laying eggs.

2. Each class has a clear and distinct responsibility, and none of the classes are responsible for more than one thing. This makes the code easy to understand, modify, and maintain.

3. Furthermore, each method within each class also has a single responsibility. For example, the **fly()** method in the **Bird** class is responsible for representing the behaviour of flying, while the **eat()** method in the **Animal** class is responsible for representing the behaviour of eating. This adherence to the single responsibility principle at the method level further contributes to the overall maintainability and readability of the code.

Open-Closed Principle (OCP)

The **Open-Closed Principle (OCP)** is a design principle that suggests that software entities (classes, modules, functions, etc.) should be open for extension but closed for modification. In other words, you should be able to add new functionality to a system without modifying its existing code, reducing the risk of introducing bugs.

The idea behind OCP is to create code that is more flexible and easier to maintain. By designing software entities to be open for extension, you can add new features to a system without having to change its existing code, reducing the risk of introducing new bugs or breaking existing functionality. This can make the codebase more stable and easier to evolve over time.

To follow the OCP, you can use techniques such as abstraction and encapsulation. Abstraction allows you to define a set of behaviours or properties that can be implemented by different classes or modules, while encapsulation allows you to hide the details of how a particular behaviour or property is implemented.

Further explain the Bird class that extends the Animal class and adds a fly() method that determines whether the bird can fly or not, based on its name. The fly() method prints a message that describes how the bird is flying, depending on its name.

Here's an example of how the OCP is violated:

```javascript
class Animal {
    constructor(name) {
        this.name = name;
    }
}

class Bird extends Animal {
    constructor(name) {
        super(name);
    }

    fly() {
        if (this.name === "Dodo") {
            console.log("The dodo is extinct and cannot fly.");
        } else if (this.name === "Penguin") {
            console.log("The penguin cannot fly.");
        } else if (this.name === "Eagle") {
            console.log("The eagle is soaring through the sky!");
```

```
        } else if (this.name === "Sparrow") {
            console.log("The sparrow is fluttering its wings!");
        }
    }
}

// Client code
const bird1 = new Bird("Eagle");
bird1.fly();

const bird2 = new Bird("Dodo");
bird2.fly();
```

Overall, this code works correctly, but it violates the Open-Closed Principle because the **fly()** method has to check the name of each bird to determine whether it can fly or not. This means that if a new species of bird is added in the future that can fly or cannot fly, the **fly()** method will need to be modified to handle it, which violates the Open-Closed principle. Now look at the next code.

Here's an example of how the OCP is followed:

```
class Bird extends Animal {
    constructor(name) {
        super(name);
    }

    fly() {
        // Abstract method, to be overridden by subclasses
    }
}

class Dodo extends Bird {
    constructor() {
        super("Dodo");
    }

    fly() {
        console.log("The dodo is extinct and cannot fly.");
    }
}

class Penguin extends Bird {
    constructor() {
        super("Penguin");
    }
```

```javascript
  fly() {
      console.log("The penguin cannot fly.");
  }

  slide() {
      console.log("The penguin is sliding on its belly!");
  }

  swim() {
      console.log("The penguin is swimming in the water!");
  }
}

class Eagle extends Bird {
    constructor() {
        super("Eagle");
    }

    fly() {
        console.log("The eagle is soaring through the sky!");
    }
}

// Client code
const bird1 = new Eagle();
bird1.fly();

const bird2 = new Dodo();
bird2.fly();
```

Output:

```
The eagle is soaring through the sky!
The dodo is extinct and cannot fly.
```

Explanation:

1. This implementation adheres to the **Open-Closed Principle**, as new species of birds can be added as new subclasses of Bird without modifying the existing code.

2. In this implementation, we have created separate subclasses for each type of bird. Each subclass inherits from the **Bird** class and overrides the **fly()** method with its own implementation specific to that bird.

3. Now, when we create instances of each bird, we simply need to create instance of the appropriate subclass. This allows us to add new types of birds by creating new subclasses without modifying the existing code.

4. This implementation adheres to the Open/Closed Principle, as it is closed for modification but open for extension. We can add new subclasses of **Bird** to extend the functionality of the program without modifying the existing code. Additionally, we can add new methods and behaviours specific to a certain bird by adding them to their corresponding subclass.

Here's an example of how the OCP is followed and code is extended:

```
class Pigeon extends Bird {
    constructor() {
        super("Pigeon");
    }

    makeCooingSound() {
        console.log("The pigeon is making a cooing sound.");
    }

    fly() {
        console.log("The pigeon is fluttering its wings!");
    }
}
```

Explanation:

1. In this implementation, we've extended the **Bird** class to create a **Pigeon** subclass. The **Pigeon** class inherits all the methods from the **Bird** class, and we've added a new method, **makeCooingSound()**, which represents a behaviour specific to pigeons.

2. Since we followed the open-closed principle when implementing the **Bird** class, we didn't have to modify the **Bird** class to add the **Pigeon** subclass. Instead, we were able to simply extend the **Bird** class to create a new subclass with its own specific behaviours.

3. This implementation adheres to the Open-Closed Principle, as new species of birds can be added as new subclasses of **Bird** without modifying the existing code.

Liskov Substitution Principle (LSP)

The **Liskov Substitution Principle (LSP)** is a fundamental principle of object-oriented design that states that objects of a superclass should be able to be replaced with objects of its subclasses without affecting the correctness of the program. In other words, a subclass should be able to substitute its superclass in any context without violating the behaviour that the client expects from the superclass.

This principle ensures that the code is modular, extensible, and maintainable. It allows for the creation of hierarchies of classes that can be reused and extended easily, without breaking existing code or introducing bugs. The LSP is closely related to other principles such as the Single Responsibility Principle (SRP), the Open-Closed Principle (OCP), and the Interface Segregation Principle (ISP), which together form the SOLID principles of object-oriented design.

By adhering to the Liskov Substitution Principle, we can write more flexible and reusable code, as we can substitute instances of subclasses for instances of their superclass wherever they are needed.

For example, if we have a superclass **Animal** with a method **makeSound()**, and a subclass **Dog** that inherits from **Animal**, **Dog** should implement the same **makeSound()** method as **Animal** and should not modify its behaviour. It does not violate the Liskov Substitution Principle.

Here's an example of how the LSP is followed:

```javascript
class Animal {
    constructor(name) {
        this.name = name;
    }

    makeSound() {
        console.log("Animal sound");
    }
}

class Dog extends Animal {
    constructor(name) {
        super(name);
    }

    makeSound() {
        console.log("woof woof!");
    }
```

```
}

class Cat extends Animal {
    constructor(name) {
        super(name);
    }

    makeSound() {
        console.log("meow!");
    }
}
```

A square should not be a derived class of a rectangle, as this violates the Liskov Substitution Principle (LSP). The reason for this is that a square has additional constraints that a rectangle does not have. Specifically, all four sides of a square must be equal in length, while a rectangle can have sides of different lengths.

If we were to create a subclass Square that inherits from the base class Rectangle and overrides its behaviour, it could cause problems when trying to substitute a square object for a rectangle object in code that expects a rectangle. For example, if the length of the square were changed, it would also change the width, violating the expectation of a rectangle. This is an example of the LSP violation.

Here's an example of how the LSP is violated:

```
class Rectangle {
    constructor(l, w) {
        this.height = l;
        this.width = w;
    }

    setWidth(w) {
        this.width = w;
    }

    setHeight(h) {
        this.height = h;
    }

    getWidth() {
        return this.width;
    }

    getHeight() {
        return this.height;
```

```javascript
    }
}

class Square extends Rectangle {
    constructor(l) {
        super(l, l);
    }

    setWidth(w) {
        super.setWidth(w);
        super.setHeight(w);
    }

    setHeight(h) {
        super.setWidth(h);
        super.setHeight(h);
    }
}

function testRect(rect) {
    rect.setHeight(10);
    rect.setWidth(20);
    if (200 === rect.getHeight() * rect.getWidth()) {
        console.log("success");
    } else {
        console.log("failure");
    }
}

// Client code
const r = new Rectangle(10, 20);
testRect(r);
const s = new Square(10);
testRect(s);
```

Explanation:

1. The code violates the Liskov Substitution Principle. The **Square** class inherits from the **Rectangle** class, but it overrides the **setWidth()** and **setHeight()** methods in a way that breaks the behaviour expected from a Rectangle.

2. In a **Rectangle**, the **setWidth()** and **setHeight()** methods should be independent, but in a **Square**, they should be coupled. For example, setting the width of a square should also set the height to the same value. The **testRectangle()** function expects the **setWidth()** and

setHeight() methods to behave independently, which is not true for a **Square**, and hence it fails when it is called with an instance of **Square**.

3. So **Square** is not a subclass of **Rectangle**. If we want to consider the property that width and length can be set independently.

Similarly, the example of Penguin not being a subclass of bird highlights another LSP violation. While it may be true that a penguin is a type of bird in the real world, in the programming world, it may have different behaviours or properties that make it incompatible with code that expects a general bird object. For example, a Penguin cannot fly, while many other types of birds can. Therefore, if we were to create a subclass Penguin that inherits from the base class Bird, it could cause issues when trying to substitute it for other types of birds in code.

Here's an another example of how the LSP is violated:

```javascript
// Animal Class
class Animal {
    constructor(name) {
        this.name = name;
    }
}


// Bird Class
class Bird extends Animal {
    constructor(name) {
        super(name);
        this.flightHeight = 0;
    }

    fly() {
        throw new Error("You have to implement the method fly!");
    }
}


// Sparrow Class
class Sparrow extends Bird {
    constructor(name) {
        super(name);
    }

    fly() {
        console.log("The sparrow is fluttering its wings.");
        this.flightHeight = 100;
    }
}
```

```javascript
}

// Penguin Class
class Penguin extends Bird {
    constructor(name) {
        super(name);
    }

    fly() {
        console.log("The penguin cannot fly.");
    }

    slide() {
        console.log("The penguin is sliding on its belly!");
    }

    swim() {
        console.log("The penguin is swimming in the water!");
    }
}

// Dodo Class
class Dodo extends Bird {
    constructor(name) {
        super(name);
    }

    fly() {
        console.log("The dodo is extinct and cannot fly.");
    }
}

// Test Function
function test(bird) {
    bird.fly();
    if (bird.flightHeight > 0) {
        console.log("Bird is flying at a positive height.");
    } else {
        console.log("Error: fly() method called; flight height is
still zero.");
    }
}

// Client code
const sparrow = new Sparrow("Sparrow");
test(sparrow);
```

```
const penguin = new Penguin("Penguin");
test(penguin);

const dodo = new Dodo("Dodo");
test(dodo);
```

Output:

```
The sparrow is fluttering its wings.
Bird is flying at a positive height.
The penguin cannot fly.
Error: fly() method called; flight height is still zero.
The dodo is extinct and cannot fly.
Error: fly() method called; flight height is still zero.
```

Explanation:

1. The above code violates the **Liskov Substitution Principle** because the subclasses of **Bird** do not behave in the same way as the superclass in the context of the **flightHeight** attribute.

2. According to the Liskov Substitution Principle, a subclass should be able to substitute the base class in any context without causing any unexpected behaviour. However, in this case, the **Sparrow** subclass updates the **flightHeight** attribute when the **fly()** method is called, while the **Penguin** and **Dodo** subclasses do not.

3. This means that if we were to substitute an instance of **Sparrow** with an instance of **Penguin** or **Dodo**, we could get unexpected behaviour if we assume that the **flightHeight** attribute will always be positive when the **fly()** method is called.

4. Finally, **Dodo** or **Penguin** is not a subclass of **Bird**, when a bird flies its height of flight should be positive.

Interface Segregation Principle (ISP)

The **Interface Segregation Principle (ISP)** is a SOLID principle that states that clients should not be forced to depend on methods they do not use. In other words, it suggests that you should break interfaces down into smaller, more specific interfaces that are easier to implement without unnecessary dependencies.

In simpler terms, it means that a class should not be forced to implement interfaces that it does not need. Instead, it should be provided with multiple smaller interfaces that only contain methods that are required by the class.

This principle is important because it helps prevent coupling between classes and reduces the impact of changes in one part of the system on other parts. It also makes code easier to maintain, test and refactor.

Here is an example to illustrate the Interface Segregation Principle. Suppose we have an interface Printer with the methods print(), scan(), and fax(). However, not all printers support all three of these methods. For example, a basic inkjet printer may only support printing, while a high-end office printer may support all three methods.

In this case, implementing the Printer interface on the basic inkjet printer would require it to have empty or useless implementations of the scan() and fax() methods. This violates the Interface Segregation Principle, as clients of the basic inkjet printer should not be forced to depend on methods that they will never use.

Consider the below code with a Printer interface:

```
// Printer Interface
class Printer {
    print(document) {
        throw new Error('You have to implement the method
print!');
    }

    scan() {
        throw new Error('You have to implement the method
scan!');
    }

    fax(document) {
        throw new Error('You have to implement the method fax!');
    }
}
```

This interface defines three methods: print(), scan(), and fax(). However, not all printers support all three methods. For example, a basic inkjet printer may only support printing, while a high-end office printer may support all three methods. To follow the Interface Segregation Principle, we should split this interface into smaller, more cohesive interfaces that are tailored to specific behaviours.

A better approach would be to split the Printer interface into smaller, more specific interfaces such as Printable, Scannable, and Faxable. Then, the inkjet printer can implement only the Printable and Scannable interfaces, while the high-end office printer can implement all three. This way, clients can depend only on the interfaces they need, rather than being forced to depend on methods they will never use.

Here's an example of how the ISP is followed:

```
// Printable Interface
class Printable {
    print(document) {
        throw new Error('You have to implement the method
print!');
    }
}


// Scannable Interface
class Scannable {
    scan() {
        throw new Error('You have to implement the method
scan!');
    }
}


// Faxable Interface
class Faxable {
    fax(document) {
        throw new Error('You have to implement the method fax!');
    }
}
```

Now, classes can implement only the interfaces they need, without being forced to implement unnecessary methods. For instance, a BasicInkjetPrinter class can implement the Printable interfaces:

```
// BasicInkjetPrinter Class
class BasicInkjetPrinter extends Printable {
    print(document) {
        console.log(`Printing ${document} using basic inkjet
printer`);
    }
}
```

Similarly, a HighEndOfficePrinter class can implement all three interfaces:

```
// HighEndOfficePrinter Class
class HighEndOfficePrinter extends Printer {
    print(document) {
        console.log(`Printing ${document} using high end office
printer`);
    }

    scan() {
        console.log("Scanning using high end office printer");
    }

    fax(document) {
        console.log(`Faxing ${document} using high end office
printer`);
    }
}
```

By splitting the original Printer interface into smaller, more cohesive interfaces, we've made our code more flexible and easier to maintain. Classes can now implement only the interfaces they need, without being forced to implement unnecessary methods.

Dependency Inversion Principle (DIP)

The Dependency Inversion Principle (DIP) is a principle of object-oriented design that states that high-level modules should not depend on low-level modules. Instead, both should depend on abstractions, which are abstract classes or interfaces that define the behaviour that the module expects. This promotes decoupling and flexibility in the design.

One example of the DIP in action is a simple email sending application. Let's say that we have two modules: a high-level EmailSender module and a low-level SmtpServer module. The SmtpServer module is responsible for sending emails using the Simple Mail Transfer Protocol (SMTP).

Without the DIP, the EmailSender module would directly depend on the SmtpServer module, making it tightly coupled. This means that any changes to the SmtpServer module would also affect the EmailSender module. This is not desirable because it reduces the flexibility and maintainability of the system.

With the DIP, both the EmailSender and SmtpServer modules depend on an abstraction, such as an interface called IMailSender. The EmailSender module would interact with the IMailSender interface, which would define the behaviour that the module expects from a mail sender. The SmtpServer module would then implement the IMailSender interface, allowing it to be used by the EmailSender module. This decouples the two modules and makes the system more flexible and maintainable.

Here's an example of how the DIP is followed:

```
class IMailSender {
    sendMail(toAddress, fromAddress, subject, body) {
        // Abstract method, to be implemented by subclasses
    }
}

class SmtpServer extends IMailSender {
    sendMail(toAddress, fromAddress, subject, body) {
        console.log(`Send mail: subject: ${subject} from: $
{fromAddress} to: ${toAddress} body: ${body}`);
    }
}

class EmailSender {
    constructor(mailSender) {
        this.mailSender = mailSender;
    }

    sendEmail(toAddress, fromAddress, subject, body) {
        // Delegate email sending to the mail sender
implementation
        this.mailSender.sendMail(toAddress, fromAddress, subject,
body);
    }
}

// Client code.
const smtpServer = new SmtpServer();
const emailSender = new EmailSender(smtpServer);

// Send an email using the EmailSender instance
emailSender.sendEmail(
    "recipient@example.com",
    "sender@example.com",
    "mail subject.",
    "This is a test email body."
);
```

Explanation:

1. The **IMailSender** interface defines the behaviour expected from a mail sender. The **SmtpServer** class implements the **IMailSender** interface to provide an implementation that sends emails using SMTP.

2. The **EmailSender** class takes an **IMailSender** object as a parameter in its constructor, which it uses to send emails. This allows the **EmailSender** class to be decoupled from any specific implementation of the mail sending functionality, making it more flexible and easier to maintain.

3. In this code, we first create an instance of the **SmtpServer** class to use as our mail sender implementation. We then create an instance of the **EmailSender** class and pass in the **SmtpServer** instance to its constructor.

4. Finally, we use the **sendEmail()** method of the **EmailSender** instance to send an email by passing in the recipient address, sender address, subject, and body of the email. The **EmailSender** instance delegates the email sending functionality to the **SmtpServer** instance, which sends the email via SMTP.

Summary

Design patterns are reusable solutions to common software development problems. The chapter discusses the benefits of using design patterns, including improved reusability, maintainability, extensibility, communication, and quality.

The five categories of design patterns are Creational, Structural, behavioural, Concurrency, and Architectural. Each category provides a set of patterns that can be used to address specific software development problems. By understanding and applying these patterns, software developers can create more modular, maintainable, and extensible software designs.

CREATIONAL PATTERNS

In this chapter, we will focus on the first category of design patterns: **Creational Patterns**. Creational patterns deal with object creation mechanisms, providing a way to create objects in a manner that is suitable for a particular situation. The patterns in this category hide the creation logic and provide flexibility in choosing which objects are created or how they are created.

We will start by exploring the **Singleton pattern**, which is one of the most commonly used Creational patterns. This pattern ensures that only one instance of a class exists in the system and provides a global point of access to that instance.

Next, we will discuss the **Factory Method pattern**, which provides an interface for creating objects in a superclass, but allows subclasses to alter the type of objects that will be created. The Factory Method pattern is useful when you want to decouple object creation from the rest of the application logic.

After that, we will cover the **Abstract Factory pattern**, which is similar to the Factory Method pattern, but it provides an interface for creating families of related or dependent objects without specifying their concrete classes. This pattern is useful when you need to create a group of related objects that should be used together.

We will then move on to the **Builder pattern**, which separates the construction of a complex object from its representation so that the same construction process can create different representations. This pattern is useful when you want to create complex objects step-by-step and have different ways to represent the final object.

Finally, we will discuss the **Prototype pattern**, which creates new objects by cloning existing ones. This pattern is useful when creating new objects is expensive or time-consuming and can be optimised by cloning an existing object.

Singleton Pattern

The **Singleton design pattern** is a Creational design pattern that ensures a class has only one instance and provides a global point of access to that instance. This pattern is commonly used when you want to restrict the instantiation of a class to a single object, ensuring that multiple instances of the class cannot be created.

Problem: The main problem that the Singleton design pattern aims to solve is controlling the number of instances created for a particular class. There are scenarios where you want to make sure that only one instance of a class exists throughout the application's lifecycle, such as global configurations, logging systems, database connections, thread pools, etc.

Solution: The Singleton design pattern provides a way to ensure that a class has only one instance and offers a global access point to that instance. There are various ways to implement the Singleton pattern, but the general idea is to make the class responsible for creating its own unique instance and ensuring that no other instance is created.

The classic implementation of the Singleton pattern involves the following steps:

1. **Private constructor**: The class's constructor is made private, so it cannot be directly instantiated from outside the class.

2. **Static method or variable**: A static method or variable is used to control access to the single instance. This method is responsible for creating the instance if it doesn't exist and returning the existing instance if it does.

3. **Lazy initialization**: The instance is created only when it is first requested. This is known as lazy initialization, and it ensures that the instance is created only when needed, not preemptively.

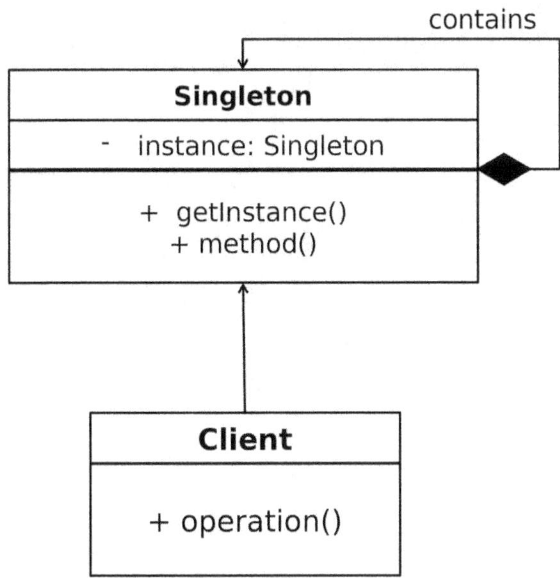

Here is an example implementation of the Singleton pattern :

```javascript
class Database {
    constructor() {
        console.log("Database created");
    }

    addData(data) {
        console.log(data);
    }
}

class Singleton {
    constructor() {
        if (!Singleton.instance) {
            Singleton.instance = this;
            this.db = new Database();
        }
        return Singleton.instance;
    }

    static getInstance() {
        if (!Singleton.instance) {
            new Singleton();
        }
        return Singleton.instance;
    }

    addData(data) {
        this.db.addData(data);
    }
}

// Client code
const s1 = Singleton.getInstance();
const s2 = Singleton.getInstance();
console.log(s1 === s2); // true, because it's the same instance
s1.addData("Hello, world!");
```

Output:

```
Database created
true
Hello, world!
```

Explanation:

1. The code defines a Singleton design pattern using a class named **Singleton**. The **Singleton** class has a private class variable **instance** which keeps a reference to the single instance of the class. If the instance does not already exist, it is created by calling `new Singleton()`.

2. The **Database** class is a helper class used by the **Singleton** class. It has a single method **addData()** that simply prints out the data passed to it.

3. When the **Singleton instance** is created, it also creates an instance of the **Database** class and assigns it to a class variable **db**. The **addData()** method of the **Singleton** class simply calls the **addData()** method of the Database instance.

4. In the code, two instances of the **Singleton** class are created (**s1** and **s2**). Since the Singleton class is designed to have only one instance, both **s1** and **s2** refer to the same object. The **addData()** method is then called on **s2**, which calls the **addData()** method of the Database instance created during the creation of the Singleton instance. This prints the string "Hello, world!" to the console.

Problem : Implement a singleton pattern for a SQLite database connection using the Singleton design pattern. The objective is to ensure that only one instance of the database connection is created, and all subsequent calls to create a database object return the same instance.

Solution: The code uses the Singleton pattern to ensure that only one instance of the `Database` class is created throughout the program's execution. The Singleton pattern restricts the instantiation of a class to a single object. The class uses a class variable `instance` to hold the single instance of the class. If no instance exists, the `instance` variable is set to `null`. If an instance does not exist, a new one is created, and the connection to the SQLite database is established. If an instance already exists, the existing instance is returned.

An example with SQLite as the database in place of a dummy database class.

```javascript
const sqlite3 = require('sqlite3').verbose();

class DatabaseSingleton {
    constructor() {
        console.log('Database created');
```

```javascript
        this.connection = new sqlite3.Database('db.sqlite3');
        this.createTable();
    }

    static getInstance() {
        if (!this._instance) {
            this._instance = new DatabaseSingleton();
        }
        return this._instance;
    }

    createTable() {
        this.connection.run(
            'CREATE TABLE IF NOT EXISTS students (id INTEGER,
name TEXT);'
        );
    }

    addData(id, name) {
        const statement = this.connection.prepare(
            'INSERT INTO students (id, name) VALUES (?, ?);'
        );
        statement.run(id, name);
    }

    display() {
        this.connection.each('SELECT * FROM students;', (err,
row) => {
            if (err) {
                console.error(err.message);
            } else {
                console.log(`${row.id} ${row.name}`);
            }
        });
    }
}

// Client code
const db1 = DatabaseSingleton.getInstance();
const db2 = DatabaseSingleton.getInstance();
console.log('Database Objects DB1:', db1);
console.log('Database Objects DB2:', db2);
db1.addData(1, 'john');
db2.addData(2, 'smith');
db1.display();
```

Explanation:

1. The code defines a Singleton design pattern using a class named **Database**. The **Database** class has a private class variable instance which keeps a reference to the single instance of the class. If the instance does not already exist, it is created by calling new **DatabaseSingleton()**.

2. When the Database instance is created, it creates a connection to an **SQLite** database and assigns it to a class variable connection.

3. The Database class has three methods. The **createTable()** method creates a table named "students" in the database if it does not already exist. The table has two columns: "id" and "name". The **addData()** method adds a row to the "students" table with the given "id" and "name". The **display()** method retrieves all rows from the "students" table and prints them to the console.

4. In the code, two instances of the **Database** class are created (**db1** and **db2**). Since the **Database** class is designed to have only one instance, both **db1** and **db2** refer to the same object. The **createTable()** method is called on **db1** to create the "students" table. The **addData()** method is called on **db1** and **db2** to add data to the "students" table. Finally, the **display()** method is called on **db1** to retrieve and print all rows from the "students" table.

Uses of Singleton Pattern

Here are some examples of situations where the singleton pattern can be used:

1. **Database connections**: In a multi-threaded application, creating multiple database connections can be expensive and cause issues such as locking and deadlocks. A singleton database connection can be used to ensure that there is only one connection to the database, which can be shared by all threads.

2. **Configuration settings**: In a large application, there may be a need for a centralised configuration store that can be accessed by various parts of the application. A singleton configuration object can be used to provide access to configuration settings.

3. **Logging**: In an application, it's often necessary to log messages to a file or database. A singleton logging object can be used to ensure that there

is only one log file or database connection, and that all log messages are written to this object.

4. **Cache**: In an application, it's often necessary to cache data in memory to improve performance. A singleton cache object can be used to provide a centralised cache that can be accessed by various parts of the application.

5. **Session management**: In a web application, it's often necessary to manage user sessions. A singleton session manager can be used to ensure that there is only one session manager object, which can manage all user sessions.

Consequence

While the Singleton pattern solves the problem of controlling the number of instances of a class and provides global access to that instance, it also has some consequences that need to be considered:

1. **Global state**: Since a Singleton instance is globally accessible, it can lead to a shared global state. This can make the code harder to test, maintain, and reason about.

2. **Thread safety**: The basic lazy initialization approach is not thread-safe. In a multi-threaded environment, multiple threads might simultaneously check if the instance is null and create multiple instances. Synchronisation or double-checked locking can be used to ensure thread safety, but they can introduce performance overhead.

3. **Testing difficulty**: Singleton can be challenging to test, as it is tightly coupled with its static method for instance retrieval. This can make it difficult to replace the Singleton instance with a mock for testing purposes.

4. **Hidden dependencies**: The Singleton pattern can introduce hidden dependencies since the instance is often accessed directly through the static method. This can make the code less modular and harder to refactor.

SOLID principle applied

SOLID principle applied to the Singleton pattern:

1. **Single Responsibility Principle (SRP)**: The Singleton pattern follows the SRP by ensuring that there is only one responsibility assigned to the Singleton class, which is to manage the single instance of the object. This way, the Singleton class does not have any additional responsibilities or concerns. SRP is the only design principle applied to the Singleton pattern.

Factory Method Pattern

The **Factory Method pattern** is a Creational design pattern that provides an interface for creating objects in a super-class but allows its subclasses to alter the type of objects that will be created. It abstracts the process of object creation and defers it to the subclasses. This pattern is useful when you want to decouple the creation of objects from the code that uses them, or when you want to provide a common interface for creating related objects that can be customised in different ways.

Problem: Consider a scenario where you have a class that needs to create objects, but the exact type of objects to be created is not known until runtime. Directly instantiating objects in this class would tightly couple it to the concrete classes, making it difficult to extend and maintain the code. Additionally, if you add new types of objects in the future, you would have to modify the existing class, violating the Open-Closed Principle (part of the SOLID principles).

Solution: The Factory Method pattern suggests defining an interface or an abstract class to declare the method (the factory method) responsible for creating objects. The super-class will use this factory method to create objects, but it won't be concerned with the actual instantiation process. Instead, subclasses will provide their implementations for the factory method, allowing them to decide the specific type of objects to create.

Here are the key elements of the Factory Method pattern:

1. **Creator**: The Creator is an abstract class or interface that defines a factory method for creating objects. This method returns an instance of a Product, but the specific class of Product to create is left to the concrete Creator subclasses.

2. **Concrete Creator**: A Concrete Creator is a subclass of Creator that implements the factory method to create a specific type of Product

3. **Product**: The Product is the object that the factory method creates. It is usually an abstract class or interface that defines the interface for the objects that the factory method creates.

4. **Concrete Product**: A Concrete Product is a subclass of Product that implements the interface defined by Product.

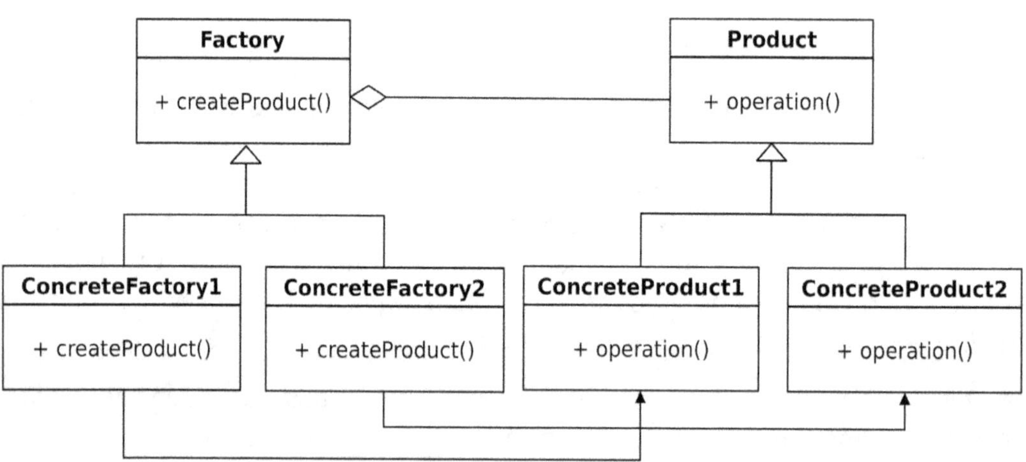

Here's an example of how the Factory Method Pattern might be used :

```javascript
// Product interface
class Product {
    operation() {
        throw new Error("Abstract method 'operation' must be
implemented.");
    }
}


// Concrete Product classes
class ConcreteProduct1 extends Product {
    operation() {
        console.log("Concrete Product1 Operation!");
    }
}


class ConcreteProduct2 extends Product {
    operation() {
        console.log("Concrete Product2 Operation!");
    }
}
```

```javascript
// Creator abstract class
class Factory {
    createProduct() {
        throw new Error("Abstract method 'createProduct' must be
implemented.");
    }
}

// Concrete Creator classes
class ConcreteFactory1 extends Factory {
    createProduct() {
        return new ConcreteProduct1();
    }
}

class ConcreteFactory2 extends Factory {
    createProduct() {
        return new ConcreteProduct2();
    }
}

// Client code
const factory1 = new ConcreteFactory1();
const product1 = factory1.createProduct();
product1.operation();

const factory2 = new ConcreteFactory2();
const product2 = factory2.createProduct();
product2.operation();
```

Output:

```
Concrete Product1 Operation!
Concrete Product2 Operation!
```

Explanation:

1. The code defines an abstract class **Product**, which is sub-classed by two concrete products, **ConcreteProduct1** and **ConcreteProduct2**. These products define their own implementation of the abstract method `operation`.

2. The **Factory** abstract class also defines an abstract method **createProduct()**, which is implemented by the **ConcreteFactory1** and **ConcreteFactory2** classes, respectively, to create instances of the **ConcreteProduct1** and **ConcreteProduct2** classes.

3. The client code uses these concrete factory classes to create instances of **ConcreteProduct1** and **ConcreteProduct2**, respectively, and calls their `operation` method.

4. In the client code, objects of **ConcreteFactory1** and **ConcreteFactory2** are created, and then **createProduct()** is called on each of them to create **ConcreteProduct1** and **ConcreteProduct2** objects respectively. Finally, the **operation()** method is called on each of these product objects to produce the output "Concrete Product1 Operation!" and "Concrete Product2 Operation!".

Problem: Implement a system that follows the Factory Method design pattern to abstract the creation of different types of animals (such as, Dogs and Cats). The goal is to enable the client code (the part of the code that uses these animals) to interact with the animals through an abstract interface, without directly instantiating the concrete animal classes.

Solution:

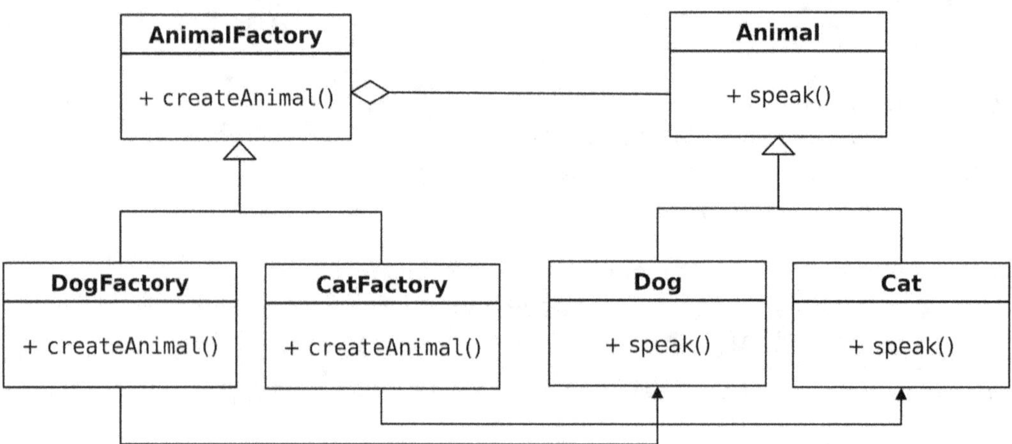

An example of how the Factory Method Pattern used to create animals:

```
// Product interface
class Animal {
    speak() {
        throw new Error("Abstract method 'speak' must be
implemented.");
    }
}

// Concrete Product classes
class Dog extends Animal {
    speak() {
```

```javascript
        console.log("Woof!");
    }
}

class Cat extends Animal {
    speak() {
        console.log("Meow!");
    }
}

// Creator abstract class
class AnimalFactory {
    createAnimal() {
        throw new Error("Abstract method 'createAnimal' must be
implemented.");
    }
}

// Concrete Creator classes
class DogFactory extends AnimalFactory {
    createAnimal() {
        return new Dog();
    }
}

class CatFactory extends AnimalFactory {
    createAnimal() {
        return new Cat();
    }
}

// Client code
const dogFactory = new DogFactory();
const dog = dogFactory.createAnimal();
dog.speak();

const catFactory = new CatFactory();
const cat = catFactory.createAnimal();
cat.speak();
```

Output:

```
Woof!
Meow!
```

Explanation:

1. The code defines an abstract class **Animal**, which is subclassed by two concrete animal classes, **Dog** and **Cat**. These concrete animal classes implement their own version of the **speak()** method.

2. The **AnimalFactory** abstract class defines an abstract method **createAnimal()**, which is implemented by **DogFactory** and **CatFactory** classes. These concrete factory classes create instances of the **Dog** and **Cat** classes, respectively.

3. The client code uses these concrete factory classes to create instances of **Dog** and **Cat**, respectively, and calls their **speak()** method.

4. This example demonstrates how the Factory Method pattern can be used to create objects (**Dog** and **Cat**) without having to specify their exact class, by using **DogFactory** and **CatFactory** to create them.

Uses of Factory Method Pattern

Here are some common uses and properties of the Factory Method pattern:

1. **Object creation**: One of the most common uses of the Factory Method pattern is to encapsulate the object creation process. This can help to decouple client code from the specific types of objects it is using, and can make it easier to change the object types being used without affecting the client code.

2. **Encapsulation of object creation logic**: The Factory Method pattern can be used to encapsulate complex object creation logic, such as the use of different parameters or settings to create different types of objects. By abstracting this logic behind a factory interface, it can be easily modified without affecting client code.

3. **Dependency injection**: The Factory Method pattern can be used as a form of dependency injection, where the factory object provides the dependencies for the client object. By using a factory to create the dependencies, the client object can be made independent of the concrete implementation of those dependencies.

4. **Dynamic object creation**: The Factory Method pattern can be used to dynamically create objects based on runtime conditions or user input. This can be useful in situations where the specific type of object needed is not known until runtime.

5. **Mocking and testing**: The Factory Method pattern can be used to create mock objects for testing purposes. By creating a factory interface for the objects being tested, it is possible to create mock objects that can be substituted for the real objects during testing. This can help to isolate the code being tested and make it easier to identify and fix bugs.

6. **Customizable**: The Factory Method pattern makes the design more customizable, since each subclass can implement the factory method in its own way to create the desired type of object.

7. **Loose coupling**: The Factory Method pattern promotes loose coupling between classes, since the superclass only depends on the interface, not on concrete implementations.

Consequence

The Factory Method pattern offers several advantages:

1. **Decoupling:** The pattern decouples the client code (super-class) from the concrete product classes, promoting flexibility and maintainability. The client code interacts with the product through the factory method interface, unaware of the specific implementation.

2. **Extensibility:** You can easily introduce new product types by creating new subclasses that implement the factory method. This adheres to the Open-Closed Principle, as you can extend the functionality without modifying the existing code.

3. **Encapsulation:** The product creation logic is encapsulated within the factory method, making the code easier to manage and understand.

4. **Code Reusability:** Common object creation logic can be shared among multiple subclasses, improving code reuse.

5. **Dependency Injection:** The Factory Method pattern can facilitate dependency injection by allowing the client code to rely on an interface rather than concrete classes.

However, there are some trade-offs:

1. **Complexity:** Introducing the Factory Method pattern can increase the complexity of the codebase, especially when dealing with a large number of product types and their corresponding factory implementations.

2. **Abstraction Overhead:** Defining interfaces and abstract classes may add some overhead, and the pattern may not be necessary if you have a simple object instantiation scenario.

SOLID principle applied

How each SOLID principle can be applied to the Factory Method pattern:

1. **Single Responsibility Principle (SRP):** Apply SRP by ensuring that each Factory Method class is responsible for creating a specific type of object. This way, the factory class has a single reason to change: if the creation process or the type of object changes. Separating creation responsibility from the client code adheres to SRP, keeping your classes focused on their intended roles.

2. **Open/Closed Principle (OCP):** Design your Factory Method pattern to be open for extension but closed for modification. New types of objects can be added by creating new factory subclasses without altering existing code. This adheres to OCP because you can introduce new behaviour (new object types) without changing the existing codebase.

3. **Liskov Substitution Principle (LSP):** Ensure that the objects created by different concrete factories can be used interchangeably. This means that the objects should adhere to a common interface or base class so that they can be substituted without causing errors. Following LSP ensures that derived objects behave as expected when passed to client code.

4. **Interface Segregation Principle (ISP):** If the Factory Method class interfaces or base classes have methods that are not used by all concrete factories, consider splitting those interfaces to adhere to ISP. This prevents clients from being forced to implement unnecessary methods.

5. **Dependency Inversion Principle (DIP):** Allow client classes to depend on abstractions (interfaces or abstract classes) instead of concrete classes. This way, the client code can remain decoupled from the specific implementations of the objects being created. The Factory Method pattern inherently encourages this by having the client code interact with the factory through an abstract creator interface.

Abstract Factory Pattern

The **Abstract Factory pattern** is a Creational design pattern that provides an interface for creating families of related or dependent objects without specifying their concrete classes. It allows the creation of objects that are part of a particular family or group, ensuring that they are compatible and work together seamlessly.

Problem: In software development, sometimes the system needs to be configured with different families of objects. For example, in a graphical user interface, you might need to create different types of buttons, windows, and other UI elements based on the operating system or the theme selected by the user. Without the Abstract Factory pattern, the code for object creation can become complex, tightly coupled, and difficult to maintain if there are multiple families of related objects.

Solution: The Abstract Factory pattern addresses the problem by providing an abstract class or interface (the "Abstract Factory") that declares methods for creating the various families of objects. Concrete implementations of this abstract factory represent different families of objects. Clients of the Abstract Factory pattern interact with these factories through the abstract interface without needing to know the specific classes of the objects being created. The Abstract Factory Pattern promotes the principle of coding to interfaces rather than concrete classes, and it provides a way to achieve the Open/Closed Principle by allowing the addition of new product variants without changing the existing code.

Implementing the Abstract Factory Pattern. The **AbstractFactory** abstract class defines the interface for creating related objects (**createProductA** and **createProductB**), which are implemented by the **ConcreteFactory1** and **ConcreteFactory2** concrete factory classes. These concrete factory classes create **ProductA1**, **ProductB1**, **ProductA2**, and **ProductB2** objects, which are related and belong to their respective product families.

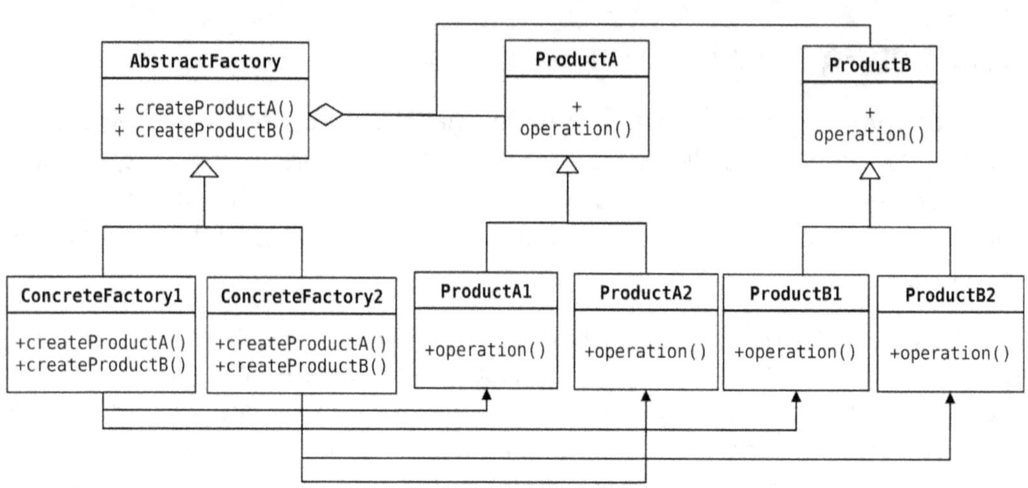

Here's an example of how the Abstract Factory Pattern might be used :

```
// Abstract ProductA
class ProductA {
    operationA() {
        console.log("ProductA operationA");
    }
}

// Concrete ProductA1
class ProductA1 extends ProductA {
    operationA() {
        console.log("ProductA1 operationA");
    }

}

// Concrete ProductA2
class ProductA2 extends ProductA {
    operationA() {
        console.log("ProductA2 operationA");
    }
}

// Abstract ProductB
class ProductB {
    operationB() {
        console.log("ProductB operationB");
    }
}
```

```javascript
// Concrete ProductB1
class ProductB1 extends ProductB {

    operationB() {
        console.log("ProductB1 operationB");
    }
}

// Concrete ProductB2
class ProductB2 extends ProductB {
    operationB() {
        console.log("ProductB2 operationB");
    }
}

// Abstract Factory
class AbstractFactory {
    createProductA() {
        throw new Error("Abstract method: createProductA");
    }

    createProductB() {
        throw new Error("Abstract method: createProductB");
    }
}

// Concrete Factory1
class ConcreteFactory1 extends AbstractFactory {
    createProductA() {
        return new ProductA1();
    }

    createProductB() {
        return new ProductB1();
    }
}

// Concrete Factory2
class ConcreteFactory2 extends AbstractFactory {
    createProductA() {
        return new ProductA2();
    }

    createProductB() {
        return new ProductB2();
```

```
    }
}

// Client code
const factory1 = new ConcreteFactory1();
const productA1 = factory1.createProductA();
const productB1 = factory1.createProductB();
productA1.operationA();
productB1.operationB();

const factory2 = new ConcreteFactory2();
const productA2 = factory2.createProductA();
const productB2 = factory2.createProductB();
productA2.operationA();
productB2.operationB();
```

Output:

```
ProductA1 operationA
ProductB1 operationB
ProductA2 operationA
ProductB2 operationB
```

Explanation:

1. In this example, **ProductA** and **ProductB** are the abstract product classes, with **operationA()** and **operationB()** methods respectively. The concrete product classes **ProductA1**, **ProductA2**, **ProductB1**, and **ProductB2** implement these methods with different functionality.

2. The abstract factory class Factory defines methods **createProductA()** and **createProductB()** that return objects of type **ProductA** and **ProductB**, respectively. The concrete factory classes **ConcreteFactory1** and **ConcreteFactory2** implement these methods to create different combinations of **ProductA** and **ProductB** objects.

3. Finally, the client code creates instances of the concrete factory classes **ConcreteFactory1** and **ConcreteFactory2**, and uses them to create **ProductA** and **ProductB** objects. These objects are then used to call their respective **operationA** and **operationB** methods to perform some functionality.

Problem: Implement the Abstract Factory Pattern. The **AbstractFactory** abstract class defines the interface for creating related objects (**getMenu** and **getButton**), which are implemented by the **WinFactory** and **MacFactory**

concrete factory classes. These concrete factory classes create **WinMenu**, **WinButton**, **MacMenu**, and **MacButton** objects, which are related and belong to their respective product families.

Solution:

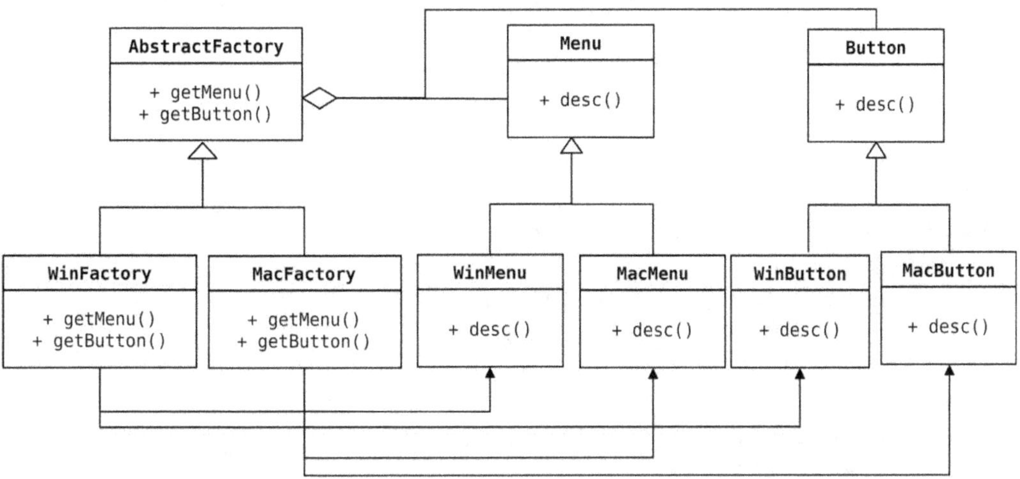

An example of Abstract Factory Pattern to create buttons and menus :

```javascript
// Menu interface
class Menu {
    desc() {
        console.log("Menu!!");
    }
}

// WinMenu class
class WinMenu extends Menu {
    desc() {
        console.log("Win Menu!!");
    }
}

// MacMenu class
class MacMenu extends Menu {
    desc() {
        console.log("Mac Menu!!");
    }
}

// Button interface
class Button {
    desc() {
```

```javascript
        console.log("Button!!");
    }
}

// WinButton class
class WinButton extends Button {
    desc() {
        console.log("Win Button!!");
    }
}

// MacButton class
class MacButton extends Button {
    desc() {
        console.log("Mac Button!!");
    }
}

// Abstract Factory interface
class AbstractFactory {
    getMenu() {
        throw new Error("Abstract method: getMenu");
    }

    getButton() {
        throw new Error("Abstract method: getButton");
    }
}

// WinFactory class
class WinFactory extends AbstractFactory {
    getMenu() {
        return new WinMenu();
    }

    getButton() {
        return new WinButton();
    }
}

// MacFactory class
class MacFactory extends AbstractFactory {
    getMenu() {
        return new MacMenu();
    }
```

```javascript
    getButton() {
        return new MacButton();
    }
}
}

// Client code
const macFactory = new MacFactory();
macFactory.getMenu().desc();
macFactory.getButton().desc();
const winFactory = new WinFactory();
winFactory.getButton().desc();
winFactory.getMenu().desc();
```

Output:

```
Mac Menu!!
Mac Button!!
Win Menu!!
Win Button!!
```

Explanation:

1. In this example, there are two abstract classes: **Menu** and **Button**. Each of these classes has two concrete implementations: **WinMenu**, **MacMenu**, **WinButton**, and **MacButton**. The **AbstractFactory** abstract class defines two abstract methods: **getMenu()** and **getButton()**, which are implemented by two concrete classes: **WinFactory** and **MacFactory**.

2. The **MacFactory** and **WinFactory** classes are responsible for creating families of related objects (**menus** and **buttons**) for their respective platforms (**Mac** and **Windows**). By calling **getMenu()** and **getButton()** methods on each factory, we can get the concrete implementations of **Menu** and **Button** classes specific to that platform.

Uses of Abstract Factory design pattern

Here are some of the common use cases for the Abstract Factory design pattern:

1. **Creating objects with different implementations:** The Abstract Factory pattern allows you to create a set of related objects with different implementations without changing the client code. For example, if you have an application that can run on multiple operating systems, you can

create a different set of UI components for each operating system using the Abstract Factory pattern.

2. **Encapsulating object creation**: The Abstract Factory pattern encapsulates object creation in a single class or set of related classes. This makes it easier to maintain and modify the code as you can change the implementation of the factory without affecting the client code.

3. **Ensuring consistency**: The Abstract Factory pattern ensures that all the objects created by the factory belong to the same family and work together. This reduces the risk of errors or inconsistencies in the application.

4. **Supporting new types of objects:** The Abstract Factory pattern makes it easier to add new types of objects to the application. You can simply create a new factory that creates the new types of objects, and the client code can use the new factory without any changes.

Consequence

The Abstract Factory pattern offers several benefits and consequences:

1. **Flexibility and Extensibility:** The pattern makes it easy to introduce new families of objects without modifying existing client code. You can add new concrete factory classes for new object families, and the clients will continue to work with the abstract interface.

2. **Loose Coupling:** Client code is decoupled from the concrete classes of the objects it uses. It only depends on the abstract interfaces provided by the factory, promoting better encapsulation and maintainability.

3. **Consistency:** Abstract Factory ensures that all objects produced by a factory belong to the same family, ensuring consistency and compatibility among the created objects.

4. **Complexity Management:** By encapsulating the object creation process within the factory, the client code becomes simpler and more focused on its primary responsibilities.

5. **Dependency Injection:** Abstract Factory can be used as a form of dependency injection. Clients can be provided with the appropriate concrete factory, allowing them to work with specific families of objects without being aware of their exact types.

SOLID principle applied

How each SOLID principle can be applied to the Abstract Factory pattern:

1. **Single Responsibility Principle (SRP)**: The Abstract Factory pattern follows the SRP by separating the creation of related objects into separate factories. Each factory has the single responsibility of creating objects that are related to each other and belong to the same family.

2. **Open-Closed Principle (OCP)**: The Abstract Factory pattern follows the OCP by allowing new families of related objects to be added without modifying the existing code. New factories can be created to produce the new objects, and the client can use the new objects without any changes to their code.

3. **Liskov Substitution Principle (LSP)**: The Abstract Factory pattern follows the LSP by ensuring that all objects produced by a factory adhere to a common interface or inheritance hierarchy. This means that the client can use any object produced by a factory interchangeably with other objects of the same family, without affecting the correctness of the program.

4. **Interface Segregation Principle (ISP)**: The Abstract Factory pattern follows the ISP by defining separate interfaces for each family of related objects. This way, the client only needs to know about the interface for the specific family of objects they need to create or use, and not about other families of objects.

5. **Dependency Inversion Principle (DIP)**: The Abstract Factory pattern follows the DIP by allowing the client to depend on the abstraction (the factory interfaces) rather than the implementation (the specific factory classes). This way, the client can easily switch between different families of related objects without affecting the rest of the code.

Builder Pattern

The **Builder design pattern** is a Creational design pattern that is used to construct complex objects step by step. It separates the construction of a complex object from its representation, allowing the same construction process to create different representations. This pattern is particularly useful when the construction process of an object is complex, and the object can have multiple valid configurations.

Problem: In software development, sometimes you need to create objects that have multiple attributes or configuration options. Instantiating such complex objects using traditional constructors with numerous parameters can be cumbersome, error-prone, and hard to maintain, especially if there are many possible combinations of properties. Also, having multiple constructors with different combinations of parameters can lead to code duplication.

Solution: The Builder design pattern addresses the above problem by defining a separate class (the Builder) responsible for creating the complex object. The Builder class provides methods for setting individual attributes or configurations of the object. Once all the necessary attributes are set, the Builder produces the final object.

The main components of the Builder Pattern are:

1. **Builder**: an abstract interface for creating parts of a complex object.

2. **ConcreteBuilder**: a concrete implementation of the Builder interface that builds and assembles parts of the complex object.

3. **Director**: responsible for managing the construction process using the Builder interface.

4. **Product**: the final object that is created by the Builder.

Implement the Builder Pattern class that builds a **Product**. The **Builder** interface would define methods for adding parts like the **partA** and **partB**. The **ConcreteBuilder** would implement these methods and assemble the product parts. The **Director** would manage the construction process by calling the appropriate methods from the **ConcreteBuilder**. Finally, the **Product** would be the completed product object with all its parts assembled.

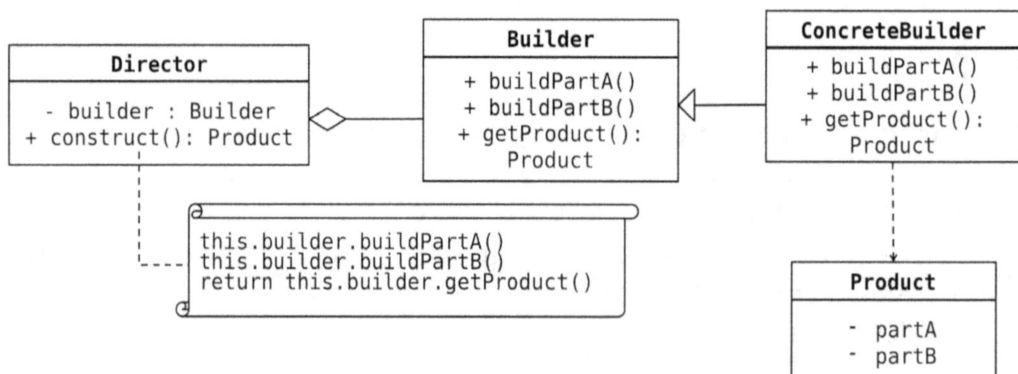

Here's an example of how the Builder Pattern might be used :

```javascript
// Define the Product class with two parts
class Product {
    constructor(A = "A default", B = "B default") {
        this.partA = A;
        this.partB = B;
    }

    setPartA(A) {
        this.partA = A;
    }

    setPartB(B) {
        this.partB = B;
    }

    toString() {
        return `Product : (${this.partA}, ${this.partB})`;
    }
}

// Define an abstract class called Builder
class Builder {
    constructor() {
        this.product = new Product();
    }

    setPartA(A) {
        throw new Error("Abstract method: setPartA");
    }

    setPartB(B) {
        throw new Error("Abstract method: setPartB");
    }

    getProduct() {
        const temp = this.product;
        this.product = new Product(); // assign new product.
        return temp;
    }
}

// Define a ConcreteBuilder class that extends Builder
class ConcreteBuilder extends Builder {
    setPartA(A) {
```

```javascript
        this.product.setPartA(A);
        return this;
    }

    setPartB(B) {
        this.product.setPartB(B);
        return this;
    }
}

// Define a Director class that takes a builder object as a
parameter
class Director {
    constructor(builder) {
        this.builder = builder;
    }

    construct() {
        return
this.builder.setPartA("A1").setPartB("B1").getProduct();
    }

    construct2() {
        this.builder.setPartA("A2");
        this.builder.setPartB("B2");
        return this.builder.getProduct();
    }

    construct3() {
        return this.builder.setPartA("A3").getProduct();
    }
}

// Client code
const builder = new ConcreteBuilder();
const director = new Director(builder);
const product = director.construct();
console.log(product.toString());

const product2 = director.construct2();
console.log(product2.toString());
const product3 = director.construct3();
console.log(product3.toString());
```

Output:

Product : (A1, B1)

```
Product : (A2, B2)
Product : (A3, B default)
```

Explanation:

1. First, a **Product** class is defined with two parts (partA and partB) that have default values if no values are provided during initialization.

2. Next, an abstract class called **Builder** is defined with two abstract methods that must be implemented by any concrete builder that extends this class. The Builder class has a **getProduct()** method that returns a **Product** object and a constructor that creates a new **Product** object.

3. A **ConcreteBuilder** class is defined that extends **Builder** and implements the **setPartA()** and **setPartB()** methods, which set the values of the parts of the **Product** object being built. These methods return self, allowing for method chaining.

4. Finally, a **Director** class is defined that takes a builder object as a parameter in its constructor. The **Director** class has three methods that use the builder object to construct different Product objects with different sets of parts.

5. In the main part of the code, a **ConcreteBuilder** object is created and passed to a Director object. The **construct()**, **construct2()**, and **construct3()** methods of the Director object are called to create three different Product objects with different sets of parts. The display method of each of the **Product** objects is called to print out the values of the parts of the **Product** objects.

Problem: Implement the Builder Pattern class that builds a house. The **HouseBuilder** interface would define methods for adding the wall and roof to the house. The **WoodenHouseBuilder** and **ConcreteHouseBuilder** would implement these methods and create the house. The **HouseDirector** would manage the construction process by calling the appropriate methods from the concrete builders. Finally, the Product would be the completed **House** object with all its parts assembled.

Solution: Example of the Builder Pattern to build different type of Houses :

```
// A class representing a house
class House {
    constructor(wall, roof) {
        this.wall = wall;
```

```javascript
        this.roof = roof;
    }

    setWall(wall) {
        this.wall = wall;
    }

    setRoof(roof) {
        this.roof = roof;
    }

    toString() {
        return `House of ${this.wall} and ${this.roof}`;
    }
}

// An abstract builder class that specifies the interface for
building a house
class HouseBuilder {
    constructor() {
        this.house = new House("", "");
    }

    setWall() {
        throw new Error("Abstract method: setWall");
    }

    setRoof() {
        throw new Error("Abstract method: setRoof");
    }

    getHouse() {
        const temp = this.house;
        this.house = new House("", ""); // assign new house.
        return temp;
    }
}

// A builder class that builds a wooden house
class WoodenHouseBuilder extends HouseBuilder {
    setWall() {
        this.house.setWall("Wooden Wall");
        return this;
    }
}
```

```javascript
    setRoof() {
        this.house.setRoof("Wooden Roof");
        return this;
    }
}

// A builder class that builds a concrete house
class ConcreteHouseBuilder extends HouseBuilder {
    setWall() {
        this.house.setWall("Concrete Wall");
        return this;
    }

    setRoof() {
        this.house.setRoof("Concrete Roof");
        return this;
    }
}

// A class that directs the building of a house
class HouseDirector {
    constructor(builder) {
        this.builder = builder;
    }

    construct() {
        return this.builder.setWall().setRoof().getHouse();
    }
}

// Client code
const builder = new ConcreteHouseBuilder();
const director = new HouseDirector(builder);
const house = director.construct();
console.log(house.toString());

// Building a wooden house using a WoodenHouseBuilder object
const builder2 = new WoodenHouseBuilder();
const director2 = new HouseDirector(builder2);
const house2 = director2.construct();
console.log(house2.toString());
```

Output:

```
House of Concrete Wall and Concrete Roof
House of Wooden Wall and Wooden Roof
```

Explanation:

1. First, there is the **House** class that represents the product being built, which has two attributes - wall and roof. It also has a **display()** method that prints the type of wall and roof for the house.

2. Then, there is the **HouseBuilder** abstract class that defines the methods for building the wall and roof of the house, as well as a **getHouse()** method for returning the final product.

3. The **WoodenHouseBuilder** and **ConcreteHouseBuilder** classes are concrete implementations of the **HouseBuilder** abstract class that set the wall and roof attributes of the **House** object with their respective materials.

4. Finally, the **HouseDirector** class is responsible for directing the construction process by passing a builder object and calling its methods to build the wall and roof of the house. It then returns the final product through the **getHouse()** method.

5. The main program creates instances of both concrete builder classes, creates houses using the director, and displays the wall and roof materials for each house.

Uses of Builder design pattern

Here are some common use cases for the Builder design pattern:

1. When a complex object needs to be created and the construction process is independent of the parts that make up the object. The builder design pattern allows you to create an object step-by-step, where each step involves creating and assembling different parts of the object.

2. When you want to create different versions of an object with the same construction process. For example, if you are creating a house-building application, you might have different types of houses (e.g., wooden, concrete, etc.) that have different parts (e.g., walls, roof, etc.), but the construction process is the same.

3. When you want to create an object in a more flexible and extensible way. The builder pattern provides a way to vary an object's internal representation, allowing you to create different types of objects from a single builder.

4. When you want to hide the complexity of object construction from the client code. By using a builder class, you can abstract away the details of how an object is constructed and only expose a simple interface to the client code.

Consequence

The Builder design pattern offers several benefits:

1. **Clear Separation of Concerns:** The pattern separates the construction logic from the final object, making the code more modular and easier to maintain.

2. **Flexible Object Construction:** Builders can create different representations of the same complex object by implementing different ConcreteBuilder classes, allowing more flexibility in the construction process.

3. **Eliminates Telescoping Constructors:** The pattern eliminates the need for constructors with a large number of parameters, which improves code readability and makes it easier to understand the object's configuration.

4. **Improved Readability:** The code that uses the Builder pattern is more readable and self-explanatory compared to using multiple constructor overloads or complex parameter lists.

5. **Encapsulation:** The details of how the complex object is constructed are hidden within the Builder, encapsulating the construction process.

SOLID principle applied

Here's how each SOLID principle can be applied to the Builder pattern:

1. **Single Responsibility Principle (SRP)**: The Builder pattern follows the SRP by separating the construction of a complex object from its representation, in order to allow for different representations to be created from the same construction process. The Builder interface and the Director class have the responsibility of constructing the object, while the ConcreteBuilder classes have the responsibility of creating a specific representation of the object.

2. **Open-Closed Principle (OCP)**: The Builder pattern follows the OCP by allowing the construction of a complex object to be separated from its representation, which allows for new representations to be added without

modifying the existing code. The Director class can work with any ConcreteBuilder that adheres to the same Builder interface, and the client can create any representation by using the Director with the appropriate ConcreteBuilder.

3. **Liskov Substitution Principle (LSP)**: The Builder pattern follows the LSP by ensuring that the ConcreteBuilder classes adhere to the same Builder interface, which means that any ConcreteBuilder can be substituted for another without affecting the correctness of the program. This allows for different representations of the same object to be created without any impact on the behaviour of the Director or the client.

4. **Interface Segregation Principle (ISP)**: The Builder pattern follows the ISP by defining a separate interface for the Builder, with methods for creating the different parts of the object. This way, the client only needs to know about the Builder interface, and not the details of each individual ConcreteBuilder.

5. **Dependency Inversion Principle (DIP)**: The Builder pattern follows the DIP by allowing the client to depend on the abstraction (the Builder interface) rather than the implementation (the specific ConcreteBuilder class). This way, the client can easily switch between different ConcreteBuilders without affecting the rest of the code.

Prototype Pattern

The **Prototype design pattern** is a Creational design pattern that is used to create new objects by copying an existing object, known as the prototype, rather than using a constructor. This pattern is useful when creating new objects is expensive in terms of time and resources. By using the Prototype pattern, you can create new objects efficiently by copying existing objects. This pattern is also useful when the number of different types of objects that need to be created is not known in advance or is too large to be handled by a conventional factory pattern.

Problem: In software development, there are situations where creating objects from scratch is inefficient and resource-consuming. For example, when creating multiple instances of similar objects with only slight variations, such as objects with identical properties but different data values. The conventional approach of creating each object individually can lead to code duplication and reduced performance.

Solution: To implement the Prototype pattern, you typically start by defining an abstract Prototype class that declares a clone method. The clone method creates and returns a copy of the current object. Concrete prototypes implement the clone method by creating a new object of the same class and copying the state of the current object to the new object.

Next, you need to define a registry or a factory class that holds references to the prototype objects. This class provides a way to retrieve a clone of a prototype object by calling a method that internally calls the clone method of the corresponding prototype.

Overall, the Prototype pattern provides a flexible and efficient way to create new objects by copying existing objects. It can reduce the number of subclasses needed in an application and can be used to create complex objects that have a complicated initialization process.

Here's an example of how the Prototype Pattern might be used :

```
class Prototype {
    constructor() {}

    clone() {
        throw new Error('clone method must be implemented');
    }
}

class ConcretePrototype1 extends Prototype {
    clone() {
        // ConcretePrototype1 clone
        return new ConcretePrototype1();
    }

    toString() {
        return "ConcretePrototype1";
    }
}

class ConcretePrototype2 extends Prototype {
    clone() {
        // ConcretePrototype2 clone
        return new ConcretePrototype2();
    }

    toString() {
        return "ConcretePrototype2";
    }
```

```javascript
}

class PrototypeRegistry {

    static addPrototype(key, value) {
        if (!PrototypeRegistry._prototypes) {
            PrototypeRegistry._prototypes = {};
        }
        if (!(key in PrototypeRegistry._prototypes)) {
            PrototypeRegistry._prototypes[key] = value;
        }
    }

    static getPrototype(key) {
        if (key in PrototypeRegistry._prototypes) {
            return PrototypeRegistry._prototypes[key].clone();
        }
        return null;
    }

    static load() {
        PrototypeRegistry.addPrototype("CP1", new
ConcretePrototype1());
        PrototypeRegistry.addPrototype("CP2", new
ConcretePrototype2());
    }
}

// Client code
PrototypeRegistry.load();
const c1 = PrototypeRegistry.getPrototype("CP1");
const c2 = PrototypeRegistry.getPrototype("CP2");
console.log(c1.toString());
console.log(c2.toString());
```

Output:

```
ConcretePrototype1
ConcretePrototype2
```

Explanation:

1. In this code, the **Prototype** class is an abstract class that defines the
   clone() method, which is implemented by the concrete prototypes
   ConcretePrototype1 and **ConcretePrototype2**. The
   PrototypeRegistry class acts as a registry for the prototypes and

provides a way to retrieve a clone of a prototype object by calling its **getObject()** method, which internally calls the `clone` method of the corresponding prototype.

2. Therefore, the Prototype pattern is used to create new objects without the need to call their constructors by copying existing objects, and the **PrototypeRegistry** acts as a central place to manage the prototypes.

Problem: Implementing the prototype-design pattern. The code defines an abstract class **Shape** with two concrete subclasses **Rectangle** and **Circle**. Additionally, there is a **ShapeRegistry** class that acts as a prototype manager and a client code section that uses the prototype pattern to create new shape objects.

Solution: Here's an example of how the Prototype Pattern might be used :

```
class Shape {
    constructor() {
        this.color = '';
    }

    toString() {
        throw new Error('toString method must be implemented');
    }

    cloneShape() {
        throw new Error('cloneShape method must be implemented');
    }

    clone() {
        return
Object.assign(Object.create(Object.getPrototypeOf(this)), this);
    }
}


class Rectangle extends Shape {
    toString() {
        return 'Rectangle.';
    }

    cloneShape() {
        return this.clone();
    }
}
```

```javascript
class Circle extends Shape {
    toString() {
        return 'Circle.';
    }

    cloneShape() {
        return this.clone();
    }
}

class ShapeRegistry {
    static addShape(key, value) {
        if(!ShapeRegistry.shapes)
        ShapeRegistry.shapes = new Map();

        ShapeRegistry.shapes.set(key, value);
    }

    static getShape(key) {
        if (ShapeRegistry.shapes.has(key)) {
            return ShapeRegistry.shapes.get(key).cloneShape();
        }
        return null;
    }

    static load() {
        ShapeRegistry.addShape('circle', new Circle());
        ShapeRegistry.addShape('rectangle', new Rectangle());
    }
}

// Client code
ShapeRegistry.load();
const c = ShapeRegistry.getShape('circle');
const r = ShapeRegistry.getShape('rectangle');
console.log(c.toString(), r.toString());
```

Output:

```
Circle. Rectangle.
```

Explanation:

1. The Prototype pattern is used to create new objects by copying existing objects, which act as prototypes. In this code, the **Shape** class is an abstract class that defines the **draw()** and **clone()** methods. The

concrete prototypes **Circle** and **Rectangle** implement the **clone()** method by creating a new object of the same class and copying the state of the current object to the new object. The **draw()** method is implemented to draw the shape.

2. The Factory pattern is used to provide a centralised way of creating objects without exposing the creation logic to the client. In this code, the **ShapeRegistry** class acts as a factory that holds references to the prototype objects. This class provides a way to retrieve a clone of a prototype object by calling a method that internally calls the **clone()** method of the corresponding prototype.

3. When the **ShapeRegistry.load()** method is called, it initialises the factory by adding the prototype objects **Circle** and **Rectangle** to the **shapes** map.

4. Finally, the code retrieves a clone of the **Circle** prototype by calling **ShapeRegistry.getShape("circle")** and a **Rectangle** prototype by calling **ShapeRegistry.getShape("rectangle")**. Both the circle and rectangle are displayed using the print function.

Uses of Prototype pattern

The Prototype pattern is used in software engineering to enable the creation of new objects by copying existing objects. Here are some common uses of the Prototype pattern:

1. When the system should be independent of how its objects are created, composed, and represented.

2. When the classes to instantiate are specified at runtime.

3. When the class instances to be created are specified by a set of parameter values.

4. When the system wants to hide the complexity of creating new objects from the client.

5. When it is more convenient to copy an existing object to create a new one rather than creating it from scratch.

6. When the number of classes required for an application is unknown in advance or large in number.

7. When the client needs to be able to dynamically add new classes at runtime.

8. When the object creation process is resource-intensive or requires a lot of time, and it is more efficient to clone an existing object rather than creating a new one.

Consequence

The Prototype pattern has several consequences:

1. **Reduced Object Creation Overhead:** Instead of creating objects from scratch, the Prototype pattern allows you to clone existing instances. This reduces the overhead of initialising and configuring new objects, leading to improved performance and reduced resource usage.

2. **Enhanced Flexibility:** With the Prototype pattern, you can easily create new objects with variations at runtime. This flexibility allows you to create complex objects based on different configurations or states.

3. **Simplified Code:** The Prototype pattern helps avoid code duplication that might occur when creating similar objects manually. The cloning process encapsulates the object creation logic, making the code cleaner and easier to maintain.

4. **Changing Class Hierarchies:** The Prototype pattern can be useful when dealing with class hierarchies where the concrete classes may change frequently. Since the client code depends on the prototype interface rather than specific classes, modifications to class hierarchies have a reduced impact on the client code.

5. **Deep vs. Shallow Cloning:** One important consideration with the Prototype pattern is how cloning is implemented. You must decide whether to perform a shallow clone (copy references) or a deep clone (copy all referenced objects recursively). The choice depends on the complexity of the objects and their relationships.

SOLID principle applied

Here's how each SOLID principle can be applied to the Prototype pattern:

1. **Single Responsibility Principle (SRP):** The Prototype pattern follows the SRP by separating the object creation and cloning logic into separate classes. The prototype interface defines a method for cloning the object,

while the concrete prototype classes implement this method to create clones of themselves.

2. **Open-Closed Principle (OCP)**: The Prototype pattern follows the OCP by allowing new objects to be added without modifying the existing code. The client can use the prototype to create objects, and new concrete prototype classes can be added without affecting the existing code.

3. **Liskov Substitution Principle (LSP)**: The Prototype pattern follows the LSP by ensuring that each concrete prototype class implements the same prototype interface, with the same cloning method. This means that any prototype class can be substituted for another prototype class without affecting the correctness of the program.

4. **Interface Segregation Principle (ISP)**: The Prototype pattern follows the ISP by defining a separate interface for the prototype, with a single method that creates clones. This way, the client only needs to know about the prototype interface, and not the details of each individual concrete prototype class.

5. **Dependency Inversion Principle (DIP)**: The Prototype pattern follows the DIP by allowing the client to depend on the abstraction (the prototype interface) rather than the implementation (the specific concrete prototype class). This way, the client can easily switch between different concrete prototype classes without affecting the rest of the code.

STRUCTURAL PATTERNS

Structural design patterns are a category of design patterns that focus on how classes and objects are structured to form larger components or structures. These patterns help define relationships between classes, simplify the organisation of code, and make the system more flexible and easier to maintain.

We will start by exploring the **Adapter Pattern**, which champions interoperability among classes with disparate interfaces. By encapsulating the conversion logic within an adapter, this pattern enables seamless integration of existing components into new systems, reducing friction and fostering code reuse.

Next, the **Bridge Pattern**, introduces an elegant solution to managing multiple dimensions of variation in software design. By decoupling abstractions from their implementations, this pattern empowers designers to handle each dimension independently, thus mitigating the explosion of class combinations that may arise from intermingling them.

The **Composite Pattern** allows you to compose objects into tree-like structures and work with those structures as if they were individual objects. This pattern is used when you have a hierarchical structure of objects and you want to treat both the individual objects and the compositions of those objects uniformly.

Our exploration continues with the **Decorator Pattern**, a hallmark of software design for the dynamic extension of functionality without altering existing code. The Decorator Pattern addresses this challenge by enabling the attachment of additional responsibilities to objects at runtime, enhancing flexibility and avoiding the pitfalls of subclass proliferation.

Next, the **Facade Pattern**, which presents a unified and simplified interface to a set of interfaces within a subsystem, shielding clients from the underlying complexities. This pattern promotes clarity, encourages best practices, and enhances the ease of use for components within the system.

Next, the **Flyweight Pattern**, which is used to optimise memory usage by sharing common data among multiple objects. It is particularly useful when dealing with a large number of similar objects that have some intrinsic (invariant) state and some extrinsic (context-dependent) state. By sharing the intrinsic state, the pattern reduces the memory footprint and improves performance.

Lastly, the **Proxy Pattern** offers a powerful mechanism for controlling access to objects and introducing additional functionalities, such as lazy initialization or access control. By interposing a proxy between clients and real objects, this pattern provides a level of indirection that can be leveraged for various purposes, such as performance optimization and security enforcement.

Adapter Pattern

The **Adapter design pattern** is a Structural design pattern that allows objects with incompatible interfaces to work together. It acts as a bridge between two interfaces, converting the interface of one class into another interface that clients expect. It involves creating an adapter class that acts as an intermediary between two objects. This pattern is useful when integrating existing systems or libraries that cannot be easily modified to match the required interface.

Problem: In software development, you may encounter situations where two existing components or classes have different interfaces and cannot directly collaborate. This incompatibility can arise due to various reasons, such as using different naming conventions, data formats, or methods. The problem is how to make these incompatible classes work together without modifying their existing code.

Solution: The Adapter design pattern provides a solution to the compatibility problem. It introduces a new adapter class that acts as an intermediary between the incompatible classes. The adapter class implements the interface expected by the client, and internally, it holds an instance of the incompatible class. The adapter then translates the requests from the client into appropriate calls to the methods of the contained object.

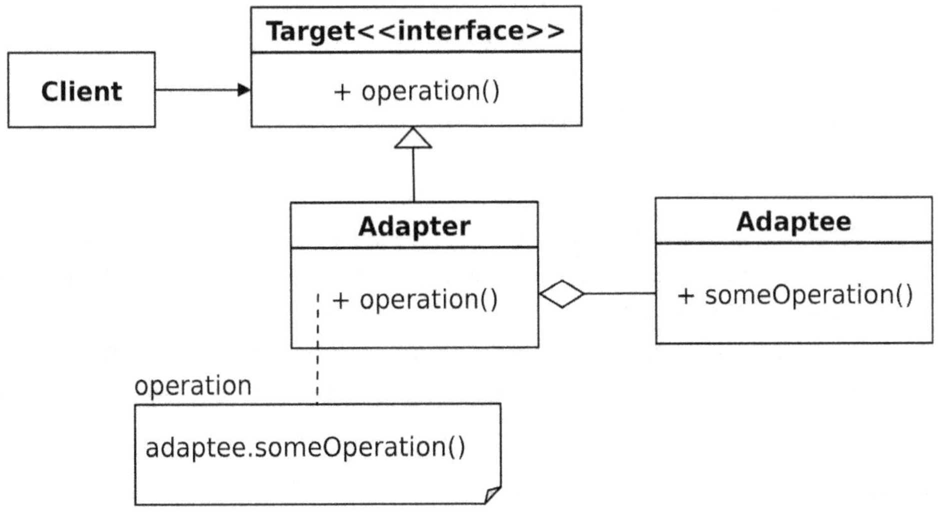

Here's an example implementation of the Adapter pattern :

```javascript
// Desired Interface
class DesiredInterface {
    operation() {
        throw new Error("Abstract method: operation");
    }
}

// Adapter class
class Adapter extends DesiredInterface {
    constructor() {
        super();
        this.adaptee = new Adaptee();
    }

    operation() {
        this.adaptee.someOperation();
    }
}

// Adaptee class
class Adaptee {
    someOperation() {
        console.log("Adaptee someOperation() function called.");
    }
}

// Client Code
const adapter = new Adapter();
adapter.operation();
```

Output:

```
Adaptee someOperation() function called.
```

Explanation:

1. In this pattern, an adapter class is created that bridges the gap between two incompatible interfaces. In this example, the **Adaptee** class has a **someOperation()** method, but the client code expects an interface with an **operation()** method. The **Adapter** class is created to provide this interface, which internally uses the **Adaptee** class to perform the actual operation.

2. The **DesiredInterface** abstract class defines the interface expected by the client code. The **Adapter** class implements this interface and

internally uses an instance of the **Adaptee** class to perform the operation. The **Adaptee** class is the class that provides the actual implementation of the operation.

3. In the client code, an instance of the **Adapter** class is created and its **operation()** method is called. The **Adapter** class internally calls the **someOperation()** method of the **Adaptee** class to perform the actual operation.

Problem: To make the existing **Rectangle** class work with the **Shape** interface by using the Adapter design pattern. The **Shape** interface is an abstract class with an abstract method **draw()**, which expects all its subclasses to implement the **draw()** method. However, the **Rectangle** class doesn't directly inherit from **Shape** and has a different method called **oldDraw()** instead.

Solution: An implementation of the Adapter pattern to adapt rectangle interface:

```javascript
// Desired Interface
class Shape {
    draw() {
        throw new Error("Abstract method: draw");
    }
}


// Circle class
class Circle extends Shape {
    constructor(x, y, radius) {
        super();
        this.x = x;
        this.y = y;
        this.radius = radius;
    }

    draw() {
        console.log("Draw the Circle.");
    }
}


// Rectangle class (Adaptee)
class Rectangle {
    constructor(x, y, length, width) {
        this.x = x;
        this.y = y;
        this.length = length;
```

```
        this.width = width;
    }

    oldDraw() {
        console.log("Drawing Rectangle.");
    }
}

// RectangleAdapter class
class RectangleAdapter extends Shape {
    constructor(x, y, length, width) {
        super();
        this.adaptee = new Rectangle(x, y, length, width);
    }

    draw() {
        this.adaptee.oldDraw();
    }
}

// Client Code
const adapter = new RectangleAdapter(1, 2, 3, 4);
adapter.draw();
```

Output:

```
Drawing Rectangle.
```

Explanation:

1. The code that implements the Adapter pattern, which adapts the interface of the **Rectangle** class to the **Shape** interface.

2. The **Shape** interface declares the **draw()** method, which is implemented by the **Circle** class. However, the **Rectangle** class doesn't implement the **Shape** interface. To make the **Rectangle** class compatible with the **Shape** interface, an adapter class **RectangleAdapter** is created that implements the **Shape** interface and internally uses the **Rectangle** class to provide the required functionality.

3. In the client code, an instance of **RectangleAdapter** is created, passing the required parameters to create an instance of **Rectangle** class. The **draw()** method is then called on the **RectangleAdapter** instance, which internally calls the **oldDraw()** method of the **Rectangle** class to draw a rectangle.

Uses of Adapter design pattern

The Adapter design pattern is useful in several scenarios where we need to make incompatible interfaces work together. Some common uses of the Adapter design pattern are:

1. **Legacy code integration**: When you need to integrate a legacy system with a modern system that uses a different interface, the Adapter pattern can be used to create a bridge between the two systems.

2. **Third-party library integration**: When you need to use a third-party library that has a different interface than what your application expects, you can create an Adapter that wraps around the library and provides the expected interface.

3. **Interface conversion**: When you have multiple components that use different interfaces, the Adapter pattern can be used to create a common interface that can be used by all the components.

4. **Interface abstraction**: When you have a complex interface, you can use the Adapter pattern to create a simplified interface that hides the complexity of the original interface.

5. **Platform independence**: When you want to make your application platform-independent, the Adapter pattern can be used to create a layer between your application and the platform-specific code. This layer can provide a common interface that works across different platforms.

Consequence

The Adapter design pattern brings several benefits and consequences:

1. **Compatibility:** It allows classes with different interfaces to work together, promoting code reuse and integration of existing components.

2. **Flexibility:** The pattern enables the integration of new classes without modifying existing client code, thus promoting flexibility and scalability.

3. **Maintainability:** By creating adapters, the changes required to incorporate new classes are localised to the adapter, keeping the core client code unchanged and easier to maintain.

4. **Complexity:** Introducing adapters may add complexity to the codebase, as it involves additional classes and indirections.

5. **Performance:** The use of adapters can introduce some performance overhead due to the extra method calls required for the translation.

SOLID principle applied

Here's how each SOLID principle can be applied to the Adapter Pattern:

1. **Single Responsibility Principle (SRP)**: The Adapter pattern follows the SRP by separating the concerns of two incompatible interfaces. The adapter class has the responsibility of adapting one interface to another. This way, the client can focus on using the target interface, while the adapter can focus on adapting the source interface.

2. **Open-Closed Principle (OCP)**: The Adapter pattern follows the OCP by allowing new classes to be adapted without modifying the existing code. The client can use the adapter to access the target interface, and the adapter can be extended to adapt new source classes without affecting the existing code.

3. **Liskov Substitution Principle (LSP)**: The Adapter pattern follows the LSP by ensuring that the adapter implements the same target interface as the objects it adapts. This means that the client can use the adapter interchangeably with the target objects, without affecting the correctness of the program.

4. **Interface Segregation Principle (ISP)**: The Adapter pattern follows the ISP by defining separate interfaces for the source and target objects. This way, the client only needs to know about the target interface, and the adapter only needs to know about the source interface.

5. **Dependency Inversion Principle (DIP)**: The Adapter pattern follows the DIP by allowing the client to depend on the abstraction (the target interface) rather than the implementation (the specific source object). This way, the client can easily switch between different source objects without affecting the rest of the code.

Bridge Pattern

The **Bridge Pattern** is a Structural design pattern that allows you to separate the abstraction (interface) from the implementation. This pattern allows the two to vary independently. In this pattern, the abstraction is a high-level component that relies on an implementation object (implementor) to perform its operations.

The implementor can be changed at runtime without affecting the client using the abstraction.

Problem: In software design, there are situations where a class or an abstraction has multiple variants, and you want to decouple the abstraction from its implementations. However, traditional inheritance can lead to an explosion of classes and make the code complex and inflexible.

Solution: The Bridge pattern solves this problem by using composition instead of inheritance. It involves separating the abstraction and the implementation into two separate hierarchies, allowing them to vary independently. The Bridge pattern promotes loose coupling between abstractions and implementations, making it easier to extend and maintain the codebase.

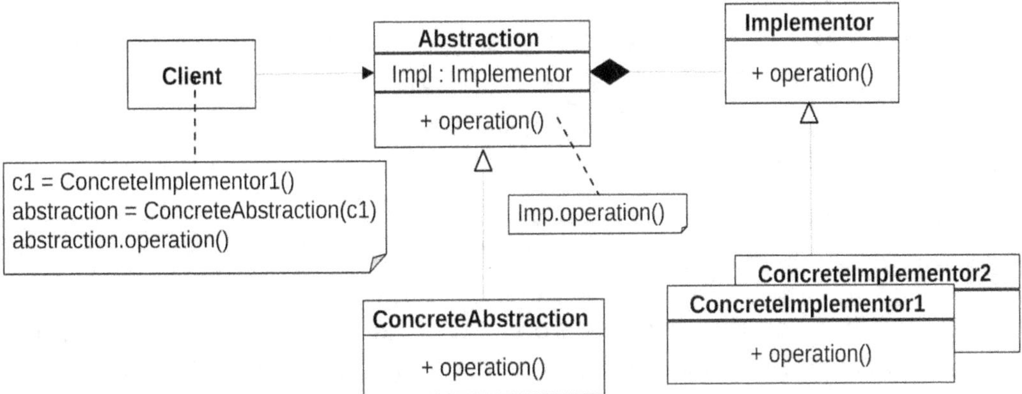

Here is an example implementation of the Bridge Pattern :

```javascript
// Abstraction interface
class Abstraction {
    constructor(imp) {
        this.imp = imp;
    }

    operation() {
        this.imp.operation();
    }
}


// Implementor interface
class Implementor {
    operation() {
        throw new Error("Abstract method: operation");
    }
}
```

```javascript
// ConcreteImplementor1 class
class ConcreteImplementor1 extends Implementor {
    operation() {
        console.log("ConcreteImplementor1 operation");
    }
}

// ConcreteImplementor2 class
class ConcreteImplementor2 extends Implementor {
    operation() {
        console.log("ConcreteImplementor2 operation");
    }
}

// Client code
const c1 = new ConcreteImplementor1();
const abstraction = new Abstraction(c1);
abstraction.operation();
```

Output:

```
ConcreteImplementor1 operation
```

Explanation:

1. In the code, **Abstraction** is the abstract class, while **ConcreteAbstraction** is the concrete implementation of the abstraction. **Implementor** is the abstract class for the implementation classes, while **ConcreteImplementor1** and **ConcreteImplementor2** are concrete implementations of the interface.

2. The **ConcreteAbstraction** class contains a reference to an instance of **Implementor**, and it calls the **operation()** method of the implementor. The **ConcreteImplementor1** and **ConcreteImplementor2** classes implement the **Implementor** interface and provide different implementations of the **operation()** method.

3. In the client code, we create an instance of **ConcreteImplementor1** and pass it to an instance of **ConcreteAbstraction**, the **operation()** method of **ConcreteImplementor1** is called when the **operation()** method of **ConcreteAbstraction** is called. This allows the **ConcreteAbstraction** to use the implementation provided by **ConcreteImplementor1** without having to know the details of its implementation.

Problem: Implement the Bridge design pattern to create a decoupled structure for shapes (Rectangle and Circle) and their colours (Red, Green, and Blue). The objective is to allow shapes and colours to vary independently, making the system flexible and easy to extend without modifying existing code.

Solution:

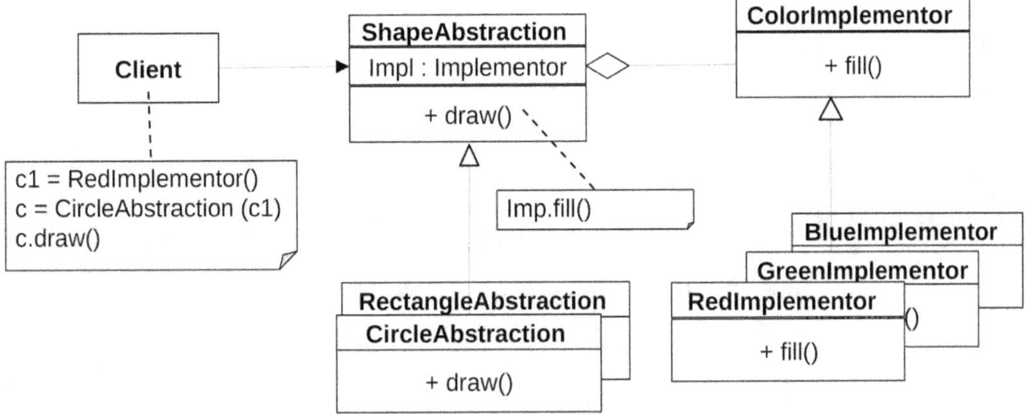

Here is an example implementation of the Bridge Pattern :

```javascript
// Abstraction abstract class
class Shape {
    constructor(imp) {
        this.imp = imp;
    }

    draw() {
        throw new Error('Method draw() must be implemented');
    }
}


// Rectangle class
class Rectangle extends Shape {
    constructor(imp) {
        super(imp);
    }

    draw() {
        console.log(`Drawing Rectangle with colour $
{this.imp.fill()}`);
    }
}
```

```javascript
// Circle class
class Circle extends Shape {
    constructor(imp) {
        super(imp);
    }

    draw() {
        console.log(`Drawing Circle with colour $
{this.imp.fill()}`);
    }
}

// Colour abstract class
class Colour {
    fill() {
        throw new Error('Method fill() must be implemented');
    }
}

// Red class
class Red extends Colour {
    fill() {
        return 'Red';
    }
}

// Green class
class Green extends Colour {
    fill() {
        return 'Green';
    }
}

// Blue class
class Blue extends Colour {
    fill() {
        return 'Blue';
    }
}

// Client code
const c1 = new Red();
let abstraction = new Circle(c1);
abstraction.draw();
```

```
const c2 = new Green();
abstraction = new Rectangle(c2);
abstraction.draw();
```

Output:

```
Drawing Circle with colour Red
Drawing Rectangle with colour Green
```

Explanation:

1. In the code example provided, the Abstraction layer is represented by the **Shape** abstract class, and its concrete subclasses **Rectangle** and **Circle**. The Implementation layer is represented by the **Colour** abstract class, and its concrete subclasses **Red**, **Green**, and **Blue**.

2. The **Shape** class has a reference to an instance of **Colour** implementor which is used to draw the shape. The draw() method is then implemented by the concrete **Rectangle** and **Circle** classes to draw the shape with the appropriate colour.

3. By separating the abstraction from its implementation, we can have multiple implementations of the same abstraction, and we can add new abstractions and implementations independently of each other. This allows for greater flexibility and maintainability in our code.

Consequence

The Bridge pattern has several consequences and advantages:

1. **Decoupling**: The primary advantage of the Bridge pattern is decoupling. It allows you to change the abstraction and implementation classes independently without affecting each other. This leads to a flexible and maintainable codebase.

2. **Flexibility**: Since the abstraction and implementation are decoupled, it becomes easier to add new variants of either without modifying the existing code.

3. **Improved Extensibility**: The Bridge pattern promotes extensibility. You can introduce new abstractions and implementations without modifying the existing codebase, making it easier to evolve the software over time.

4. **Reduced Complexity**: The Bridge pattern avoids the problem of a class explosion that can arise with traditional inheritance hierarchies. This results in a more manageable and cleaner codebase.

5. **Enhanced Testability**: By separating abstractions and implementations, it becomes easier to test each component in isolation, leading to better unit testing.

6. **Run-time Binding**: The Bridge pattern allows for dynamic binding of the abstraction and implementation at runtime, enabling you to switch implementations during the program's execution.

However, the Bridge pattern also comes with some trade-offs:

1. **Complexity of Initial Implementation**: Implementing the Bridge pattern may initially introduce some complexity due to the need for separate abstraction and implementation hierarchies.

2. **Increased Indirection**: The Bridge pattern adds an extra level of indirection, which may lead to a slight performance overhead.

3. **Increased Code Size**: Since the pattern involves creating additional abstraction and implementation classes, the codebase might increase in size.

SOLID principle applied

Here's how each SOLID principle can be applied to the Bridge pattern:

1. **Single Responsibility Principle (SRP)**: The Bridge pattern follows the SRP by separating the abstraction (interface) from its implementation (implementation classes). This way, each class has a single responsibility - the abstraction defines the interface, and the implementation classes provide the concrete implementation.

2. **Open-Closed Principle (OCP)**: The Bridge pattern follows the OCP by allowing the abstraction and implementation to vary independently. The client can use the abstraction and its methods, and new implementation classes can be added without modifying the abstraction or the client code.

3. **Liskov Substitution Principle (LSP)**: The Bridge pattern follows the LSP by ensuring that the implementation classes conform to the same interface as the abstraction. This means that any implementation class can be used interchangeably with the abstraction, without affecting the correctness of the program.

4. **Interface Segregation Principle (ISP):** The Bridge pattern follows the ISP by defining a separate interface for the abstraction and the

implementation. This way, the client only needs to know about the abstraction interface, and the implementation classes only need to implement the necessary methods of that interface.

5. **Dependency Inversion Principle (DIP):** The Bridge pattern follows the DIP by allowing the client to depend on the abstraction, rather than the implementation. This way, the client can easily switch between different implementations, without affecting the rest of the code.

Composite Pattern

The **Composite pattern** is a Structural design pattern that allows you to compose objects into tree-like structures and work with those structures as if they were individual objects. This pattern is used when you have a hierarchical structure of objects and you want to treat both the individual objects and the compositions of those objects uniformly.

Problem: When dealing with complex hierarchical structures made up of objects and groups of objects, it becomes challenging to treat individual objects and compositions of objects uniformly. The problem is that clients of these structures often need to interact with individual objects and collections of objects in the same way, without distinguishing between them.

Solution: The Composite Design Pattern is a Structural design pattern that addresses this problem by creating a unified interface for individual objects and composite objects (combinations of objects). It allows clients to treat both types of objects uniformly, making it easier to work with complex hierarchical structures.

The basic idea behind the Composite pattern is to create a tree-like structure of objects where each object can be either a composite or a leaf. Composites have a list of children (which can be either composites or leaves) and can delegate work to their children. Leaves do not have children and perform the actual work.

The Composite pattern allows you to treat composite and leaf nodes uniformly, which makes it easy to work with complex hierarchical structures. It also makes it easy to add new types of nodes to the structure without affecting the existing code.

The key components of the Composite pattern are:

1. **Component**: an abstract class or interface that defines the common methods for both composite and leaf nodes.

2. **Composite**: a class that represents a composite node and can have child components. It implements the methods defined in the Component interface by delegating the work to its child components.

3. **Leaf**: a class that represents a leaf node and cannot have child components. It implements the methods defined in the Component interface directly.

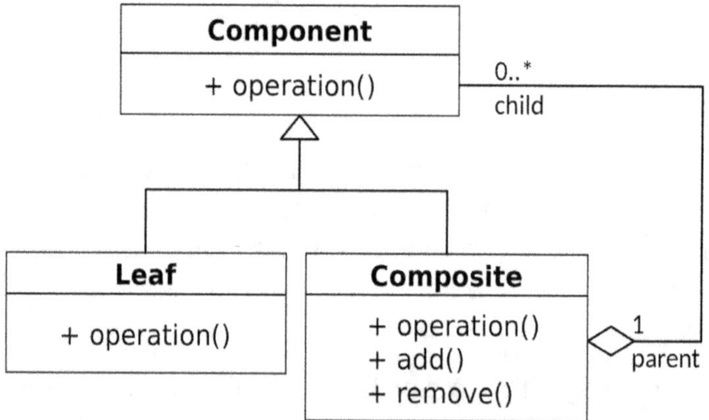

Here is an example implementation of the Composite Design Pattern :

```javascript
// Component
class Component {
    operation() {
        throw new Error("Abstract method: operation");
    }
}

// Composite
class Composite extends Component {
    constructor() {
        super();
        this.children = new Set();
    }

    operation() {
        console.log("Composite Operation");
        for (const child of this.children) {
            child.operation();
        }
    }

    add(component) {
        this.children.add(component);
    }
```

```
    remove(component) {
        this.children.delete(component);
    }
}

// Leaf
class Leaf extends Component {
    operation() {
        console.log("Leaf Operation");
    }
}

// Client code
const composite = new Composite();
composite.add(new Leaf());

const composite2 = new Composite();
composite2.add(new Leaf());

composite.add(composite2);
composite.operation();
```

Output:

```
Composite Operation.
Composite Operation.
Leaf Operation.
Leaf Operation.
```

Explanation:

1. This code that implements the Composite pattern, which allows for the creation of hierarchical structures of objects where each object can be treated uniformly as a Component, regardless of whether it's a composite or a leaf.

2. In this code, there are two classes: **Component** and **Composite**. **Component** is an abstract class that defines the interface for all components, whether they are leaves or composites. **Composite** is a class that represents the composite object in the structure, which can contain other components.

3. **Composite** has a set of children components and provides operations for adding and removing children. Composite also implements the **operation()** method, which performs an operation on all of its children.

4. There is also a **Leaf** class that represents the leaf object in the structure. Leaf implements the **operation()** method, which performs an operation specific to the leaf object.

5. The code creates a **Composite** object and adds a **Leaf** to it. Then it creates another **Composite** object, adds a **Leaf** to it, and adds the second composite to the first composite. Finally, it calls the **operation()** method on the first composite, which recursively calls the **operation()** method on all of its children, including the second composite and the Leaf object.

Problem: Implement a simple code of the Composite Design Pattern to manage geometric shapes (rectangles and circles) in a hierarchical manner. The problem is to create a unified interface for individual shapes (rectangles and circles) and collections of shapes (a group of shapes) so that clients can work with them uniformly without distinguishing between individual shapes and groups of shapes.

Solution:

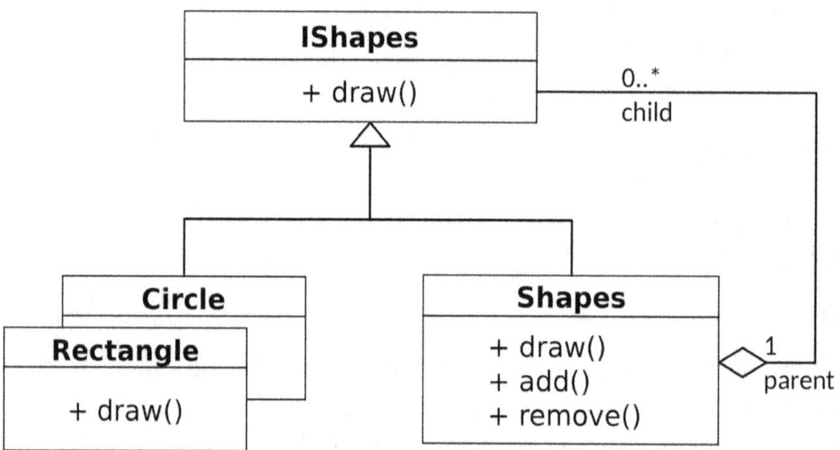

Here is an example implementation of the Composite Design Pattern :

```
// IShape interface
class IShape {
    move(x, y) {
        throw new Error("Abstract method: move");
    }

    draw() {
        throw new Error("Abstract method: draw");
    }
}
```

```javascript
// Rectangle class
class Rectangle extends IShape {
    constructor(x, y, length, breadth) {
        super();
        this.x = x;
        this.y = y;
        this.length = length;
        this.breadth = breadth;
    }

    move(x, y) {
        this.x += x;
        this.y += y;
    }

    draw() {
        console.log(`Draw a Rectangle at (${this.x},${this.y}).`);
        return "<Rectangle>";
    }
}

// Circle class
class Circle extends IShape {
    constructor(x, y, radius) {
        super();
        this.x = x;
        this.y = y;
        this.radius = radius;
    }

    move(x, y) {
        this.x += x;
        this.y += y;
    }

    draw() {
        console.log(`Draw a Circle of radius ${this.radius} at ($
{this.x}, ${this.y}).`);
        return "<Circle>";
    }
}

// CompoundShape class
class CompoundShape extends IShape {
    constructor() {
```

```javascript
        super();
        this.children = new Set();
    }

    add(child) {
        this.children.add(child);
    }

    remove(child) {
        this.children.delete(child);
    }

    move(x, y) {
        for (const child of this.children) {
            child.move(x, y);
        }
    }

    draw() {
        let st = "Shapes(";
        for (const child of this.children) {
            st += child.draw();
        }
        st += ")";
        return st;
    }
}

// Client code
const all = new CompoundShape();
all.add(new Rectangle(1, 2, 1, 2));
all.add(new Circle(5, 3, 10));
const group = new CompoundShape();
group.add(new Rectangle(5, 7, 1, 2));
group.add(new Circle(2, 1, 2));
all.add(group);
console.log(all.draw());
```

Output:

```
Draw a Circle of radius 10 at (5, 3).
Draw a Circle of radius 2 at (2, 1).
Draw a Rectangle at (5, 7).
Draw a Rectangle at (1, 2).
Shapes(<Circle>Shapes(<Circle><Rectangle>)<Rectangle>)
```

Explanation:

1. This code that implements the Composite Pattern, which allows the creation of complex objects by combining simpler objects into a tree-like structure.

2. In this code, there is an abstract class **Shapes** which declares the common methods that all shapes should have - **move()** and **draw()**. The **Rectangle** and **Circle** classes implement these methods with their specific implementation.

3. The **CompoundShape** class is the composite class which also implements the **move()** and **draw()** methods, but it also has the ability to add or remove child shapes. The **add()** and **remove()** methods are used to manage the children of a Shapes object.

4. Finally, an object of **CompoundShape** is created which contains two child shapes - a **Rectangle** and a **Circle**. Another **CompoundShape** object is created which contains a **Rectangle** and a **Circle**. This second **CompoundShape** object is added as a child to the first one. The **draw()** method is called on the root **Shapes** object which returns a string representation of the entire tree of shapes.

Consequence

The Composite design pattern offers several advantages and consequences:

1. **Uniformity:** The pattern provides a unified way of treating individual objects and compositions, simplifying client code and reducing the need for duplicated logic.

2. **Flexibility:** New types of components can be easily added to the existing structure without affecting the client code.

3. **Nested Structure:** You can create complex tree-like structures with components, allowing you to represent part-whole hierarchies effectively.

4. **Complexity:** While the pattern simplifies client code, it might increase the complexity of managing the hierarchy within the Composite objects.

5. **Performance:** Depending on the complexity of the hierarchy, traversing the composite structure may impact performance, especially if it is deep and contains many elements.

6. **Safety Concerns:** It may be necessary to add safeguards or additional checks to ensure that certain operations are supported only for specific types of components (e.g., attempting to add a child to a leaf node).

SOLID principle applied

Here's how each SOLID principle can be applied to the Composite pattern:

1. **Single Responsibility Principle (SRP):** The Composite pattern follows the SRP by separating the individual components of the composite object into separate classes. Each component has the responsibility of performing a specific task or providing specific functionality. This way, each component has a single responsibility.

2. **Open-Closed Principle (OCP):** The Composite pattern follows the OCP by allowing new components to be added without modifying the existing code. The client can interact with the composite object without knowing the specific types of its components.

3. **Liskov Substitution Principle (LSP):** The Composite pattern follows the LSP by ensuring that all components of the composite object adhere to the same interface or inheritance hierarchy. This means that the client can interact with the composite object and its components interchangeably, without affecting the correctness of the program.

4. **Interface Segregation Principle (ISP):** The Composite pattern follows the ISP by defining a separate interface for the composite object and its components. This way, the client only needs to know about the composite interface, and not the details of each individual component.

5. **Dependency Inversion Principle (DIP):** The Composite pattern follows the DIP by allowing the client to depend on the abstraction (the composite interface) rather than the implementation (the specific component classes). This way, the client can easily switch between different types of composite objects and components without affecting the rest of the code.

Decorator Pattern

The **Decorator design pattern** is a Structural design pattern that allows behaviour to be added to individual objects dynamically, without affecting other objects of the same class. It is used to extend the functionality of objects at runtime, providing a flexible alternative to subclassing for extending functionality.

Problem: The problem that the Decorator design pattern addresses is the need to add new responsibilities or behaviour to objects without modifying their code directly. In traditional object-oriented programming, this can be achieved through subclassing, but this approach has limitations:

1. **Class Explosion:** When using subclassing to add new functionality, a large number of subclasses can emerge, leading to a "class explosion" problem. For each new combination of features, a new subclass needs to be created.

2. **Rigid Class Hierarchy:** Subclassing leads to a rigid class hierarchy, making it difficult to combine different behaviours or features dynamically.

3. **Open-Closed Principle Violation:** Subclassing requires modifying the existing code, which violates the Open-Closed Principle, a fundamental principle in software design that states classes should be open for extension but closed for modification.

Solution: The Decorator design pattern solves the problem by introducing a set of decorator classes that wrap concrete components (objects) and add new functionality to them. The pattern uses composition rather than inheritance, allowing dynamic behaviour extension. The pattern involves creating a set of decorator classes that are used to wrap concrete components. Decorator classes mirror the interface of the components they decorate and add new behaviours or operations to them.

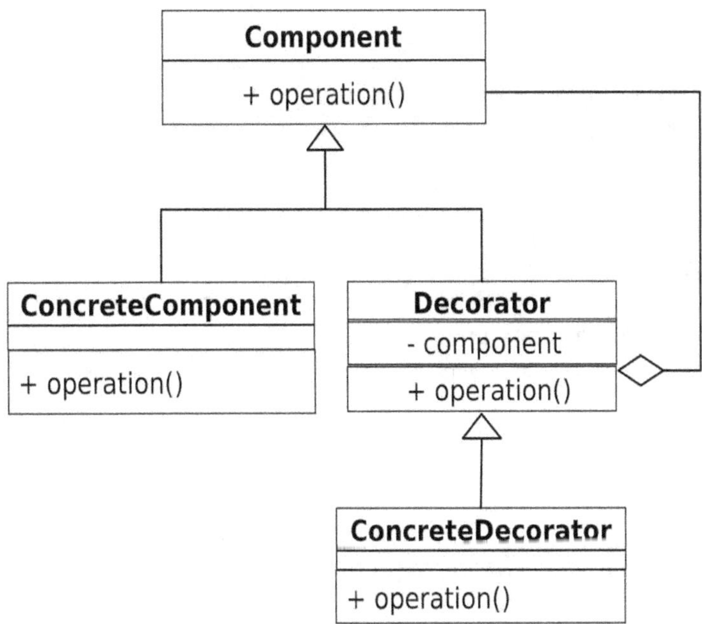

Here's an example implementation of the Decorator Pattern:

```
// Component interface
class Component {
    operation() {
        throw new Error("Abstract method: operation");
    }
}

// ConcreteComponent class
class ConcreteComponent extends Component {
    operation() {
        console.log("ConcreteComponent operation.");
    }
}

// Decorator class
class Decorator extends Component {
    constructor(component) {
        super();
        this.component = component;
    }

    operation() {
        this.component.operation();
    }
}

// ConcreteDecorator1 class
class ConcreteDecorator1 extends Decorator {
    constructor(component) {
        super(component);
    }

    operation() {
        console.log("ConcreteDecorator1 operation start.");
        super.operation();
        console.log("ConcreteDecorator1 operation end.");
    }
}

// ConcreteDecorator2 class
class ConcreteDecorator2 extends Decorator {
    constructor(component) {
        super(component);
    }
```

```
    operation() {
        console.log("ConcreteDecorator2 operation start.");
        super.operation();
        console.log("ConcreteDecorator2 operation end.");
    }
}

// Client code
const component = new ConcreteComponent();
const decorator1 = new ConcreteDecorator1(component);
const decorator2 = new ConcreteDecorator2(decorator1);
decorator2.operation();
```

Output:

```
ConcreteDecorator2 operation start.
ConcreteDecorator1 operation start.
ConcreteComponent operation.
ConcreteDecorator1 operation end.
ConcreteDecorator2 operation end.
```

Explanation:

1. This is an example of the Decorator pattern, where the **ConcreteComponent** class is the core component that performs the main operation. The **Decorator** abstract class provides the interface for adding functionality to the core component. The **ConcreteDecorator1** and **ConcreteDecorator2** classes are concrete decorators that add specific behaviour to the core component.

2. In the code, the **decorator2** object is created with **decorator1** object as its component. When **decorator2.operation()** is called, the **ConcreteDecorator2** class adds its own behaviour before and after calling the operation of **decorator1**. Similarly, **decorator1.operation()** adds its own behaviour before and after calling the operation of the core **component**. Finally, the **operation()** method of **ConcreteComponent** is called, which simply prints a message.

Problem: The problem is that the client needs to enhance the behaviour of a simple window object by adding vertical and horizontal scroll bars. However, directly modifying the SimpleWindow class would violate the Open/Closed Principle, which states that classes should be open for extension but closed for modification. The client wants to add scroll bars to the window without changing the existing code for the SimpleWindow class.

Solution: The solution is to use the Decorator Design Pattern. This pattern allows behaviour to be added to individual objects dynamically, without affecting other objects of the same class. It involves creating a set of decorator classes that wrap the original class (in this case, the SimpleWindow class) and provide additional functionality.

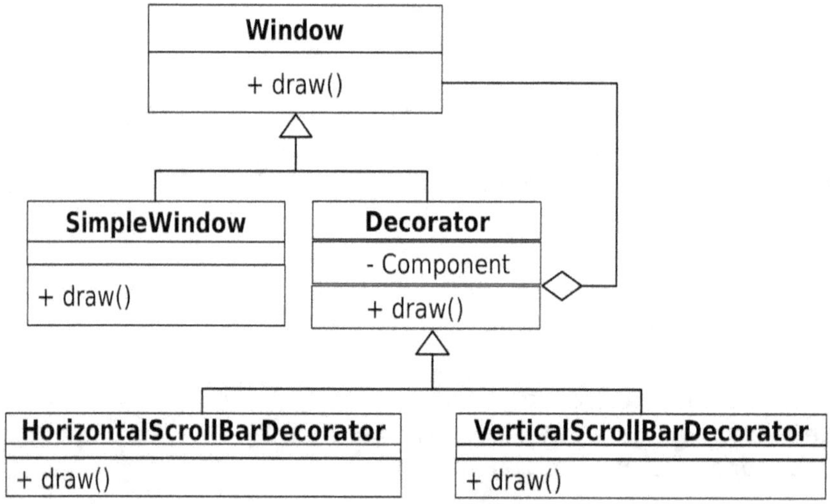

Here's an example implementation of the Decorator Pattern:

```javascript
// Window (Component)
class Window {
    draw() {
        throw new Error("Abstract method: draw");
    }
}

// SimpleWindow (ConcreteComponent)
class SimpleWindow extends Window {
    draw() {
        console.log("SimpleWindow draw.");
    }
}

// Decorator (Decorator)
class Decorator extends Window {
    constructor(component) {
        super();
        this.component = component;
    }

    draw() {
        this.component.draw();
```

```javascript
        }
}

// VerticalScrollBarDecorator (ConcreteDecorator)
class VerticalScrollBarDecorator extends Decorator {
    constructor(component) {
        super(component);
    }

    draw() {
        super.draw();
        console.log("VerticalScrollBarDecorator draw");
    }
}

// HorizontalScrollBarDecorator (ConcreteDecorator)
class HorizontalScrollBarDecorator extends Decorator {
    constructor(component) {
        super(component);
    }

    draw() {
        super.draw();
        console.log("HorizontalScrollBarDecorator draw");
    }
}

// Client code
const component = new SimpleWindow();
const decorator1 = new VerticalScrollBarDecorator(component);
const decorator2 = new HorizontalScrollBarDecorator(decorator1);
decorator2.draw();
```

Output:

```
SimpleWindow draw.
VerticalScrollBarDecorator draw
HorizontalScrollBarDecorator draw
```

Explanation:

1. **Window Interface**: Defines the interface for objects that can be decorated. In this case, it only contains a **draw()** method.

2. **SimpleWindow Class**: Implements the **Window** interface. It represents the basic window without any additional features.

3. **Decorator Abstract Class**: Implements the **Window** interface as well. It is an abstract class that serves as the base class for all decorators. It contains a reference to a **Window** object, which it decorates. It delegates the **draw()** method to the component it decorates.

4. **VerticalScrollBarDecorator** and **HorizontalScrollBarDecorator** Classes: Concrete decorators that add vertical and horizontal scroll bars, respectively, to the window. They extend the **Decorator** class and override the **draw()** method to add their specific behavior after calling the **draw()** method of the component they decorate.

5. **Client Code**: In the **DecoratorPatternWindow** class, the main method serves as the client code. It creates a **SimpleWindow** object and then wraps it with two decorators (**VerticalScrollBarDecorator** and **HorizontalScrollBarDecorator**). When the **draw()** method is called on the final decorator, it triggers a cascade of draw calls through the decorators, each adding its behavior to the drawing process.

Consequence

1. **Flexible Extension:** The Decorator pattern allows for flexible and dynamic extension of object behaviour. New decorators can be created to add new features or combinations of features without modifying existing code.

2. **Reduced Subclassing:** The pattern reduces the need for a large number of subclasses since the functionality can be achieved by combining different decorators.

3. **Open-Closed Principle Compliance:** The Decorator pattern adheres to the Open-Closed Principle, as it allows behaviour extension without modifying existing code.

4. **Complexity:** The pattern may introduce an increased number of small classes, which can lead to increased complexity in the codebase.

5. **Order of Wrapping:** The order in which decorators are applied can affect the final behaviour. Developers need to be cautious about the order of decorators to get the desired outcome.

6. **Performance Impact:** Depending on the complexity of decorators and the number of decorations applied, there might be a slight performance impact due to multiple levels of indirection.

SOLID principle applied

Here's how each SOLID principle can be applied to the Decorator pattern:

1. **Single Responsibility Principle (SRP):** The Decorator pattern follows the SRP by separating the responsibilities of the original object and the decorators into separate classes. Each decorator has a single responsibility, and the original object has its own responsibilities, resulting in a clear separation of concerns.

2. **Open-Closed Principle (OCP):** The Decorator pattern follows the OCP by allowing new behaviours to be added to the original object without modifying its source code. Instead, new decorators can be created and wrapped around the original object to add new functionality.

3. **Liskov Substitution Principle (LSP):** The Decorator pattern follows the LSP by ensuring that the decorators adhere to the same interface as the original object. This means that any decorator can be substituted for the original object, and vice versa, without affecting the correctness of the program.

4. **Interface Segregation Principle (ISP):** The Decorator pattern follows the ISP by defining separate interfaces for the original object and its decorators. This way, the original object only needs to expose the methods that it is responsible for, while the decorators only need to expose the methods that they add to the object.

5. **Dependency Inversion Principle (DIP):** The Decorator pattern follows the DIP by allowing the client to depend on the abstraction (the original object interface) rather than the concrete implementation (the specific object or decorator class). This means that the client can work with the original object or any of its decorators without knowing the details of their implementation.

Flyweight Pattern

The **Flyweight design pattern** is a Structural pattern used to optimise memory usage by sharing common data among multiple objects. It is particularly useful when dealing with a large number of similar objects that have some intrinsic (invariant) state and some extrinsic (context-dependent) state. By sharing the intrinsic state, the pattern reduces the memory footprint and improves performance.

Problem: The problem that the Flyweight pattern aims to address is the excessive memory usage and inefficiency caused by creating large numbers of similar objects, each with its own unique data. This is especially common in situations where objects have some shared characteristics and a significant portion of their state can be reused across multiple instances.

Solution: The solution involves creating a FlyweightFactory that manages a pool of shared flyweight objects. These objects are shared by multiple clients, and each object is designed to be immutable and stateless. This means that the object's properties cannot be changed once it has been created, which makes it safe for sharing. When a client requests a flyweight object, the factory class checks if an instance of that object already exists in the pool. If so, it returns the existing object. If not, it creates a new object, adds it to the pool, and returns it to the client.

By using the Flyweight pattern, an application can reduce memory usage and improve performance, especially in situations where a large number of objects are created and used repeatedly. However, it's important to note that the pattern may not be suitable for all situations, and careful consideration should be given to the specific requirements of the application before implementing it.

The Flyweight pattern proposes dividing an object's state into two parts:

1. **Intrinsic State:** Represents the data that is shared among multiple objects and remains constant throughout their lifetime.

2. **Extrinsic State:** Represents the data that is unique to each individual object and can vary depending on the context.

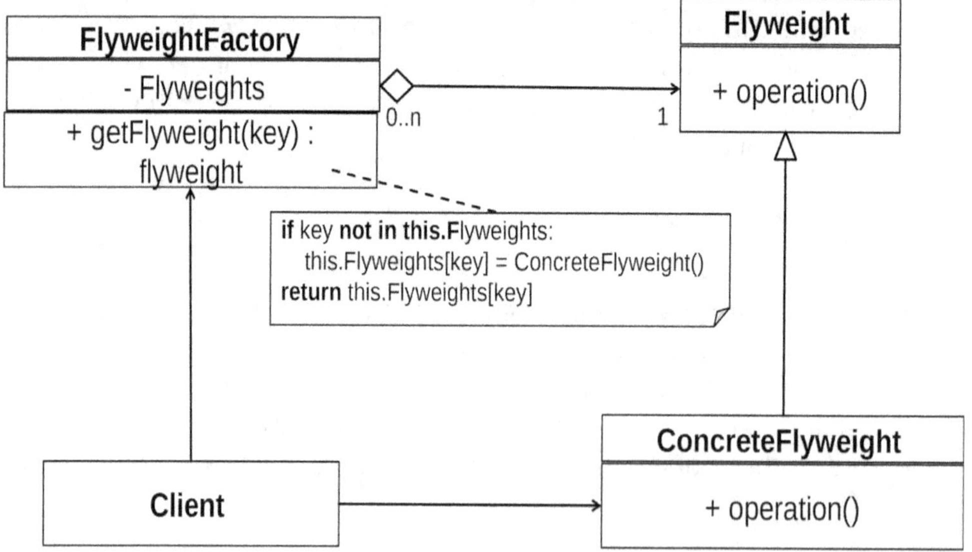

Here's an example implementation of the Flyweight Pattern:

```javascript
// Flyweight interface
class Flyweight {
    constructor(intrinsicState) {
        this.intrinsicState = intrinsicState;
    }

    // Common operation for all flyweight instances
    operation(extrinsicState) {
        console.log(`Operation inside concrete flyweight with
intrinsic state: ${this.intrinsicState}`);
    }
}

// FlyweightFactory class
class FlyweightFactory {
    constructor() {
        this.flyweights = new Map();
    }

    getFlyweight(key) {
        if (!this.flyweights.has(key)) {
            this.flyweights.set(key, new Flyweight(key));
            console.log(`Creating a new flyweight with key: $
{key}`);
        } else {
            console.log(`Reusing existing flyweight with key: $
{key}`);
        }
        return this.flyweights.get(key);
    }

    getCount() {
        return this.flyweights.size;
    }
}

// Client code
// Create a flyweight factory
const factory = new FlyweightFactory();

// Obtain flyweight instances
const flyweight1 = factory.getFlyweight("key");
const flyweight2 = factory.getFlyweight("key");
```

```
// Perform operations on flyweights
flyweight1.operation("fw1");

// Display flyweight instances and count
console.log(`Flyweight instances: ${flyweight1.intrinsicState}, $
{flyweight2.intrinsicState}`);
console.log("Object count: " + factory.getCount());
```

Output:

```
Operation inside concrete flyweight
ConcreteFlyweight@73d16e93 ConcreteFlyweight@73d16e93
Object count: 1
```

Explanation:

1. This is an example of code that implements the Flyweight pattern. The **Flyweight** class is defined as an abstract class with an abstract method **operation()**. The **ConcreteFlyweight** class is a subclass of **Flyweight** that provides the implementation for the **operation()** method.

2. The **FlyweightFactory** class acts as the flyweight factory, responsible for creating and managing flyweight objects. It maintains a dictionary **flyweights** to store the created flyweight objects. The **getFlyweight()** method retrieves the flyweight object corresponding to the given key. If the flyweight doesn't exist, it creates a new **ConcreteFlyweight** object and stores it in the dictionary before returning it.

3. In the client code, an instance of **FlyweightFactory** is created. Two flyweight objects (**flyweight1** and **flyweight2**) are obtained from the factory using the same key. The **operation()** method is called on **flyweight1**, which simply prints a message. The print statements display the memory addresses of **flyweight1** and **flyweight2** to demonstrate that they are referring to the same object. Finally, the **getCount()** method of the factory is called to display the number of flyweight objects currently stored in the factory's dictionary.

Problem: The problem is to create a program that generates random rectangles of different colours and different positions and draws them. The challenge is to efficiently manage the creation and reuse of rectangle objects with the same colour to minimise memory usage and optimise object creation.

Solution:

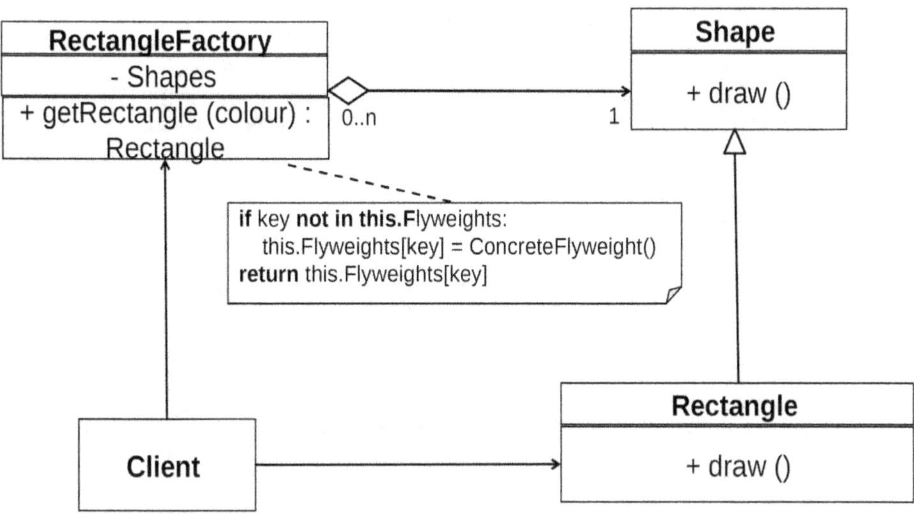

The code implementations the Flyweight Design Pattern:

```
// Shape interface
class Shape {
    draw(x1, y1, x2, y2) {
        //Common operation logic
    }
}


// ColouredShape class implementing Shape
class ColouredShape extends Shape {
    constructor(color) {
        super();
        this.color = color;
    }

    draw(x1, y1, x2, y2) {
        console.log(`Draw ColouredShape color: ${this.color},
topleft: (${x1},${y1}), rightBottom: (${x2},${y2})`);
    }
}


// ColouredShapeFactory class
class ColouredShapeFactory {
    constructor() {
        this.shapes = {};
    }
```

```javascript
    getColouredShape(color) {
        if (!this.shapes[color]) {
            this.shapes[color] = new ColouredShape(color);
            console.log("Creating a new ColouredShape with color:
" + color);
        } else {
            console.log("Reusing existing ColouredShape with
color: " + color);
        }
        return this.shapes[color];
    }

    getCount() {
        return Object.keys(this.shapes).length;
    }
}


// Client code
const factory = new ColouredShapeFactory();
const random = () => Math.floor(Math.random() * 100);


for (let i = 0; i < 100; i++) {
    // Generate a random color for the ColouredShape
    const randomColor = random().toString();

    // Obtain a ColouredShape with the specified color
    const ColouredShape = factory.getColouredShape(randomColor);

    // Generate random coordinates for drawing the ColouredShape
    const x1 = random();
    const y1 = random();
    const x2 = random();
    const y2 = random();
    // Draw the ColouredShape
    ColouredShape.draw(x1, y1, x2, y2);
}

// Display the total number of unique ColouredShapes created
console.log("Total unique ColouredShapes created: " +
factory.getCount());
```

Explanation:

1. **Shape** is an abstract class defining the common interface for shapes. It
   has an abstract method **draw()**, which will be implemented by concrete
   shape classes.

2. **Rectangle** is a concrete shape class that extends **Shape**. It implements the **draw()** method to print the details of the rectangle, including its colour and coordinates.

3. **RectangleFactory** is a flyweight factory responsible for managing and reusing instances of **Rectangle**. It maintains a dictionary **shapes** to store instances of rectangles based on their colours. When a request for a rectangle of a particular colour is made, the factory checks if an instance of that colour already exists. If it does, it returns the existing instance; otherwise, it creates a new one and stores it in the dictionary for future reuse.

4. The client code creates an instance of **RectangleFactory** and then generates 1000 random rectangles using a loop. For each rectangle, a random colour and random coordinates are generated. The factory is used to get the appropriate rectangle instance based on the colour, and the **draw()** method is called to display the rectangle's details.

Consequence

The Flyweight pattern provides several benefits and consequences:

1. **Memory Efficiency:** By sharing the intrinsic state among multiple objects, the pattern reduces the memory footprint and makes the application more memory-efficient.

2. **Performance Improvement:** Since shared flyweight objects are reused, object creation and initialization are minimised, leading to improved performance, especially when dealing with a large number of objects.

3. **Trade-off with Processing Time:** While the Flyweight pattern reduces memory usage, it can potentially increase processing time. Accessing and managing shared flyweight objects might introduce some additional overhead. However, this trade-off is usually worthwhile when memory optimization is a crucial concern.

4. **Thread Safety Consideration:** Care must be taken to ensure thread safety, especially in a multithreaded environment. If multiple threads access and modify the same flyweight object, proper Synchronisation mechanisms need to be implemented to prevent data corruption.

5. **Immaturity Data Modification:** As flyweight objects are shared among multiple clients, any modification to the intrinsic state affects all the

objects using that state. Thus, flyweight objects should be immutable or carefully managed to prevent unintended side effects.

SOLID principle applied

Here's how each SOLID principle can be applied to the Flyweight pattern:

1. **Single Responsibility Principle (SRP):** The Flyweight pattern follows the SRP by separating intrinsic state (shared state) from extrinsic state (unique state) of objects. The intrinsic state is managed by a flyweight factory, while the extrinsic state is managed by the client. This separation of responsibilities allows for more efficient use of memory and faster object creation.

2. **Open-Closed Principle (OCP):** The Flyweight pattern follows the OCP by allowing new flyweight objects to be added without modifying the existing code. The flyweight factory can be extended to create new flyweight objects without affecting the client code that uses them.

3. **Liskov Substitution Principle (LSP):** The Flyweight pattern follows the LSP by ensuring that all flyweight objects adhere to the same interface, which defines the intrinsic state. This means that any flyweight object can be substituted for another flyweight object without affecting the correctness of the program.

4. **Interface Segregation Principle (ISP):** The Flyweight pattern follows the ISP by defining a clear interface for flyweight objects that only includes methods related to intrinsic state. This way, the client only needs to know about the flyweight interface, and not the details of each individual flyweight object.

5. **Dependency Inversion Principle (DIP):** The Flyweight pattern follows the DIP by allowing the client to depend on the abstraction (the flyweight interface) rather than the implementation (the specific flyweight class). This way, the client can easily switch between different flyweight objects without affecting the rest of the code.

Facade Pattern

The **Facade design pattern** is a Structural design pattern that provides a simplified interface to a complex system, making it easier to interact with and use. It is used to hide the complexities of a subsystem and present a unified and simplified interface to the client code. In the Facade pattern, a single class acts as a simple interface for a group of classes, and the client uses this interface to access the functionality of the group of classes. The Facade class simplifies the interface and reduces the complexity of the system, making it easier to use.

Problem: In software development, complex systems can often consist of many interdependent classes and subsystems. When clients interact directly with these subsystems, it can lead to tight coupling, increased complexity, and difficulty in understanding and maintaining the codebase. Changes in the subsystems' implementation can also have a ripple effect on the client code, making it hard to adapt to changes.

Solution: The Facade design pattern introduces a new class called the "Facade" that serves as an entry point to the subsystems. The Facade class provides a simple, high-level interface that shields the client from the underlying complexities of the subsystems. It encapsulates the interactions with the subsystems and provides a unified interface that clients can easily work with.

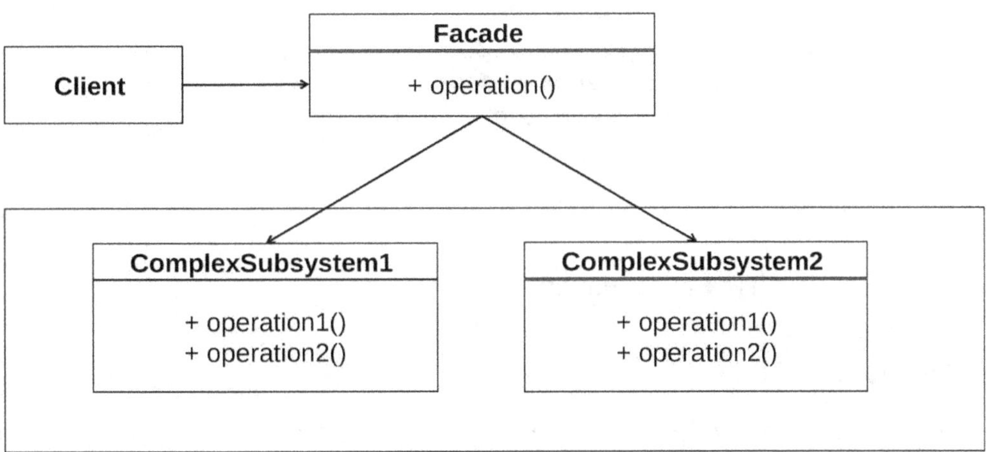

Here is an example implementation of the Facade pattern :

```javascript
// Subsystem1
class Subsystem1 {
    operation1() {
        console.log("Subsystem1 operation1");
    }

    operation2() {
        console.log("Subsystem1 operation2");
    }
}
```

```javascript
// Subsystem2
class Subsystem2 {
    operation1() {
        console.log("Subsystem2 operation1");
    }

    operation2() {
        console.log("Subsystem2 operation2");
    }
}

// SystemManagerFacade
class SystemManagerFacade {
    constructor() {
        this.subsystem1 = new Subsystem1();
        this.subsystem2 = new Subsystem2();
    }

    operation() {
        this.subsystem1.operation1();
        this.subsystem1.operation2();
        this.subsystem2.operation1();
        this.subsystem2.operation2();
    }
}

// Client code
const facade = new SystemManagerFacade();
facade.operation();
```

Explanation:

1. **Subsystem1** and **Subsystem2**: These are two classes representing two complex subsystems. Each subsystem has two operations (**operation1** and **operation2**).

2. **SystemManagerFacade**: This class serves as the facade. It creates instances of **Subsystem1** and **Subsystem2** in its constructor. The **operation()** method acts as the simplified interface that clients can use to interact with the subsystems.

3. **operation()**: This method is the simplified interface provided by the facade. When called, it internally calls the relevant methods of **Subsystem1** and **Subsystem2** in a coordinated manner to execute the required functionality.

4. **Client code**: The client code creates an instance of `SystemManagerFacade` (the facade), and it interacts with the subsystems using the `operation()` method. The client is unaware of the complexity of interactions between `Subsystem1` and `Subsystem2`.

Consequences

1. **Simplified Interface:** Facade pattern provides a straightforward and easy-to-understand interface to the client, hiding the complexities of the subsystems. This makes it easier for clients to use the system without needing to understand the intricate details of how it works.

2. **Decoupling:** By introducing a facade layer, the client code is decoupled from the internal subsystems. This reduces dependencies and allows for more flexible and independent development of both the client and subsystems.

3. **Code organisation:** The pattern improves code organisation by segregating the complex subsystem code into a separate facade class. This promotes a clear separation of concerns and makes the codebase more maintainable.

4. **Encapsulation:** The facade class encapsulates the interactions with the subsystems, providing a controlled and consistent interface. Changes to the subsystems can be confined within the facade, minimising the impact on client code.

5. **Reduced Learning Curve:** Developers who work with the facade do not need to understand the complexities of the entire system. This reduces the learning curve for new team members and allows them to focus on their specific tasks.

6. **Trade-offs:** While the Facade pattern simplifies the usage of a complex system, it may hide certain advanced functionalities of the subsystems. Developers should strike a balance between simplicity and exposing enough capabilities for specialised use cases.

SOLID principle applied

Here's how each SOLID principle can be applied to the Facade pattern:

1. **Single Responsibility Principle (SRP)**: The Facade pattern follows the SRP by providing a simplified interface to a complex subsystem. The

facade class has the responsibility of hiding the complexity of the subsystem and providing a single point of contact for the client.

2. **Open-Closed Principle (OCP):** The Facade pattern follows the OCP by allowing new functionality to be added to the subsystem without affecting the facade class or the client code. The facade class only needs to be updated if the interface to the subsystem changes.

3. **Interface Segregation Principle (ISP):** The Facade pattern follows the ISP by defining a separate interface for the subsystem and a separate interface for the facade. The client code only needs to know about the facade interface, which simplifies the overall design.

4. **Dependency Inversion Principle (DIP):** The Facade pattern follows the DIP by allowing the client code to depend on the abstraction (the facade interface) rather than the implementation (the subsystem classes). This way, the client code is decoupled from the implementation details of the subsystem, which makes it easier to modify and maintain.

Proxy Pattern

The **Proxy design pattern** is a Structural design pattern that provides a surrogate or placeholder for another object to control its access. It allows you to add an extra layer of indirection to an object, enabling you to control and manage access to the real object. This pattern is especially useful when you want to add additional functionalities or control access to an object without modifying its core logic.

The Proxy pattern is useful in situations where creating and initialising the real object is expensive, or where the real object needs to be protected from unauthorised access or manipulation. By using a Proxy object, the client code can access the real object indirectly, without needing to create or initialise it directly.

Problem: The Proxy pattern addresses several common scenarios and problems:

1. **Access Control:** You need to control access to an object, either to restrict certain clients from accessing it or to add authentication and authorization mechanisms.

2. **Lazy Initialization:** You want to delay the creation or loading of a resource-intensive object until it is actually needed, improving performance and resource usage.

3. **Remote Proxy:** When dealing with distributed systems or remote services, you may want to represent an object that exists in a different address space.

4. **Logging and Auditing:** You might need to log method calls and access patterns to an object for debugging or auditing purposes.

Solution: The Proxy pattern introduces a new class, the **Proxy**, which acts as an intermediary between the client and the real subject (the object being proxied). The Proxy implements the same interface as the real subject, so clients can interact with it seamlessly without knowing whether they are dealing with the real subject or the proxy.

The Proxy may perform additional operations before or after forwarding the request to the real subject. Depending on the use case, different types of proxies can be implemented:

1. **Virtual Proxy:** Lazy loads the real subject only when it is required, avoiding the unnecessary creation of heavyweight objects until necessary.

2. **Remote Proxy:** Acts as a representative for a real subject residing in a different address space, like in a remote server.

3. **Protection Proxy:** Controls access to the real subject by adding authentication and authorization checks before forwarding the request.

4. **Logging Proxy:** Records method invocations and other relevant information for logging or auditing purposes.

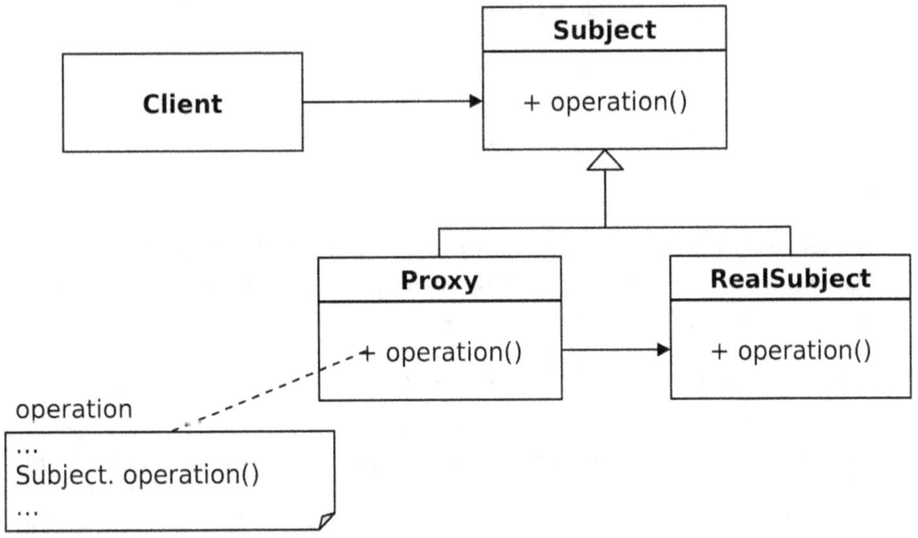

Here is an example implementation of the Proxy pattern :

```javascript
// Interface
class Subject {
    request() {
        throw new Error('request method must be implemented');
    }
}

// RealSubject class
class RealSubject extends Subject {
    request() {
        console.log("Concrete Subject Request Method");
    }
}

// Proxy class
class Proxy extends Subject {
    constructor() {
        super();
        this.realSubject = new RealSubject();
    }

    request() {
        this.realSubject.request();
    }
}

// Client code
const proxy = new Proxy();
proxy.request();
```

Output:

Concrete Subject Request Method

Explanation:

1. In this example, the **RealSubject** class represents the real object that the client code wants to access. The **Proxy** class is the surrogate object that controls access to the **RealSubject** object.

2. When the **Proxy** object is created then the **Proxy** object creates and initialises the **RealSubject** object. Then, the **Proxy** object handles the request itself, and delegates the actual work to the **RealSubject** object.

3. The Client code creates a **Proxy** object and calls its **request()** method. The **Proxy** object controls access to the **RealSubject** object, and the

client code does not need to create or initialise the **RealSubject** object directly.

Problem : Implement the Proxy design pattern with lazy initialization. The problem it addresses is how to create a Proxy that acts as an intermediary for the RealSubject. The Proxy should control access to the RealSubject and ensure that the RealSubject is instantiated only when needed (lazy initialization).

Solution: Here is an lazy initialization implementation of the Proxy pattern

```
// Interface
class Subject {
    request() {
        throw new Error('request method must be implemented');
    }
}


// RealSubject class
class RealSubject extends Subject {
    request() {
        console.log("Concrete Subject Request Method");
    }
}


// Proxy class
class Proxy extends Subject {
    constructor() {
        super();
        this.realSubject = null;
    }

    request() {
        if (!this.realSubject) {
            this.realSubject = new RealSubject(); // Lazy
Initialization
        }
        this.realSubject.request();
    }
}

// Client code
const proxy = new Proxy();
proxy.request();
```

Explanation:

1. The Proxy pattern is used to provide a surrogate or placeholder for an object to control access to it. In the example provided, we have an abstract **Subject** class with a **request()** method, a **RealSubject** class that implements the **request()** method, and a **Proxy** class that acts as a surrogate for **RealSubject**.

2. In the first example, the **Proxy** class has a reference to a **RealSubject** instance that is created when the **Proxy** instance is created. This is called "eager initialization" because the **RealSubject** instance is created right away, whether it is needed or not.

3. In this example, the **Proxy** class has a reference to a **RealSubject** instance that is created only when the **request()** method of the **Proxy** class is called for the first time. This is called "lazy initialization" because the **RealSubject** instance is created only when it is needed.

4. Lazy initialization is useful when creating the **RealSubject** object is expensive or time-consuming, or when it is uncertain whether the **RealSubject** object will be needed at all. By delaying the creation of the **RealSubject** object until it is actually needed, we can improve the performance of our program and reduce unnecessary resource usage.

Problem : The problem is to implement a Proxy design pattern to create a **LazyBookParserProxy**, which acts as a surrogate or placeholder for a **ConcreteBookParser**. The **ConcreteBookParser** is a heavy object that calculates the number of pages in a book. The goal is to delay the instantiation and initialization of the **ConcreteBookParser** until the number of pages is actually requested, to improve performance and resource usage.

Solution: The solution involves creating a `LazyBookParserProxy` class that implements the same `BookParser` interface. This proxy class acts as a placeholder for the real `ConcreteBookParser` object. The actual `ConcreteBookParser` object is only created (and the heavy calculation performed) when the client explicitly requests the number of pages. Until then, the proxy defers the creation.

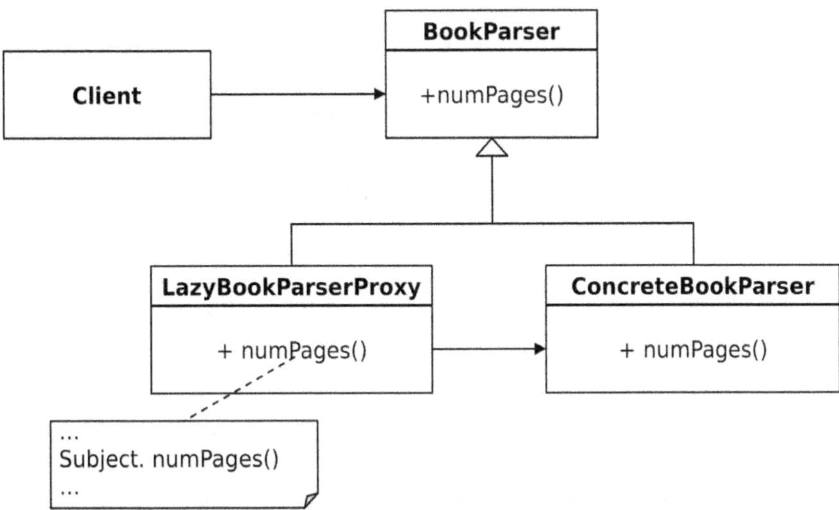

Here is an lazy initialization implementation of the Proxy pattern :

```javascript
// Interface
class BookParser {
    numPages() {
        throw new Error('numPages method must be implemented');
    }
}

// ConcreteBookParser class
class ConcreteBookParser extends BookParser {
    constructor() {
        super();
        console.log("Concrete Book Parser Created");
        // Number of pages calculation heavy operation.
        // Suppose this calculation results in 1000 pages.
        this.numPagesValue = 1000;
    }

    numPages() {
        console.log("Concrete Book Parser Request Method");
        return this.numPagesValue;
    }
}

// LazyBookParserProxy class
class LazyBookParserProxy extends BookParser {
    constructor() {
        super();
        this.subject = null;
    }
```

```
    numPages() {
        if (!this.subject) {
            this.subject = new ConcreteBookParser();
        }
        return this.subject.numPages();
    }
}

// Client code
const proxy = new LazyBookParserProxy();
console.log(proxy.numPages());
```

Explanation:

1. The code is an implementation of the Proxy design pattern, where the **LazyBookParserProxy** acts as a proxy for the **ConcreteBookParser**. The **ConcreteBookParser** is a heavy object that takes time to instantiate and is only created when needed. The **LazyBookParserProxy** is a lightweight object that is used to access the **ConcreteBookParser**.

2. The **BookParser** is an abstract class that defines the interface for the **ConcreteBookParser** and the **LazyBookParserProxy**. The **ConcreteBookParser** implements the **BookParser** interface and performs the heavy task of calculating the number of pages in a book. The **LazyBookParserProxy** also implements the **BookParser** interface and acts as a proxy for the **ConcreteBookParser**. It creates the **ConcreteBookParser** object only when the **numPages()** method is called for the first time.

3. The client code creates an instance of the **LazyBookParserProxy** and calls the **numPages()** method. The **LazyBookParserProxy** object creates an instance of the **ConcreteBookParser** object when the **numPages()** method is called for the first time, and then returns the number of pages in the book.

Consequence

The Proxy pattern offers several benefits and consequences:

1. **Security Enhancement:** With the help of a Protection Proxy, you can implement access controls, adding an additional layer of security to the real subject.

2. **Performance Optimization:** By using a Virtual Proxy, you can defer the creation or initialization of the real subject until it is actually needed, improving performance and resource utilisation.

3. **Abstraction of Remote Resources:** Remote Proxies allow you to hide the complexity of dealing with remote resources, making it appear as if the resource is local.

4. **Flexibility:** The Proxy pattern allows you to modify or extend the behaviour of the real subject without altering its core implementation, promoting a separation of concerns and code reusability.

5. **Resource Management:** Proxies can help in managing shared resources, controlling their usage and avoiding excessive allocation.

SOLID principle applied

Here's how each SOLID principle can be applied to the Proxy pattern:

1. **Single Responsibility Principle (SRP)**: The Proxy pattern follows the SRP by separating the proxy object from the real object, so that the proxy can handle additional responsibilities such as caching, security, and logging without affecting the real object.

2. **Open-Closed Principle (OCP):** The Proxy pattern follows the OCP by allowing the real object to be modified without affecting the code that uses the proxy. The proxy provides a consistent interface to the client, regardless of changes to the real object.

3. **Liskov Substitution Principle (LSP):** The Proxy pattern follows the LSP by ensuring that the proxy and the real object implement the same interface. This allows the proxy to be used interchangeably with the real object, without affecting the correctness of the program.

4. **Interface Segregation Principle (ISP):** The Proxy pattern follows the ISP by defining a separate interface for the proxy, with methods that mimic the real object's interface. This way, the client only needs to know about the proxy interface, and not the details of the real object.

5. **Dependency Inversion Principle (DIP):** The Proxy pattern follows the DIP by allowing the client to depend on the abstraction (the proxy interface) rather than the implementation (the real object). This way, the client can interact with the proxy object without knowing anything about the real object, which can be loaded lazily or remotely.

BEHAVIOURAL PATTERNS

Behavioural design patterns are a category of design patterns that focus on the interaction and collaboration between objects to define the behaviour and communication flow within a software system. These patterns help manage the responsibilities and interactions of objects, making the system more flexible and dynamic.

We will start by exploring the **Chain of Responsibility Pattern**, which creates a chain of handler objects that sequentially attempt to handle a request. If one handler cannot handle the request, it passes the request to the next handler in the chain. This pattern decouples sender and receiver, allowing multiple objects to potentially process the request.

Next, the **Command Pattern**, which encapsulates commands as objects, enabling their execution, undoing, and queuing. This design decouple sender and receiver, and it can be useful for implementing undo functionality.

Further, we explore the **Interpreter Pattern**, which provides a way to evaluate language grammar or expressions. It involves defining a grammar representation for a language and providing an interpreter that parses and evaluates expressions in that language.

The **Iterator Pattern**, which provides a way to access elements of a collection sequentially without exposing the underlying representation. It decouples the traversal algorithm from the collection, making the code more flexible and reusable.

Moving forward, the **Mediator Pattern**, which defines an object that controls communication between a set of objects (colleagues). Instead of direct communication between colleagues, they communicate through the mediator, which promotes loose coupling and centralises control.

Then, the **Memento Pattern** which captures and externalises an object's internal state so that it can be restored to that state later. This pattern is useful for implementing undo functionality or maintaining a history of changes.

The **Observer Pattern** which defines a dependency between objects so that when one object changes state, all its dependents are notified and updated automatically. This pattern promotes loose coupling and enhances maintainability.

Then the **State Pattern**, which allows an object to change its behaviour when its internal state changes. It involves defining a set of state classes, each representing a different behaviour, and allowing the object to transition between states.

Next, the **Strategy Pattern**, which defines a family of algorithms, encapsulates each algorithm, and makes them interchangeable. This pattern allows clients to choose an algorithm from the available set without altering the client's structure.

Then the **Template Method Pattern**, which defines the structure of an algorithm in a superclass but allows subclasses to override specific steps of the algorithm. It promotes code reuse and provides a framework for implementing similar algorithms with varying details.

Finally, the **Visitor Pattern**, which separates the operations on an object structure from the objects themselves. It involves defining visitor classes that encapsulate operations, and objects accept these visitors to perform operations without modifying their own structure.

Chain of Responsibility Pattern

The **Chain of Responsibility pattern** is a Behavioural design pattern that allows a set of objects to handle a request or message in a chain-like fashion. Each object in the chain has the ability to handle the request or pass it along to the next object in the chain.

Problem: The Chain of Responsibility design pattern addresses the issue of coupling the sender of a request to its receiver, where there may be multiple potential receivers for the request, but the sender should not know which receiver will handle the request. This leads to a rigid and inflexible design, making it difficult to add or remove new handlers without modifying the sender's code. The problem arises when a request must be processed by multiple objects, but the specific handler is not known at compile-time.

Solution: The Chain of Responsibility design pattern promotes a decoupled and flexible solution to the above problem. It allows multiple objects to have the chance to handle a request without the sender needing to know the exact receiver.

The pattern creates a chain of handler objects, where each handler has a reference to the next handler in the chain. When a request is made, it is passed through the chain until a handler can process it. The request is either handled by one of the handlers or passes through the entire chain if no handler can process it.

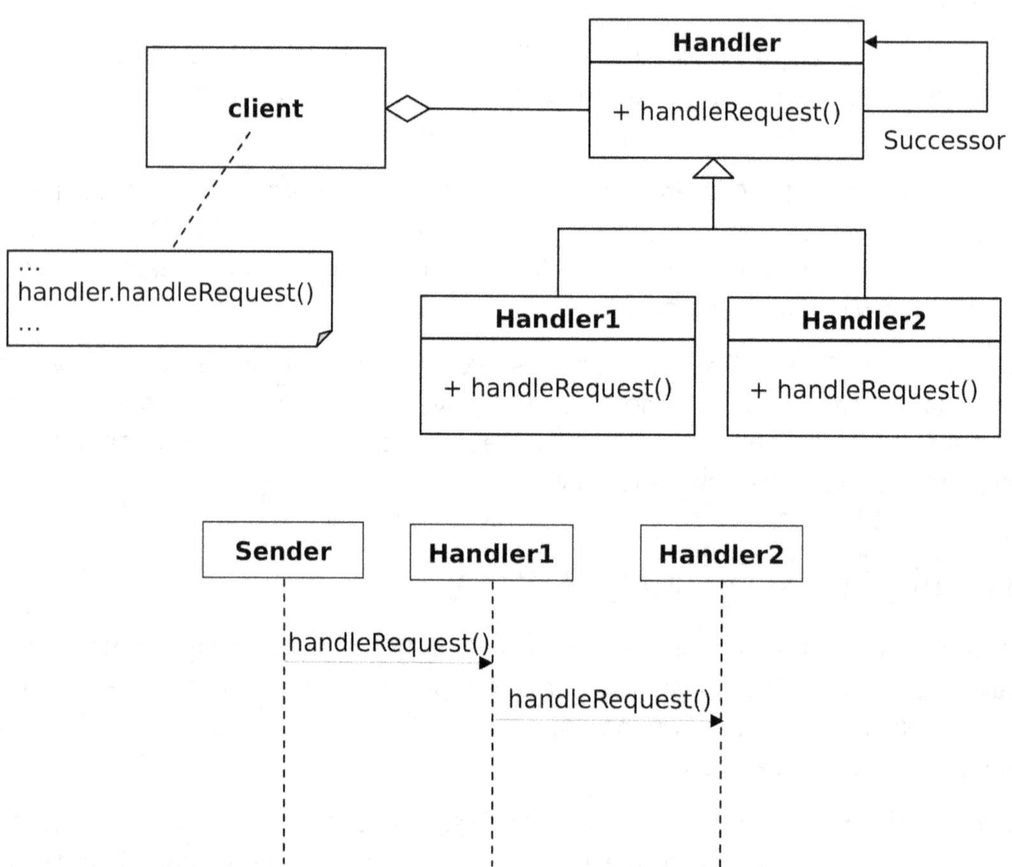

Here's an example implementation of the Chain of Responsibility pattern :

```
// Handler abstract class
class Handler {
    constructor(successor) {
        this.successor = successor;
    }

    handleRequest(request) {
        throw new Error('Method handleRequest() must be
implemented');
    }
}
```

```javascript
// ConcreteHandler1 class
class ConcreteHandler1 extends Handler {
    constructor(successor) {
        super(successor);
    }

    handleRequest(request) {
        if (request === "request1") {
            console.log("ConcreteHandler1 handles the
request1.");
        } else if (this.successor !== null) {
            this.successor.handleRequest(request);
        }
    }
}

// ConcreteHandler2 class
class ConcreteHandler2 extends Handler {
    constructor(successor) {
        super(successor);
    }

    handleRequest(request) {
        if (request === "request2") {
            console.log("ConcreteHandler2 handles the
request2.");
        } else if (this.successor !== null) {
            this.successor.handleRequest(request);
        }
    }
}

// ConcreteHandler3 class
class ConcreteHandler3 extends Handler {
    constructor(successor) {
        super(successor);
    }

    handleRequest(request) {
        if (request === "request3") {
            console.log("ConcreteHandler3 handles the
request3.");
        } else if (this.successor !== null) {
            this.successor.handleRequest(request);
        }
    }
```

```
}

// Client code
const ch1 = new ConcreteHandler1(null);
const ch2 = new ConcreteHandler2(ch1);
const ch3 = new ConcreteHandler3(ch2);

ch3.handleRequest("request1");
ch3.handleRequest("request2");
ch3.handleRequest("request3");
ch3.handleRequest("request4");
```

Output:

```
ConcreteHandler1 handles the request1.
ConcreteHandler2 handles the request2.
ConcreteHandler3 handles the request3.
```

Explanation:

1. The **Handler** class is an abstract class that defines the interface for handling requests. It has a reference to the next Handler object in the chain. The concrete **Handler** classes (**ConcreteHandler1**, **ConcreteHandler2**, and **ConcreteHandler3**) implement the **handleRequest()** method and check if they can handle the request. If they can't, they pass the request on to the next Handler in the chain.

2. In the client code, we create instances of the concrete **Handler** classes and chain them together by passing a reference to the next Handler in the constructor. We then call the **handleRequest()** method on the first Handler in the chain (ch3), passing in different requests. The **handleRequest()** method is responsible for determining if it can handle the request or if it needs to pass the request on to the next Handler in the chain.

3. The first three requests are handled by **ConcreteHandler1**, **ConcreteHandler2**, and **ConcreteHandler3**, respectively. The fourth request is not handled by any of the Handler objects in the chain, so it is ignored.

Problem: Implements the Chain of Responsibility design pattern for an ATM cash withdrawal scenario. It aims to handle a withdrawal request and dispense the amount using a combination of different denominations (e.g., 1000, 100, 50,

10) based on the availability of each denomination. The goal is to ensure the minimal number of notes is used to fulfil the withdrawal request.

Solution:

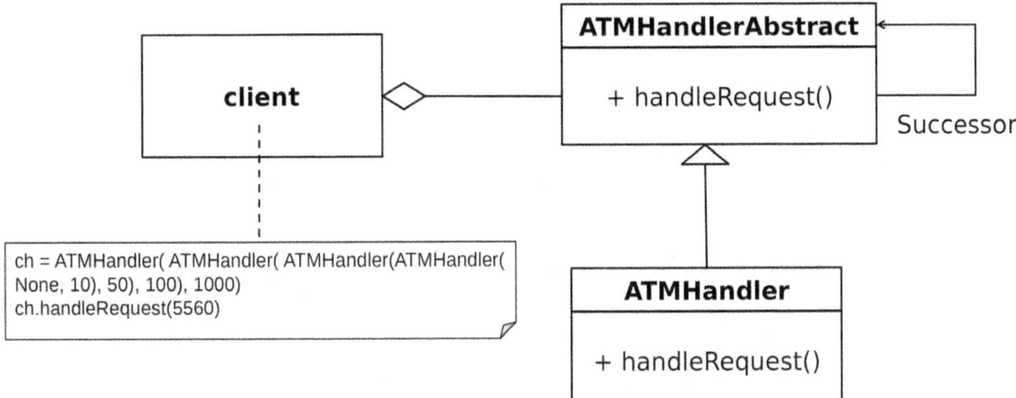

Here's an example implementation of the Chain of Responsibility pattern :

```javascript
class ATMHandlerAbstract {
    constructor(successor, denomination) {
        this.successor = successor;
        this.denomination = denomination;
    }

    handleRequest(amount) {
        throw new Error("Abstract method: handleRequest");
    }
}

class ATMHandler extends ATMHandlerAbstract {
    constructor(successor, denomination) {
        super(successor, denomination);
    }

    handleRequest(amount) {
        const q = Math.floor(amount / this.denomination);
        const r = amount % this.denomination;

        if (q !== 0) {
            console.log(`${q} notes of ${this.denomination}`);
        }

        if (r !== 0 && this.successor !== null) {
            this.successor.handleRequest(r);
        }
```

```
        }
}

// Client code
const handler = new ATMHandler(
    new ATMHandler(
        new ATMHandler(
            new ATMHandler(null, 10), 50
        ), 100
    ), 1000
);

handler.handleRequest(5560);
```

Output:

```
5 notes of 1000
5 notes of 100
1 notes of 50
1 notes of 10
```

Explanation:

1. **ATMHandlerAbstract**: This is an abstract class defining the interface for the handler. It has an abstract method **handleRequest()** that all concrete handler classes must implement. The constructor takes two parameters: **successor**, which holds the next handler in the chain, and **denomination**, which stores the denomination of the current handler.

2. **ATMHandler**: This class extends **ATMHandlerAbstract** and provides the concrete implementation for handling the withdrawal request based on the provided denomination. It overrides the **handleRequest()** method to process the request.

3. **handleRequest** (ATMHandler): In this method, the amount passed as a parameter is processed to determine the number of notes of the current denomination that can be dispensed. It then calculates the remaining amount that still needs to be processed. If there is a remaining amount and a successor handler exists, the remaining amount is passed to the successor for further processing.

4. Client Code: In the client code, a chain of responsibility is created, starting from the highest denomination (1000) and going down to the lowest (10). The **ATMHandler** objects are linked together using the **successor** parameter in the constructor.

5. `handler.handleRequest(5560)`: The client code calls the **handleRequest()** method on the chain's first element (`handler`), passing the withdrawal amount (5560). The chain then processes the amount and calculates the number of notes needed for each denomination to fulfil the withdrawal request.

Consequence

The Chain of Responsibility pattern offers several benefits and consequences:

1. **Decoupling:** The pattern decouples the sender of a request from its receivers, allowing different handlers to be added, modified, or removed without affecting the client code that sends the request.

2. **Flexibility:** The pattern allows dynamic addition or removal of handlers, providing flexibility in handling different types of requests and varying request chains.

3. **Reduce Coupling:** By removing explicit dependencies between the sender and receiver, it reduces tight coupling and makes the code more maintainable and adaptable.

4. **Fallback Mechanism:** If none of the handlers in the chain can handle the request, there should be a default fallback mechanism to handle such cases.

SOLID principle applied

Here's how each SOLID principle can be applied to the Chain of Responsibility pattern:

1. **Single Responsibility Principle (SRP):** The Chain of Responsibility pattern follows the SRP by separating the different processing steps into separate handler classes, each with a single responsibility. Each handler class has a specific task that it can perform and passes the request to the next handler in the chain if it cannot handle the request.

2. **Open-Closed Principle (OCP):** The Chain of Responsibility pattern follows the OCP by allowing new handlers to be added to the chain without modifying the existing code. The client can send requests to the first handler in the chain, and the chain can be extended to handle new types of requests without affecting the existing code.

3. **Liskov Substitution Principle (LSP):** The Chain of Responsibility pattern follows the LSP by ensuring that each handler class adheres to the same interface. This means that any handler class can be substituted for another handler class without affecting the correctness of the program.

4. **Interface Segregation Principle (ISP):** The Chain of Responsibility pattern follows the ISP by defining a separate interface for the handlers, with a single method that handles the request. This way, the client only needs to know about the handler interface, and not the details of each individual handler.

5. **Dependency Inversion Principle (DIP):** The Chain of Responsibility pattern follows the DIP by allowing the client to depend on the abstraction (the handler interface) rather than the implementation (the specific handler class). This way, the client can easily switch between different handlers without affecting the rest of the code.

Command Pattern

The **Command Design Pattern** is a Behavioural design pattern that allows you to encapsulate a request as an object, thereby decoupling the sender of the request from the receiver of the request. This pattern enables you to parameterize objects with different requests, queue or log requests, and support undoable operations.

Problem: In some software applications, there is a need to decouple the sender and receiver of a request. For example, you might want to implement a system where different objects can request different actions without needing to know the specifics of how those actions are carried out. Also, you might need to support undo and redo functionality in your application.

A direct coupling between sender and receiver can lead to the following issues:

- The sender becomes dependent on the implementation details of the receiver.

- Adding or modifying new functionalities becomes cumbersome as it requires changing both the sender and receiver.

- Implementing undo and redo functionalities can be complex and error-prone if not handled properly.

Solution: The Command Design Pattern addresses the above problem by introducing an intermediate object called the "command" that encapsulates the request details and the associated action. The pattern typically consists of the following components:

1. **Command:** This is an interface or abstract class defining a common interface for all concrete command objects. It declares an **execute()** method that contains the logic for performing the action.

2. **ConcreteCommand:** These are the implementations of the **Command** interface. Each **ConcreteCommand** binds a specific action to a receiver. It contains a reference to the receiver and implements the **execute()** method by invoking the corresponding operation on the receiver.

3. **Invoker:** This is the class that holds the **Command** object and triggers the execution of the command by calling the **execute()** method.

4. **Receiver:** This is the class that knows how to perform the actual action associated with the command.

5. **Client:** This is the class that creates the **ConcreteCommand** objects, sets the appropriate receivers, and binds them to Invokers.

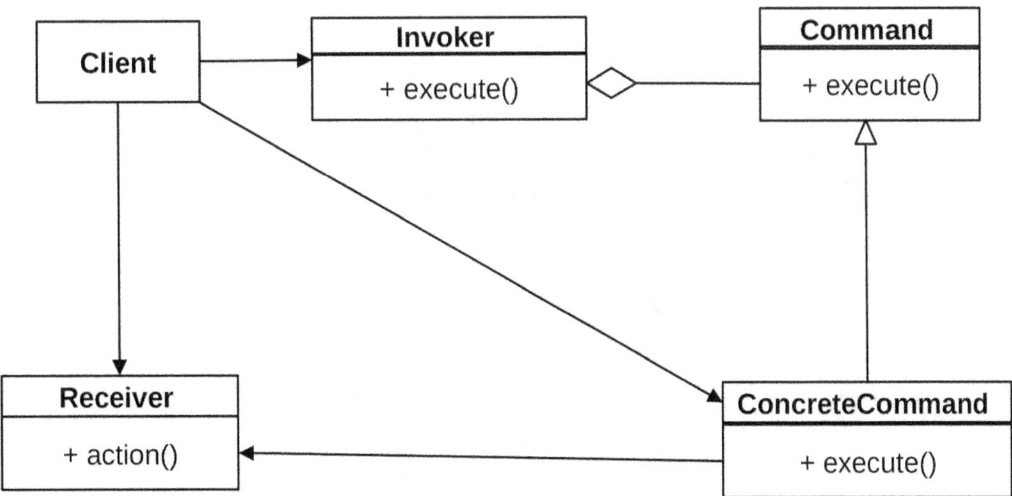

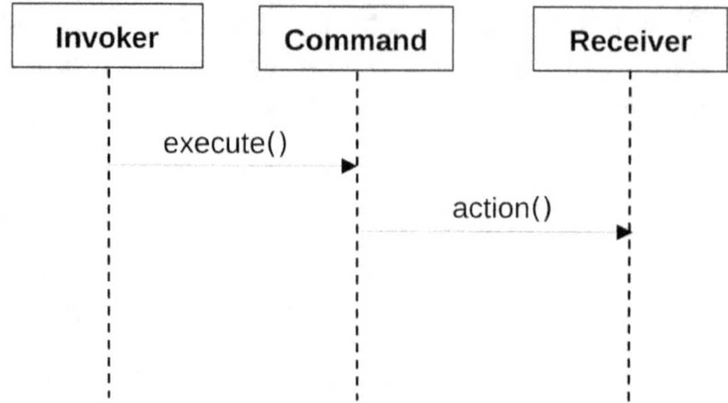

Here's an example implementation of the Command pattern :

```
// Invoker
class Invoker {
    constructor() {
        this.commands = [];
    }

    setCommand(command) {
        this.commands.push(command);
    }

    executeCommands() {
        for (const command of this.commands) {
            command.execute();
        }
    }

    unexecuteCommands() {
        for (const command of this.commands) {
            command.unexecute();
        }
    }
}

// Command
class Command {
    execute() {
        throw new Error("Abstract method: execute");
    }

    unexecute() {
        throw new Error("Abstract method: unexecute");
    }
}
```

```javascript
// ConcreteCommand
class ConcreteCommand extends Command {
    constructor(receiver) {
        super();
        this.receiver = receiver;
    }

    execute() {
        this.receiver.action("Action 1");
    }

    unexecute() {
        this.receiver.action("Action 2");
    }
}

// Receiver
class Receiver {
    action(action) {
        console.log(action);
    }
}

// Client Code
const receiver = new Receiver();
const concreteCommand = new ConcreteCommand(receiver);
const invoker = new Invoker();
invoker.setCommand(concreteCommand);
invoker.executeCommands();
invoker.unexecuteCommands();
```

Output:

```
Action 1
Action 2
```

Explanation: The code implements the Command Design Pattern, which separates the sender and receiver of a request using the **Invoker**, **Command**, and **Receiver** classes. Let's go through the code step by step and explain its functionality:

1. **Invoker (Remote):** The **Invoker** class acts as a remote control that holds a list of commands. It has two main methods: **setCommand()** to add commands to its list and **executeCommands()** and **unexecuteCommands()** to execute and unexecute (undo) the commands, respectively.

2. **Command (abstract class):** The **Command** class is an abstract class that defines the common interface for all commands. It declares two abstract methods, **execute()** and **unexecute()**, which will be implemented by concrete commands.

3. **ConcreteCommand:** The **ConcreteCommand** class is a concrete implementation of the **Command** interface. It represents a specific action to be performed on the **Receiver**. It holds a reference to the Receiver and implements the **execute()** and **unexecute()** methods, which call the **action()** method on the **Receiver**.

4. **Receiver:** The **Receiver** class is responsible for executing the actual action. It has an **action()** method that takes an action string as input and prints it.

5. **Client Code:**

   - An instance of the **Receiver** class is created.

   - An instance of the **ConcreteCommand** class is created, passing the **Receiver** object as an argument.

   - An instance of the **Invoker** class is created.

   - The **ConcreteCommand** instance is set as the command for the **Invoker**.

   - The **executeCommands()** method of the **Invoker** is called, which triggers the execution of the command. In this case, it calls the **execute()** method of the **ConcreteCommand**, which, in turn, calls the **action()** method of the **Receiver** with the action string "Action 1". The output will be "Action 1" printed on the console.

   - The **unexecuteCommands()** method of the **Invoker** is called, which triggers the unexecution (undo) of the command. In this case, it calls the **unexecute()** method of the **ConcreteCommand**, which, in turn, calls the **action()** method of the **Receiver** with the action string "Action 2". The output will be "Action 2" printed on the console.

Problem : Implement a simple stock trading system where we can place "buy" and "sell" orders for stocks. However, we want to decouple the code responsible for executing the orders from the code that initiates the orders. We also want to support the possibility of adding more types of orders in the future without modifying the existing code.

Solution:

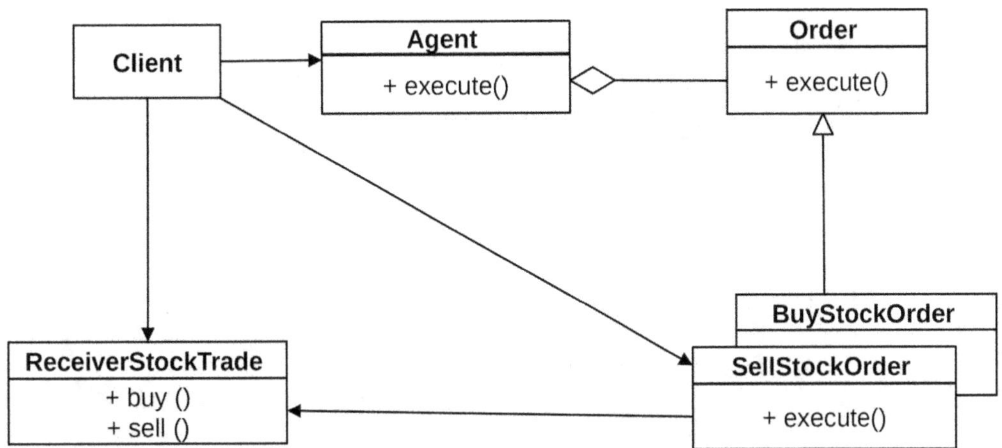

Here's an example implementation of the Command pattern :

```
// Agent (Invoker)
class Agent {
    placeOrder(command) {
        command.execute();
    }
}


// Order (Command)
class Order {
    execute() {
        throw new Error("Abstract method: execute");
    }
}


// BuyStockOrder (ConcreteCommand)
class BuyStockOrder extends Order {
    constructor(stock) {
        super();
        this.stock = stock;
    }

    execute() {
        this.stock.buy();
    }
}


// SellStockOrder (ConcreteCommand)
class SellStockOrder extends Order {
    constructor(stock) {
```

```javascript
        super();
        this.stock = stock;
    }

    execute() {
        this.stock.sell();
    }
}

// Receiver
class ReceiverStockTrade {
    buy() {
        console.log("Buy stocks");
    }

    sell() {
        console.log("Sell stocks");
    }
}

// Client code
const trader = new ReceiverStockTrade();
const buyStock = new BuyStockOrder(trader);
const sellStock = new SellStockOrder(trader);

const agent = new Agent();
agent.placeOrder(buyStock);
agent.placeOrder(sellStock);
```

Output:

```
Buy stocks
Sell stocks
```

Explanation: This code that implements the Command Design Pattern to address the problem statement. Let's break down the code step by step:

1. **Agent class (Invoker):**

    ○ The **Agent** class acts as the invoker, responsible for placing orders.

    ○ It has a method called **placeOrder**, which takes a command as an argument and calls the **execute()** method of that command.

2. **Order class (Command - abstract):**

    ○ The **Order** class is an abstract class representing the command interface.

- It defines a single abstract method, **execute()**, which must be implemented by its subclasses.

3. **BuyStockOrder class (ConcreteCommand)**:

   - The **BuyStockOrder** class is a concrete implementation of the Order interface.

   - It takes a **stock** object as an argument during initialization.

   - The **execute()** method of **BuyStockOrder** calls the **buy()** method on the stock object.

4. **SellStockOrder class (ConcreteCommand)**:

   - The **SellStockOrder** class is another concrete implementation of the Order interface.

   - It takes a **stock** object as an argument during initialization.

   - The execute() method of **SellStockOrder** calls the **sell()** method on the stock object.

5. **ReceiverStockTrade class (Receiver)**:

   - The **ReceiverStockTrade** class acts as the receiver, which knows how to perform the actual "buy" and "sell" operations.

   - It has two methods, **buy()** and **sell()**, which simply print out appropriate messages for demonstration purposes.

6. **Client Code**:

   - The client code begins by creating an instance of **ReceiverStockTrade** called trader, which will act as the receiver.

   - Next, it creates two concrete command objects, **BuyStockOrder** and **SellStockOrder**, passing the trader as a parameter to each of them.

   - Then, it creates an instance of the **Agent** class called agent.

   - Finally, the client code calls agent.**placeOrder(buyStock)** and agent.**placeOrder(sellStock)** to execute the "buy" and "sell" operations, respectively.

Consequence

The Command Design Pattern has several advantages and consequences:

1. **Decoupling:** It decouples the sender from the receiver, allowing them to evolve independently. The sender does not need to know the details of how a request is handled.

2. **Undo/Redo functionality:** Since commands encapsulate actions, it becomes easier to implement undo and redo functionalities by maintaining a history of executed commands.

3. **Flexibility:** New commands can be added without modifying existing code, making the system more flexible and extensible.

4. **Logging and auditing:** Commands can be logged for auditing purposes, allowing you to keep track of operations executed in the system.

5. **Complexity:** The pattern introduces additional classes and abstraction, which can increase code complexity and maintenance effort.

SOLID principle applied

Here's how each SOLID principle can be applied to the Command pattern:

1. **Single Responsibility Principle (SRP):** The Command pattern follows the SRP by encapsulating each action or command in a separate object, which has the responsibility of executing that command. Each command object has a single responsibility, which is to perform one specific action.

2. **Open-Closed Principle (OCP):** The Command pattern follows the OCP by allowing new commands to be added without modifying the existing code. The client can use the invoker to execute commands, and new commands can be added by creating new command classes that implement the command interface.

3. **Liskov Substitution Principle (LSP):** The Command pattern follows the LSP by ensuring that each command object implements the same command interface, with the same execution method. This means that any command object can be substituted for another command object without affecting the correctness of the program.

4. **Interface Segregation Principle (ISP):** The Command pattern follows the ISP by defining a separate interface for the commands, with a single method that executes the command. This way, the client only needs to

know about the command interface, and not the details of each individual command.

5. **Dependency Inversion Principle (DIP):** The Command pattern follows the DIP by allowing the client to depend on the abstraction (the command interface) rather than the implementation (the specific command class). This way, the client can easily switch between different commands without affecting the rest of the code.

Interpreter Pattern

The **Interpreter pattern** is a Behavioural design pattern that is used to define a grammar for a language and provide an interpreter to interpret sentences in that language. It allows you to define a language or grammar in a domain-specific language (DSL) and then implement an interpreter to evaluate expressions or statements written in that DSL.

Problem: The Interpreter pattern is useful when you have a domain-specific language or expressions that need to be evaluated, and you want to avoid complex, nested conditional statements or if-else blocks. It can be challenging to implement a grammar efficiently and maintainable without the use of the Interpreter pattern. For example, consider creating a simple language to handle date expressions like "today," "tomorrow," "next week," "last month," etc. Manually processing each of these expressions with multiple conditional statements would quickly become unmanageable and less readable.

Solution: The Interpreter pattern suggests creating classes for each grammar rule or terminal/non-terminal expression. These classes implement an `interpret()` method that evaluates or processes the expression. The expressions can then be combined in a way that represents the grammar of the language.

The pattern typically includes the following components:

1. **Context:** Contains the information on which the expressions operate.

2. **AbstractExpression:** An interface or abstract class that defines the `interpret()` method.

3. **TerminalExpression:** Concrete classes implementing the `AbstractExpression` for terminal expressions in the grammar.

4. **NonTerminalExpression:** Concrete classes implementing the `AbstractExpression` for non-terminal expressions in the grammar.

5. **Client:** Builds the abstract syntax tree (AST) of the expressions and invokes the `interpret()` method on the root of the tree.

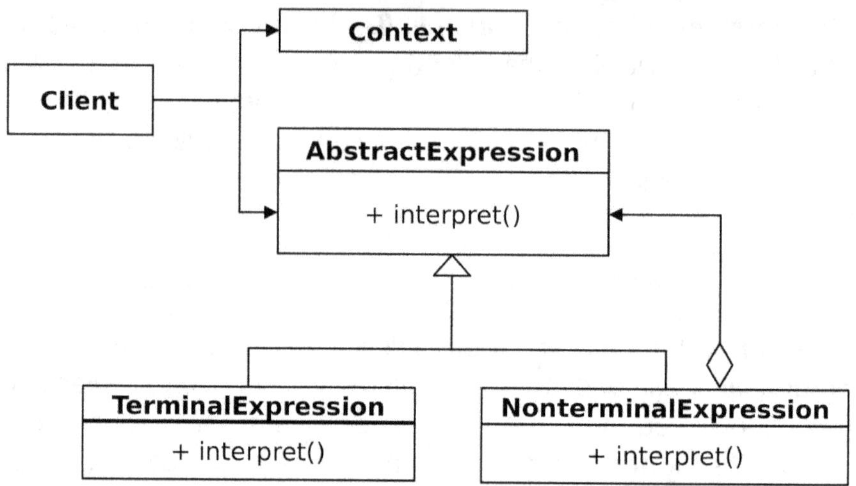

Here's an example implementation of the Interpreter pattern :

```javascript
// Abstract Expression
class AbstractExpression {
    interpret() { }
}

// Nonterminal Expression
class NonterminalExpression extends AbstractExpression {
    constructor(expression) {
        super();
        this.expression = expression;
    }

    interpret() {
        console.log("NonTerminalExpression:interpret");
        this.expression.interpret();
    }
}

// Terminal Expression
class TerminalExpression extends AbstractExpression {
    interpret() {
        console.log("TerminalExpression:interpret");
    }
}
```

```
// Client Code
const tree = new NonterminalExpression(new TerminalExpression());
tree.interpret();
```

Output:

```
NonTerminalExpression:interpret
TerminalExpression:interpret
```

Explanation: This code demonstrates the implementation of the Interpreter design pattern. Let's go through the explanation of each part of the code:

1. **AbstractExpression (Interface):**

   - **AbstractExpression** is an interface that must be implemented by all expressions in the grammar. It declares a method **interpret()**, which must be implemented by its concrete expressions. This method defines how the expression is interpreted or evaluated.

2. **NonterminalExpression (Concrete Class):**

   - **NonterminalExpression** is a concrete class that represents a non-terminal expression in the grammar. It takes an **AbstractExpression** as input during initialization, which can be either a **NonterminalExpression** or a **TerminalExpression**.

   - The **interpret()** method of NonterminalExpression simply delegates the interpretation to the contained expression (**this.expression.interpret()**). This allows the non-terminal expression to evaluate itself by recursively interpreting its subexpressions.

3. **TerminalExpression (Concrete Class):**

   - **TerminalExpression** is another concrete class that represents a terminal expression in the grammar. A terminal expression is an expression that cannot be further decomposed.

   - The **interpret()** method of **TerminalExpression** just print text since a terminal expression does not have any further interpretation to perform.

4. **Client Code:**

   - In the client code section, an instance of NonterminalExpression is created with **TerminalExpression()** passed as an argument during initialization.

- ○ **`tree.interpret()`** is called on the **`NonterminalExpression`** instance, which starts the interpretation process.

- ○ The interpretation process starts from the root (**`NonterminalExpression`**) and recursively interprets its subexpressions (in this case, the **`TerminalExpression`**).

Problem : Create an interpreter for a simple mathematical language to evaluate expressions involving addition. The language supports two types of expressions: terminal expressions (numbers) and non-terminal expressions (addition of two expressions). The task is to implement the interpreter design pattern to interpret these expressions and provide the result.

Solution: An example implementation of the Interpreter pattern :

```javascript
// Abstract Expression
class Expression {
    interpret(context) { }
}

// Terminal Expression
class NumberExpression extends Expression {
    constructor(number) {
        super();
        this.number = number;
    }

    interpret() {
        return this.number;
    }
}

// Non-terminal Expression
class AddExpression extends Expression {
    constructor(leftExpression, rightExpression) {
        super();
        this.leftExpression = leftExpression;
        this.rightExpression = rightExpression;
    }

    interpret(context) {
        return this.leftExpression.interpret(context) +
this.rightExpression.interpret(context);
    }
}
```

```javascript
// Context
class Context {
    constructor() {
        this.variables = new Map();
    }

    setVariable(variable, value) {
        this.variables.set(variable, value);
    }

    getVariable(variable) {
        return this.variables.get(variable) || 0;
    }
}

// Client code
const context = new Context();
context.setVariable("x", 10);
context.setVariable("y", 5);

// Create the expression tree: x + (y + 2)
const expression = new AddExpression(
    new NumberExpression(context.getVariable("x")),
    new AddExpression(
        new NumberExpression(context.getVariable("y")),
        new NumberExpression(2)));

const result = expression.interpret(context);
console.log("Result:", result);
```

Output:

```
Result: 17
```

Explanation:

1. **Abstract Expression (Expression):**

   - The code defines a interface **Expression**, which acts as the base template for all expressions in the grammar.

   - The interfaces **Expression** declares a single method **interpret()**, which must be implemented the classes that Implements it.

   - This method defines how the expression is interpreted or evaluated.

2. **Terminal Expression (NumberExpression):**

   - The **NumberExpression** is a concrete class representing a terminal expression in the grammar. It corresponds to a numeric value in the mathematical language.

   - The **NumberExpression** class takes a number as input during initialization and stores it as an instance variable `number`.

   - The **interpret()** method of **NumberExpression** returns the stored number when evaluated.

3. **Non-terminal Expression (AddExpression):**

   - The **AddExpression** is a concrete class representing a non-terminal expression in the grammar. It corresponds to the addition of two expressions.

   - The **AddExpression** class takes two `Expression` objects, **leftExpression** and **rightExpression**, as input during initialization.

   - The **interpret()** method of **AddExpression** evaluates the addition by calling the **interpret()** method on both **leftExpression** and **rightExpression** and returning their sum.

4. **Context:**

   - The **Context** class is a simple class that acts as a context for the interpreter. It holds variables and their corresponding values.

   - The **Context** class has methods to set and get variables and their values.

5. **Client Code:**

   - In the client code section, a **Context** instance `context` is created.

   - Two variables, "x" and "y," are set in the `context` object with the values 10 and 5, respectively.

   - The expression tree for the mathematical expression x + (y + 2) is created using the **AddExpression** and **NumberExpression** classes.

   - The result of the expression is obtained by calling the **interpret()** method on the root of the expression tree.

- The final result (17) is printed as the output.

Consequence

The Interpreter pattern offers several benefits and trade-offs:

Benefits:

1. **Flexibility:** You can easily change or extend the grammar by adding new classes for new expressions.

2. **Readability:** It simplifies the representation of complex grammatical rules, making the code more readable and maintainable.

3. **Separation of Concerns:** The pattern separates the grammar from the parsing logic, which improves code organisation.

Trade-offs:

1. **Complexity:** The pattern can become complex and hard to manage if the grammar is extensive or changes frequently.

2. **Performance:** Depending on the complexity of the grammar and the size of the AST, the Interpreter pattern might not be the most efficient solution for some cases.

SOLID principle applied

Here's how each SOLID principle can be applied to the Interpreter pattern:

1. **Single Responsibility Principle (SRP):** The Interpreter pattern adheres to the SRP by separating the parsing of the input language into a separate class (the parser), which has the responsibility of interpreting the input and creating the AST (Abstract Syntax Tree). The interpreter then operates on the AST. This way, the parser is responsible for parsing the input, while the interpreter is responsible for executing the code.

2. **Open-Closed Principle (OCP):** The Interpreter pattern follows the OCP by allowing new grammar rules to be added without modifying the existing code. The parser can be extended to handle new grammar rules, and the interpreter can be extended to handle new AST nodes without affecting the existing code.

3. **Liskov Substitution Principle (LSP)**: The Interpreter pattern follows the LSP by ensuring that each AST node implements the same interface or inheritance hierarchy. This means that any AST node can be substituted for another AST node without affecting the correctness of the program.

4. **Interface Segregation Principle (ISP)**: The Interpreter pattern follows the ISP by defining a separate interface for each AST node, with a single method that returns the result of the interpretation. This way, the interpreter only needs to know about the AST node interfaces, and not the details of each individual AST node.

5. **Dependency Inversion Principle (DIP):** The Interpreter pattern follows the DIP by allowing the client to depend on the abstraction (the AST node interfaces) rather than the implementation (the specific AST node classes). This way, the client can easily switch between different AST node classes without affecting the rest of the code.

Iterator Pattern

The **Iterator design pattern** is a Behavioural design pattern that provides a way to access the elements of a collection without exposing its underlying representation. It allows sequential access to the elements of an aggregate (collection) object without knowing its internal structure. This pattern decouples the collection from the iteration logic, making the code more flexible, maintainable, and reusable.

Problem: The Iterator design pattern addresses the problem of accessing elements in a collection (e.g., a list, array, or tree) without exposing the underlying representation of the collection. Traditional iteration using loops can become cumbersome, especially when dealing with complex data structures or when the structure of the collection changes. Directly accessing elements of a collection can also lead to code duplication and increased coupling between the collection and its clients.

Solution: The Iterator design pattern provides a way to access elements in a collection sequentially without exposing the underlying data structure. It separates the responsibility of traversing the collection from the collection itself.

The pattern involves two main components:

1. **Iterator:** This is an interface that defines methods like **hasNext()** to check if there are more elements in the collection, and **next()** to retrieve the next element.

2. **ConcreteIterator:** This is a specific implementation of the Iterator interface for a particular collection. It keeps track of the current position during iteration.

3. **Iterable (Aggregate):** This is an interface that defines a method createIterator() to instantiate an Iterator for the collection.

4. **ConcreteIterable (ConcreteAggregate):** This is a specific implementation of the Iterable interface that creates and returns a ConcreteIterator for the collection.

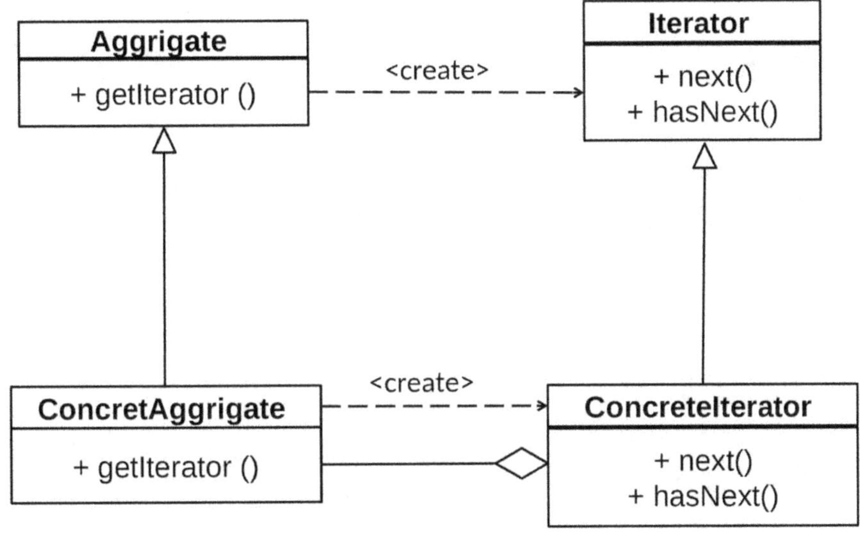

Here's an example implementation of the Iterator pattern :

```
class Aggregate {
    getIterator() {}
}

class ConcreteAggregate extends Aggregate {
    constructor() {
        super();
        this._data = [];
    }
```

```
    addData(val) {
        this._data.push(val);
    }

    getIterator() {
        return new ConcreteIterator(this);
    }
}

class Iterator {
    next() {}
    hasNext() {}
}

class ConcreteIterator extends Iterator {
    constructor(aggregate) {
        super();
        this._aggregate = aggregate;
        this._index = 0;
    }

    next() {
        if (this._index >= this._aggregate._data.length) {
            throw new Error("StopIteration");
        }
        const val = this._aggregate._data[this._index];
        this._index++;
        return val;
    }

    hasNext() {
        return this._index < this._aggregate._data.length;
    }
}

// Client code
const aggregate = new ConcreteAggregate();
aggregate.addData("Item 1");
aggregate.addData("Item 2");
aggregate.addData("Item 3");

const iterator = aggregate.getIterator();

while (iterator.hasNext()) {
    console.log(iterator.next());
}
```

Output:

```
Item 1
Item 2
Item 3
```

Explanation:

1. The code defines the **Aggregate** interface and the **ConcreteAggregate** class which implements the **Aggregate** interface. The **Aggregate** interface has one method, **getIterator()**, which is implemented by the **ConcreteAggregate** class. The **ConcreteAggregate** class maintains a list of data and provides the iterator over that data through the **getIterator()** method which returns a **ConcreteIterator** object.

2. The code also defines the **Iterator** interface and the **ConcreteIterator** class which implements the **Iterator** interface. The **Iterator** interface has two methods, **next()** and **hasNext()**, which are implemented by the **ConcreteIterator** class. The **ConcreteIterator** class provides the actual implementation of iterating over the data in the **ConcreteAggregate** object.

3. Finally, in the last few lines of code, the **ConcreteAggregate** object is created and populated with some data. The **ConcreteIterator** object is created using the **getIterator()** method of the **ConcreteAggregate** object, and then used to iterate over the data in the **ConcreteAggregate** object using a while loop that checks for the existence of the next element using the **hasNext()** method and retrieves the next element using the **next()** method.

4. Overall, this code demonstrates how the Iterator Pattern can be used to traverse the elements of a collection without exposing the underlying representation of the collection.

Problem : The problem addressed by the given code is to implement a simple linked list data structure with the ability to iterate over its elements using the Iterator design pattern.

Solution: The code defines a **LinkedList** class that represents a linked list with **addTail()** and **addHead()** methods for adding elements to the list. It also implements an Iterator named **LinkedListIterator** to allow the client code to traverse the linked list sequentially using a for loop.

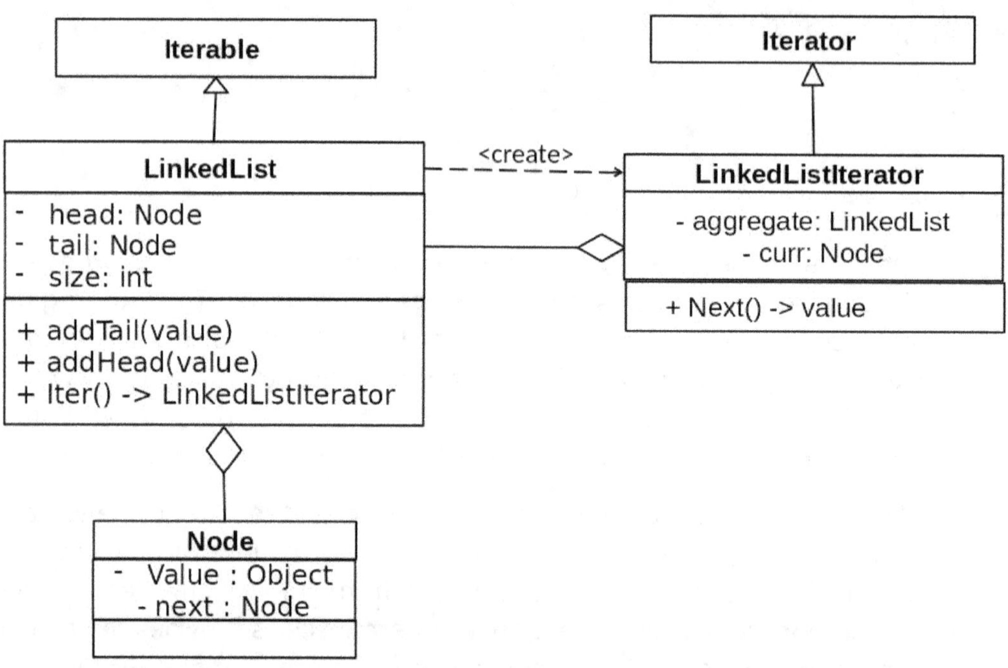

Here's an example implementation of the Iterator pattern :

```
class Node {
    constructor(value, next) {
        this.value = value;
        this.next = next;
    }
}

class Iterator {
    next() {}
    hasNext() {}
}

class LinkedListIterator extends Iterator {
    constructor(aggregate) {
        super();
        this.aggregate = aggregate;
        this.current = aggregate.head;
    }

    hasNext() {
        return this.current !== null;
    }
}
```

```javascript
    next() {
        if (!this.hasNext()) {
            throw new Error("No such element");
        }
        const value = this.current.value;
        this.current = this.current.next;
        return value;
    }
}

class Iterable {
    iterator() {}
}

class LinkedList extends Iterable {
    constructor() {
        super();
        this.head = null;
        this.tail = null;
        this.size = 0;
    }

    addHead(value) {
        const newNode = new Node(value, this.head);
        if (!this.head) {
            this.tail = newNode;
        }
        this.head = newNode;
        this.size++;
    }

    iterator() {
        return new LinkedListIterator(this);
    }

    getSize() {
        return this.size;
    }
}

// Client code
const linkedList = new LinkedList();
linkedList.addHead(1);
linkedList.addHead(2);
linkedList.addHead(3);
```

```
const iterator = linkedList.iterator();
while (iterator.hasNext()) {
    console.log(iterator.next());
}
```

Output:

```
3
2
1
```

Explanation:

1. Iterator Interface (**Iterator**): The **Iterator** interface is an abstract class for iterators. The **LinkedListIterator** class implements the standard Iterator interface.

2. Concrete Iterator (**LinkedListIterator**): The **LinkedListIterator** class implements the Iterator interface.

   - It maintains a reference to the **LinkedList** aggregate and a current node pointer to keep track of the position during iteration.

   - The **hasNext()** method checks if there is a next element in the linked list.

   - The **next()** method returns the next element in the iteration and advances the iterator to the next position.

3. Aggregate Interface (**Iterable**): The **Iterable** interface is an abstract class. The **Iterable** interface is implemented by the **LinkedList** class, indicating that instances of the class can be iterated over.

4. Concrete Aggregate (**LinkedList**): The **LinkedList** class represents the aggregate object containing elements (integer values) in a linked list structure.

   - It implements the Iterable interface, providing an **iterator()** through the iterator method. The iterator method returns a new instance of **LinkedListIterator**, which acts as the iterator for the linked list.

5. Client Code (IteratorPatternLinkedList Class):

   - In the main method, a **LinkedList** object (aggregate) is created and populated with elements.

- ○ The enhanced for loop (for (int val : aggregate)) demonstrates the use of the iterator to traverse the elements of the linked list without exposing its internal structure.

- ○ This client code highlights the decoupling between the client and the specific implementation of the linked list, allowing for easy iteration over the elements.

6. Together, these four classes implement the iterator pattern, which separates the mechanism for iterating over a collection from the collection itself. The **LinkedList** class represents the collection, and the **LinkedListIterator** class represents the iterator. By separating these two concerns, the iterator pattern allows for more flexible and modular code.

Consequence

The Iterator design pattern has several advantages and consequences:

1. **Decoupling:** It decouples the client code from the underlying collection, as the client interacts only with the Iterator interface. This enhances the flexibility and maintainability of the codebase.

2. **Single Responsibility Principle:** The pattern separates the iteration logic from the collection, adhering to the Single Responsibility Principle, making the code more modular.

3. **Simplified Client Code:** The Iterator pattern simplifies client code by providing a consistent way to access elements, regardless of the collection's specific implementation.

4. **Support for Multiple Iterators:** The pattern allows multiple iterators to work on the same collection concurrently without interfering with each other.

5. **Easier Extension:** Adding new types of collections or custom iterators becomes more manageable since the iteration logic is isolated.

6. **Performance Considerations:** While the Iterator pattern simplifies access to elements, it might introduce a slight overhead due to the additional interface and objects involved. However, the trade-off usually justifies the advantages it brings.

SOLID principle applied

Here's how each SOLID principle can be applied to the Iterator pattern:

1. **Single Responsibility Principle (SRP)**: The Iterator pattern follows the SRP by separating the traversal logic from the collection class. The iterator has the responsibility of iterating over the elements in the collection, while the collection has the responsibility of storing the elements.

2. **Open-Closed Principle (OCP)**: The Iterator pattern follows the OCP by allowing new collections to be added without modifying the existing code. The iterator can be used to iterate over any collection that implements the same interface, without needing to modify the iterator code.

3. **Liskov Substitution Principle (LSP)**: The Iterator pattern follows the LSP by ensuring that any collection that implements the iterator interface can be used with the iterator class, without affecting the correctness of the program.

4. **Interface Segregation Principle (ISP)**: The Iterator pattern follows the ISP by defining a separate interface for the iterator, with a set of methods for iterating over the collection. This way, the client only needs to know about the iterator interface, and not the details of the collection implementation.

5. **Dependency Inversion Principle (DIP)**: The Iterator pattern follows the DIP by allowing the client to depend on the abstraction (the iterator interface) rather than the implementation (the specific iterator class). This way, the client can easily switch between different iterators without affecting the rest of the code.

Mediator Pattern

The **Mediator design pattern** is a behavioural pattern that promotes loose coupling between components by centralising their communication through a mediator object. It is used to reduce direct dependencies between objects, making the system more maintainable and easier to extend. Let's discuss the problem it addresses, its solution, and the consequences of using this pattern.

Problem: In a complex software system, when objects or components need to interact with each other, direct communication can lead to a tightly coupled design. When multiple objects depend on each other, any change in one object can cause a ripple effect of changes in related objects, making the codebase difficult to maintain and extend. Additionally, having direct references between objects can make it challenging to understand the overall flow of the system.

Solution: The Mediator pattern addresses this problem by introducing a mediator object that acts as a central hub for communication between the components. Instead of the components communicating directly with each other, they communicate only through the mediator. The mediator encapsulates the communication logic, reducing the interdependencies between the components.

The Mediator pattern has four main components:

1. **Mediator**: Defines the interface for communication between objects and implements the communication logic.

2. **Concrete Mediator**: Implements the Mediator interface and coordinates the communication between the objects.

3. **Colleague**: Defines the interface for objects that need to communicate with each other.

4. **Concrete Colleague**: Implements the Colleague interface and communicates with other objects through the Mediator.

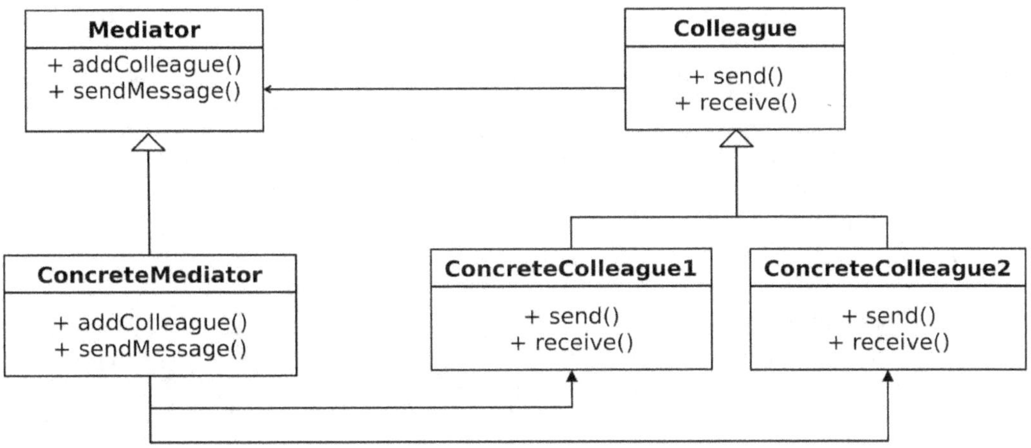

Here's an example implementation of the Mediator pattern :

```
class Mediator {
    constructor() {
        this.colleagues = new Map();
    }
```

```javascript
    addColleague(colleague) {
        this.colleagues.set(colleague.getId(), colleague);
    }

    sendMessage(message, colleagueId) {
        console.log(`Mediator pass Message : ${message}`);
        this.colleagues.get(colleagueId).receive(message);
    }
}

class Colleague {
    constructor(mediator, id) {
        this.mediator = mediator;
        this.id = id;
    }

    send(message, to) {
        console.log(`${this.id} Sent Message : ${message}`);
        this.mediator.sendMessage(message, to);
    }

    receive(message) {
        console.log(`${this.id} Received Message : ${message}`);
    }

    getId() {
        return this.id;
    }
}

class ConcreteColleague1 extends Colleague {
    constructor(mediator) {
        super(mediator, "First");
    }

    send(message, to) {
        console.log(`${this.id} Sent Message : ${message}`);
        this.mediator.sendMessage(message, to);
    }

    receive(message) {
        console.log(`${this.id} Received Message : ${message}`);
    }
}
```

```javascript
class ConcreteColleague2 extends Colleague {
    constructor(mediator) {
        super(mediator, "Second");
    }

    send(message, to) {
        console.log(`${this.id} Sent Message : ${message}`);
        this.mediator.sendMessage(message, to);
    }

    receive(message) {
        console.log(`${this.id} Received Message : ${message}`);
    }
}

// Client code
const mediator = new Mediator();
const first = new ConcreteColleague1(mediator);
mediator.addColleague(first);
const second = new ConcreteColleague2(mediator);
mediator.addColleague(second);

first.send("Hello, World!", "Second");
```

Output:

```
First Sent Message : Hello, World!
Mediator pass Message : Hello, World!
Second Received Message Hello, World!
```

Explanation:

1. This is an example implementation of the Mediator Pattern. The code defines the **Mediator** interface and the **ConcreteMediator** class which implements the **Mediator** interface. The **Mediator** interface has two methods, addColleague() and sendMessage(), which are implemented by the **ConcreteMediator** class.

2. The code also defines the **Colleague** interface and the **ConcreteColleague1** and **ConcreteColleague2** classes which implement the **Colleague** interface. The **Colleague** interface has two methods, send() and receive(), which are implemented by the **ConcreteColleague** classes.

3. In the client code, the **ConcreteMediator** object is created and two **ConcreteColleague** objects are created and added to the mediator using the addColleague() method. Finally, a message is sent from the

first **ConcreteColleague** to the second using the send() method which in turn calls the sendMessage() method of the mediator.

4. Overall, this code demonstrates how the Mediator Pattern can be used to facilitate communication between objects in a loosely coupled manner.

Problem : Implement the Mediator design pattern for a simple chat room application. The objective is to create a system where participants in the chat room can communicate with each other through a central mediator (the **ChatRoom** class) without directly interacting with each other. The **ChatRoom** acts as a hub for communication, and participants (instances of the **Participant** class) can send messages to specific participants or broadcast messages to all participants.

Solution:

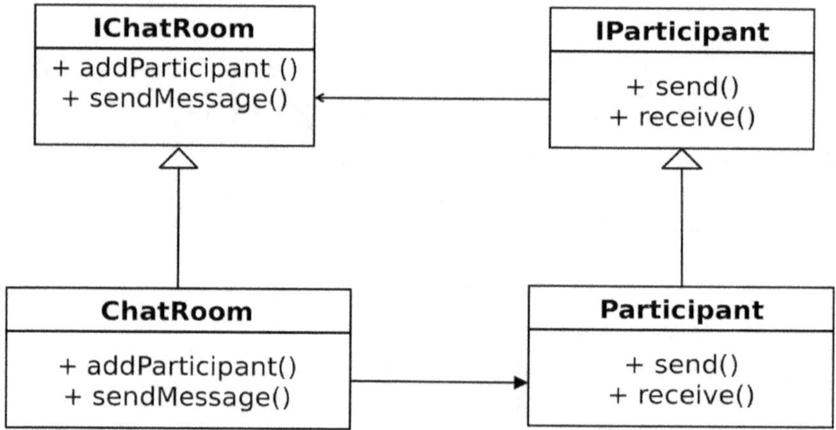

Here's an example implementation of the chatroom using Mediator pattern :

```javascript
class ChatRoom {
    constructor() {
        this.participants = new Map();
    }

    addParticipant(participant) {
        this.participants.set(participant.getName(),
participant);
    }

    broadcast(message, origin) {
        console.log(`ChatRoom broadcast Message : ${message}`);
        for (const [name, participant] of this.participants) {
            if (name !== origin) {
                participant.receive(message);
```

```javascript
            }
        }
    }

    sendMessage(message, to) {
        this.participants.get(to).receive(message);
    }
}

class Participant {
    constructor(name, chatRoom) {
        this.name = name;
        this.chatRoom = chatRoom;
        chatRoom.addParticipant(this);
    }

    getName() {
        return this.name;
    }

    broadcast(message) {
        console.log(`${this.name} broadcast Message : $
{message}`);
        this.chatRoom.broadcast(message, this.name);
    }

    send(message, to) {
        console.log(`${this.name} sent Message : ${message}`);
        this.chatRoom.sendMessage(message, to);
    }

    receive(message) {
        console.log(`${this.name} received Message : $
{message}`);
    }
}

// Client code
const chatRoom = new ChatRoom();
const james = new Participant("James", chatRoom);
const michael = new Participant("Michael", chatRoom);
const robert = new Participant("Robert", chatRoom);

michael.send("Good Morning.", "James");
james.broadcast("Hello, World!");
```

Output:

```
Michael sent Message : Good Morning.
James received Message : Good Morning.
James broadcast Message : Hello, World!
ChatRoom broadcast Message : Hello, World!
Michael received Message : Hello, World!
Robert received Message : Hello, World!
```

Explanation:

1. **IChatRoom** (Interface): Defines the interface for the chat room. It has three methods:

   - **addParticipant**(participant): Adds a participant to the chat room.

   - **broadcast**(message, origin): Broadcasts a message to all participants except the one who sent the message (the origin).

   - **sendMessage**(message, to): Sends a message to a specific participant (the one specified by to).

2. **ChatRoom** (Class):

   - Implements the **IChatRoom** interface.

   - Maintains a dictionary **participants** to keep track of all participants in the chat room.

   - Implement the methods from **IChatRoom**:

     - **addParticipant**(participant): Adds the participant to the participants dictionary.

     - **broadcast**(message, origin): Broadcasts the message to all participants (except the one specified by origin) by calling the receive() method of each participant.

     - **sendMessage**(message, to): Sends the message to a specific participant (the one specified by to) by calling the receive() method of that participant.

3. **IParticipant** (Interface): Defines the interface for participants in the chat room. It has three methods:

- **broadcast**(message): Broadcasts a message on behalf of the participant.

- **send**(message, to): Sends a message to a specific participant (the one specified by to).

- **receive**(message): Receives a message from the chat room.

4. **Participant** (Class): Implements the **IParticipant** interface.

- Takes a participant's name and a reference to the chat room (chatRoom) during initialization.

- Implement the methods from **IParticipant**:

    - **broadcast**(message): Broadcasts the message by calling the broadcast() method of the chat room.

    - **send**(message, to): Sends the message to a specific participant (the one specified by to) by calling the sendMessage() method of the chat room.

    - **receive**(message): Receives the message and prints it along with the participant's name.

5. **Client Code**:

- Creates an instance of the **ChatRoom** class (chatRoom).

- Creates three participants (James, Michael, and Robert) and adds them to the chat room by instantiating the **Participant** class.

- Demonstrates communication between participants using the **broadcast()** and **send()** methods.

Consequences

1. **Decoupling**: The Mediator pattern helps to decouple the components from each other, promoting a more flexible and maintainable design. Each component only needs to know about the mediator and not about other components, which simplifies the system's architecture.

2. **centralised control**: With a mediator in place, the control over the communication between components is centralised. This can make the

system easier to understand and debug since all communication logic is confined to a single location.

3. **Scalability and extensibility**: Adding new components to the system becomes easier as they only need to interact with the mediator to communicate with existing components. This promotes scalability and reduces the risk of introducing bugs when extending the system.

4. **Complexity**: Introducing a mediator can add an extra layer of complexity to the system, especially for smaller projects where direct communication between components might be sufficient. It's important to use the pattern judiciously and only when the complexity of direct interactions becomes a problem.

5. **Single point of failure**: Since the mediator becomes the central point of communication, it can become a single point of failure. If the mediator fails or becomes overloaded, the entire system's communication may be affected.

SOLID principle applied

Here's how each SOLID principle can be applied to the Mediator pattern:

1. **Single Responsibility Principle (SRP)**: The Mediator pattern follows the SRP by separating the communication between objects into a separate class (the mediator), which has the responsibility of coordinating the interactions between objects. This way, each object has a single responsibility, and the mediator handles the communication between them.

2. **Open-Closed Principle (OCP)**: The Mediator pattern follows the OCP by allowing new objects to be added without modifying the existing code. The mediator can handle communication between new objects without requiring changes to the existing objects.

3. **Liskov Substitution Principle (LSP)**: The Mediator pattern follows the LSP by ensuring that each object adheres to the same interface or inheritance hierarchy, and communicates with the mediator using the same methods. This means that the mediator can handle communication between objects interchangeably, without affecting the correctness of the program.

4. **Interface Segregation Principle (ISP)**: The Mediator pattern follows the ISP by defining a separate interface for the mediator, which specifies the

methods that each object can use to communicate with the mediator. This way, the objects only need to know about the mediator interface, and not the details of each other.

5. **Dependency Inversion Principle (DIP)**: The Mediator pattern follows the DIP by allowing the objects to depend on the abstraction (the mediator interface) rather than the implementation (the specific mediator class). This way, the objects can communicate with any mediator that adheres to the same interface, without affecting the rest of the code.

Memento Pattern

The **Memento pattern** is a Behavioural design pattern that allows an object's state to be saved and restored later. The pattern is useful when we need to save and restore the state of an object, for example, when we need to implement undo-redo functionality in an application.

Problem: The problem of maintaining the internal state of an object and providing the ability to restore that state at a later time without violating encapsulation. In some scenarios, objects need to be able to undo or revert to previous states, track changes, or implement rollback mechanisms.

Solution: In this pattern, the object whose state needs to be saved is called the "originator". The state of the originator is saved in an object called the "memento". The memento object contains the necessary state information to restore the originator to its previous state. The memento object is then saved in a "caretaker" object, which is responsible for managing the memento objects.

The Memento pattern consists of three main components:

1. **Originator**: This is the object whose state needs to be saved and restored. The originator creates a memento object that contains a snapshot of its current state.

2. **Memento**: This is the object that contains the state of the originator. The memento object can be created only by the originator, which ensures that the memento object contains a valid snapshot of the originator's state.

3. **Caretaker**: This object is responsible for storing and managing the memento objects. The caretaker can store multiple memento objects, which allows the originator to restore to different states.

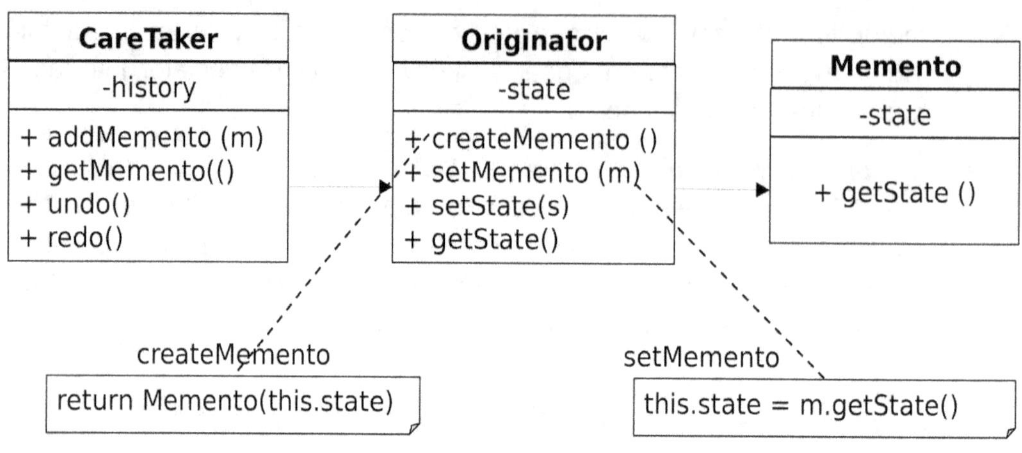

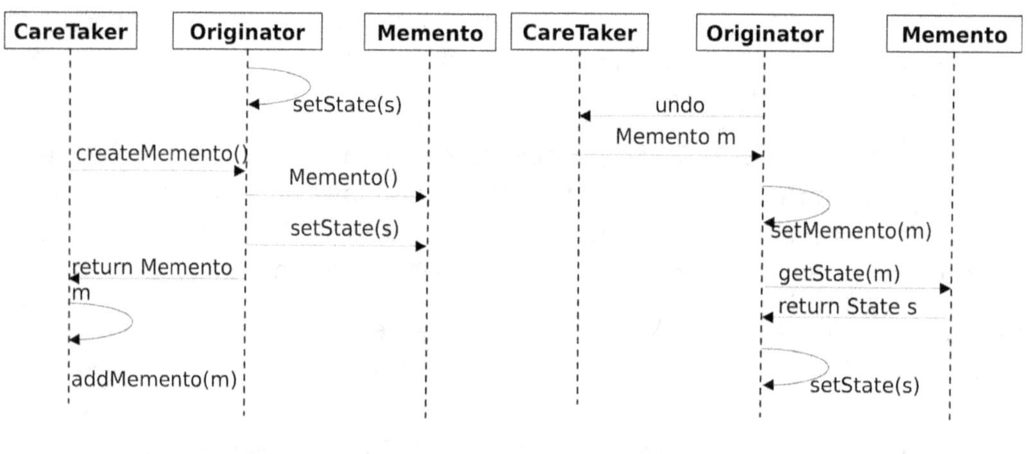

Saving State   **Restoring State**

Here's an example implementation of the Memento pattern :

```javascript
// Memento
class Memento {
    constructor(state) {
        this.state = state;
    }

    getState() {
        return this.state;
    }
}

// CareTaker
class CareTaker {
    constructor() {
        this.history = [];
```

```javascript
        this.top = -1;
        this.max = -1;
    }

    addMemento(m) {
        this.top += 1;
        this.max = this.top;
        if (this.top <= this.history.length - 1) {
            this.history[this.top] = m;
        } else {
            this.history.push(m);
        }
    }

    getMemento(index) {
        return this.history[index];
    }

    undo() {
        console.log("Undoing state.");
        if (this.top <= 0) {
            this.top = 0;
            return this.getMemento(0);
        }

        this.top -= 1;
        return this.getMemento(this.top);
    }

    redo() {
        console.log("Redoing state.");
        if (this.top >= this.history.length - 1 || this.top >=
this.max) {
            return this.getMemento(this.top);
        }

        this.top += 1;
        return this.getMemento(this.top);
    }

    getStatesCount() {
        return this.history.length;
    }
}
```

```javascript
// Originator
class Originator {
    setState(state) {
        this.state = state;
    }

    getState() {
        return this.state;
    }

    createMemento() {
        return new Memento(this.state);
    }

    setMemento(m) {
        this.setState(m.getState());
    }
}

// Client code
const originator = new Originator();
const careTaker = new CareTaker();

originator.setState("State 1");
careTaker.addMemento(originator.createMemento());
console.log(originator.getState());

originator.setState("State 2");
careTaker.addMemento(originator.createMemento());
console.log(originator.getState());

originator.setState("State 3");
careTaker.addMemento(originator.createMemento());
console.log(originator.getState());

originator.setMemento(careTaker.undo());
console.log(originator.getState());

originator.setMemento(careTaker.undo());
console.log(originator.getState());

originator.setMemento(careTaker.redo());
console.log(originator.getState());

originator.setMemento(careTaker.redo());
console.log(originator.getState());
```

Output:

```
State 1
State 2
State 3
Undoing state.
State 2
Undoing state.
State 1
Redoing state.
State 2
Redoing state.
State 3
```

Explanation:

1. This is an implementation of the Memento pattern. It consists of three classes: **Originator**, **Memento**, and **CareTaker**.

2. The **Originator** class is the class whose object state needs to be saved and restored. It has methods for setting and getting the state, creating a **Memento** object with the current state, and restoring the state from a **Memento** object.

3. The **Memento** class represents the saved state of the **Originator**. It has a **getState()** method for getting the saved state.

4. The **CareTaker** class is responsible for managing the saved states. It has a history list to store the **Memento** objects and methods for adding a new **Memento**, getting a **Memento** at a specified index, undoing the last state change, redoing the last undone state change, and getting the number of saved states.

5. In the usage example, we create an instance of **Originator**, set its initial state to "State 1", and save it using the **createMemento()** method. We add the **Memento** object to the **CareTaker** using the **addMemento()** method.

6. We then change the state of the **Originator** to "State 2" and save it again, followed by changing it to "State 3" and saving it again.

7. We then call the **undo()** method of the **CareTaker** twice to restore the **Originator** to its previous states. We call the **redo()** method of the **CareTaker** twice to redo the last undone state changes.

8. This implementation demonstrates how the Memento pattern can be used to implement undo and redo functionality.

Consequence

The Memento pattern brings several benefits to the design of a system:

1. **Encapsulation:** The Memento pattern ensures that the internal state of the originator is encapsulated and not exposed to external clients. This helps in maintaining the integrity of the object and its state.

2. **Undo/Redo:** The pattern allows easy implementation of undo and redo functionality by keeping a stack of mementos. It enables objects to revert to previous states and track state history efficiently.

3. **Isolation of State:** The state is isolated within memento objects, which makes it easier to manage different snapshots of an object's state and manage their lifecycle independently.

4. **Flexibility:** Clients can request to save the state of an object at any point in time, providing a flexible mechanism for state management.

5. **Snapshot Support:** The pattern facilitates taking snapshots of the object's state at regular intervals or at specific events, which can be useful in various scenarios, such as versioning systems or data recovery.

However, using the Memento pattern may also introduce some potential downsides:

1. **Memory Overhead:** If the state of the originator is large or complex, storing multiple mementos can consume a significant amount of memory.

2. **Performance Concerns:** Creating and managing mementos can add some overhead, especially if the state is frequently changing or if there are many state transitions.

3. **Managing Memento Lifecycles:** Caretaker classes need to manage the lifecycle of mementos properly to avoid resource leaks or unexpected behaviour.

SOLID principle applied

Here's how each SOLID principle can be applied to the Memento pattern:

1. **Single Responsibility Principle (SRP)**: The Memento pattern adheres to the SRP by separating the responsibility of maintaining the state of an object from the object itself. The object is responsible for its own behaviour, while the memento is responsible for storing and restoring the object's state.

2. **Open-Closed Principle (OCP)**: The Memento pattern follows the OCP by allowing for easy extension without modification of the existing code. The memento can be extended to store additional information about the object's state without affecting the object's behaviour.

3. **Liskov Substitution Principle (LSP)**: The Memento pattern follows the LSP by ensuring that the memento can be used interchangeably with the original object. The memento should be able to restore the object's state without affecting its behaviour.

4. **Interface Segregation Principle (ISP)**: The Memento pattern follows the ISP by defining separate interfaces for the originator (the object that will be saved and restored) and the memento. This way, the originator only needs to know about the memento interface, and not the details of the memento implementation.

5. **Dependency Inversion Principle (DIP)**: The Memento pattern follows the DIP by allowing the originator to depend on the abstraction (the memento interface) rather than the implementation (the specific memento class). This way, the originator can easily switch between different memento implementations without affecting the rest of the code.

Observer Pattern

The **Observer design pattern** is a Behavioural pattern in software design that allows an object, called the subject, to notify its dependents, known as observers, about changes in its state. When the subject's state changes, all registered observers are automatically notified and updated accordingly. This pattern promotes loose coupling between the subject and its observers, as they are unaware of each other's existence.

Problem: In software development, there are scenarios where multiple objects need to be informed about the changes that occur in another object. However, direct coupling between these objects can lead to several issues:

1. **Tight coupling**: If objects are directly dependent on each other, any change in one object may require modifications in multiple other objects, making the codebase less flexible and maintainable.

2. **Scalability**: As the number of objects that need to be notified increases, managing the dependencies becomes complex, and adding new observers can be cumbersome.

3. **Inefficiency**: In the absence of a proper mechanism to notify observers, they might resort to inefficient polling methods to check for updates, leading to performance issues.

Solution: The Observer design pattern addresses these issues by decoupling the subject and its observers. The Observer pattern is useful when you have a one-to-many relationship between objects, such that the state of one object affects the state of several others. It is commonly used in GUI programming, where components need to be notified of changes in other components. It is also useful in event-driven systems, where events trigger changes in the state of the system.

The main components of this pattern are:

1. **Subject**: It is the object whose state is being monitored for changes. It contains a list of registered observers and provides methods to add, remove, and notify them.

2. **Observer**: It is the interface that defines the contract for the objects that need to be notified of changes in the subject's state. It typically includes an **update()** method that is called by the subject when a change occurs.

3. **Concrete Subject**: It is an implementation of the subject interface that maintains the state and sends notifications to the registered observers when the state changes.

4. **Concrete Observer**: It is an implementation of the observer interface and defines how the observer reacts to the updates received from the subject.

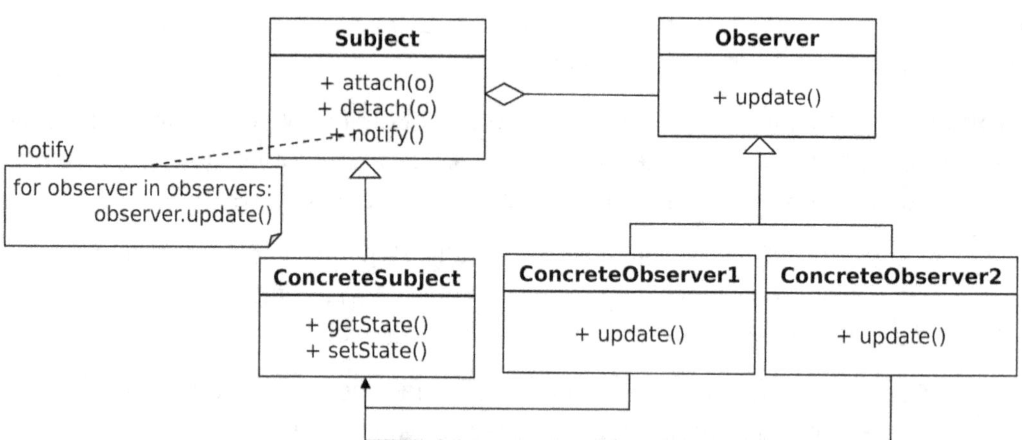

Here's an example implementation of the Observer pattern :

```javascript
class Subject {
    constructor() {
        this.observers = [];
    }

    attach(observer) {
        observer.setSubject(this);
        this.observers.push(observer);
    }

    detach(observer) {
        observer.setSubject(null);
        this.observers = this.observers.filter(obs => obs !==
observer);
    }

    notifyObservers() {
        this.observers.forEach(observer => observer.update());
    }
}

class ConcreteSubject extends Subject {
    constructor() {
        super();
        this.state = "";
    }

    getState() {
        return this.state;
    }

    setState(state) {
        this.state = state;
        this.notifyObservers();
    }
}

class Observer {
    setSubject(subject) {
        this.subject = subject;
    }

    update() {
        // To be implemented by concrete observers
```

```javascript
        }
}

class ConcreteObserver1 extends Observer {
    constructor(subject) {
        super();
        this.setSubject(subject);
        subject.attach(this);
    }

    update() {
        if (this.subject instanceof ConcreteSubject) {
            console.log(`${this.subject.getState()} notified to
Observer1`);
        }
    }
}

class ConcreteObserver2 extends Observer {
    constructor(subject) {
        super();
        this.setSubject(subject);
        subject.attach(this);
    }

    update() {
        if (this.subject instanceof ConcreteSubject) {
            console.log(`${this.subject.getState()} notified to
Observer2`);
        }
    }
}

// Client code
const subject = new ConcreteSubject();
const observer1 = new ConcreteObserver1(subject);
const observer2 = new ConcreteObserver2(subject);
subject.setState("First state");
subject.setState("Second state");
```

Output:

```
First state notified to Observer1
First state notified to Observer2
Second state notified to Observer1
Second state notified to Observer2
```

Explanation:

1. This is an implementation of the Observer pattern. The pattern defines a one-to-many dependency between objects where when one object (the **subject**) changes its state, all its dependents (**observers**) are notified and updated automatically.

2. The code defines an abstract **Subject** class that has a list of observers and methods to **attach()**, **detach()** and **notifyObservers()** the observers. The **ConcreteSubject** class inherits from the **Subject** class and has a state attribute that can be changed with the **setState()** method. When the state changes, the **notify()** method is called, which in turn calls the **update()** method on all attached observers.

3. The **Observer** class is also an abstract class that defines an **update()** method. The **ConcreteObserver1** and **ConcreteObserver2** classes inherit from the **Observer** class and implement the **update()** method, which simply prints the new state of the subject.

4. Finally, the client code creates a **ConcreteSubject** object and two **ConcreteObserver** objects. The observers are attached to the subject, and then the state of the subject is changed twice, which triggers the observers to be notified and updated.

Problem : The provided code implements a simple Publisher-Subscriber pattern, where a Publisher class manages a set of subscribers that are interested in specific topics. When the publisher publishes a message on a topic, all subscribers registered for that topic receive the message.

Solution: Code demonstrate publisher subscriber pattern

```
class Publisher {
    constructor() {
        this.topicSubscribers = new Map();
    }

    subscribe(subscriber, topic) {
        this.topicSubscribers.set(topic,
(this.topicSubscribers.get(topic) || []).concat(subscriber));
        console.log(`Subscribing: ${subscriber.getId()} to topic:
${topic}`);
    }
```

```javascript
    unsubscribe(subscriber, topic) {
        const subscribers = this.topicSubscribers.get(topic) ||
[];
        this.topicSubscribers.set(topic, subscribers.filter(sub
=> sub !== subscriber));
        console.log(`Unsubscribing: ${subscriber.getId()} to
topic: ${topic}`);
    }

    notifySubscribers(data, topic) {
        if (this.topicSubscribers.has(topic)) {
            console.log(`Publishing: ${data} in topic: $
{topic}`);
            for (const subscriber of
this.topicSubscribers.get(topic)) {
                subscriber.update(data);
            }
        }
    }
}

class Subscriber {
    constructor(id) {
        this.id = id;
    }

    getId() {
        return this.id;
    }

    update(data) {
        console.log(`Subscriber ${this.id} got :: ${data}`);
    }
}

// Client code
const pub = new Publisher();

const sub1 = new Subscriber("Subscriber1");
const sub2 = new Subscriber("Subscriber2");
const sub3 = new Subscriber("Subscriber3");
console.log();
pub.subscribe(sub1, "topic1");
pub.subscribe(sub2, "topic2");
pub.subscribe(sub3, "topic2");
```

```
console.log();
pub.notifySubscribers("Topic 1 data", "topic1");
console.log();
pub.notifySubscribers("Topic 2 data", "topic2");
console.log();
pub.unsubscribe(sub3, "topic2");
pub.notifySubscribers("Topic 2 data", "topic2");
```

Output:

```
Subscribing: Subscriber1 to topic: topic1
Subscribing: Subscriber2 to topic: topic2
Subscribing: Subscriber3 to topic: topic2

Publishing: Topic 1 data in topic: topic1
Subscriber Subscriber1 got :: Topic 1 data

Publishing: Topic 2 data in topic: topic2
Subscriber Subscriber2 got :: Topic 2 data
Subscriber Subscriber3 got :: Topic 2 data

Unsubscribing: Subscriber3 to topic: topic2
Publishing: Topic 2 data in topic: topic2
Subscriber Subscriber2 got :: Topic 2 data
```

Explanation:

1. The **Publisher** class acts as the central entity that maintains a list of subscribers for each topic. It provides methods to subscribe and unsubscribe a subscriber from a specific topic, and to notify all subscribers about new data being published on a topic.

2. The **Subscriber** class represents a subscriber that is interested in receiving notifications for a particular topic. It has an **update()** method that gets called by the publisher whenever new data is published on the subscribed topic.

3. In the client code, we create a **Publisher** object and several **Subscriber** objects. We then subscribe the subscribers to different topics using the Publisher's **subscribe()** method. After that, we publish some data on the topics using the Publisher's **notifySubscribers()** method, which causes the subscribers to be notified.

4. Finally, we unsubscribe one of the subscribers using the Publisher's **unsubscribe()** method, and publish some more data to see that the unsubscribed subscriber does not receive any further notifications.

Problem: The provided code implements a simple Publisher-Subscriber pattern, where a Publisher class manages a set of subscribers that are interested in specific topics. When the publisher publishes a message on a topic, all subscribers registered for that topic receive the message.

Solution: Publisher subscriber pattern code for courses and students.

```javascript
class Courses {
    constructor() {
        this.courseStudents = new Map();
    }

    subscribe(subject, student) {
        if (!this.courseStudents.has(subject)) {
            this.courseStudents.set(subject, new Set());
        }
        this.courseStudents.get(subject).add(student);
    }

    unsubscribe(subject, student) {
        const students = this.courseStudents.get(subject);
        if (students) {
            students.delete(student);
        }
    }

    publish(subject, message) {
        if (!this.courseStudents.has(subject)) {
            console.log(`No subscribers for subject '$
{subject}'.`);
            return;
        }
        for (const student of this.courseStudents.get(subject)) {
            student.notify(subject, message);
        }
    }
}

class Student {
    constructor(name) {
        this.name = name;
    }

    notify(subject, message) {
        console.log(`${this.constructor.name} received message on
subject '${subject}': ${message}`);
```

```javascript
    }
}

// Client code
const courses = new Courses();
const john = new Student("John");
const eric = new Student("Eric");
const jack = new Student("Jack");

courses.subscribe("English", john);
courses.subscribe("English", eric);
courses.subscribe("Maths", eric);
courses.subscribe("Science", jack);

courses.publish("English", "Tomorrow class at 11");
courses.publish("Maths", "Tomorrow class at 1");

// Unsubscribe Eric from English
courses.unsubscribe("English", eric);
courses.publish("English", "Updated schedule for English");
```

Output:

```
Student received message on subject 'English': Tomorrow class at
11
Student received message on subject 'English': Tomorrow class at
11
Student received message on subject 'Maths': Tomorrow class at 1
Student received message on subject 'English': Updated schedule
for English
```

Explanation:

1. The code above implements the Observer pattern, where the **Courses** class is the subject and the **Student** class is the observer.

2. The **Courses** class has three main methods: **subscribe()**, **unsubscribe()**, and **publish()**. When a student subscribes to a course, the **subscribe()** method adds the student to the list of observers for that course. When a student unsubscribes from a course, the **unsubscribe()** method removes the student from the list of observers. When new information is available for a course, the **publish()** method is called to send the information to all the observers subscribed to that course.

3. The **Student** class is the observer that receives the information published by the **Courses** class. The **update()** method is called by the **Courses** class to notify the students of any new information.

4. In the client code, **Student** objects are created and subscribed to courses. The **publish()** method of the **Courses** class is called with new information to be published to the students subscribed to that course.

Consequence

The Observer design pattern offers several benefits:

1. **Loose coupling**: The subject and observers are decoupled, making it easy to add or remove observers without affecting the subject's code.

2. **Reusability**: The observers can be reused in different contexts, as they are independent of the subject's implementation.

3. **Maintainability**: Modifying the subject's state does not require changes in the observer classes, promoting better code maintainability.

4. **Real-time updates**: Observers receive updates in real-time whenever there is a change in the subject, allowing for synchronous communication.

However, the pattern can lead to some potential challenges:

1. **Potential performance impact**: If there are many observers, notifying all of them on each state change can lead to performance overhead.

2. **Ordering of notifications**: The order in which observers are notified may not always be guaranteed, which might be a concern in some scenarios.

3. **Memory management**: Care must be taken to manage the lifecycle of observers properly to avoid memory leaks.

SOLID principle applied

Here's how each SOLID principle can be applied to the Observer pattern:

1. **Single Responsibility Principle (SRP)**: The Observer pattern adheres to the SRP by separating the responsibilities of the subject and the observers. The subject is responsible for maintaining the state and notifying the observers, while the observers are responsible for updating their own state based on the changes in the subject.

2. **Open-Closed Principle (OCP)**: The Observer pattern follows the OCP by allowing new observers to be added without modifying the existing

code. The subject can notify any number of observers, and new observers can be added without affecting the existing code.

3. **Liskov Substitution Principle (LSP)**: The Observer pattern follows the LSP by ensuring that all observers implement the same interface, which defines the method for receiving updates from the subject. This means that any observer can be substituted for another observer without affecting the correctness of the program.

4. **Interface Segregation Principle (ISP)**: The Observer pattern follows the ISP by defining a separate interface for the subject and the observer, with a clear method for updating the observers. This way, the subject can notify the observers without the need for the observers to know the details of the subject.

5. **Dependency Inversion Principle (DIP)**: The Observer pattern follows the DIP by allowing the subject and the observers to depend on abstractions, rather than concrete implementations. The subject depends on the observer interface, while the observers depend on the subject interface. This way, the subject and the observers can be easily switched out for different implementations without affecting the rest of the code.

State Pattern

The **State design pattern** is a Behavioural design pattern that allows an object to alter its behaviour when its internal state changes. This pattern can be used when an object has multiple possible states, and each state requires a different behaviour from the object. Instead of including all the behaviour in the object itself, the State pattern encapsulates the behaviour of each state in a separate class.

Problem: In software design, certain objects can have multiple states and their behaviour changes based on these states. Managing the transitions and interactions between these states can lead to complex and error-prone code, especially as the number of states and state-dependent behaviours increases. In such cases, the code becomes difficult to maintain, understand, and extend.

Solution: The State Pattern is a Behavioural design pattern that addresses this problem by encapsulating each state of an object into a separate class, making it easier to manage and maintain state-specific behaviour. The pattern allows an object to alter its behaviour when its internal state changes, without changing its class. It promotes a clean separation between state-related logic and the core functionality of the object.

The pattern consists of four main components: the Context, the State, the ConcreteState, and the Client.

1. **Context**: This is the class that contains the state and the behaviour that depends on the state. It delegates the behaviour to the current state object.

2. **State**: This is an abstract class or interface that defines the behaviour for each state. It contains methods that are implemented by ConcreteState classes.

3. **ConcreteState**: This is a class that implements the behaviour for a specific state.

4. **Client**: This is the class that uses the Context and the State objects to perform some actions.

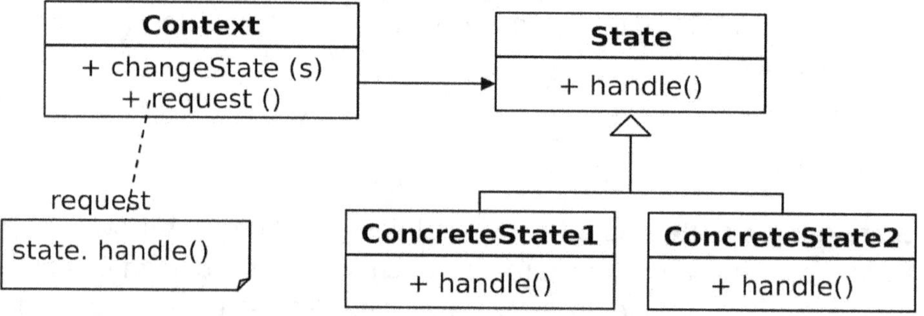

Here is an example implementation of the State pattern:

```
// Define State interface
class State {
    handle(context) {
        throw new Error("handle method must be implemented");
    }
}

// Define Context class
class Context {
    constructor(state) {
        this.currentState = state;
    }
```

```javascript
    changeState(state) {
        this.currentState = state;
    }

    request() {
        this.currentState.handle(this);
    }
}

// Define ConcreteState1 class implementing State
class ConcreteState1 extends State {
    handle(context) {
        console.log("ConcreteState1 handle");
        context.changeState(new ConcreteState2());
    }
}

// Define ConcreteState2 class implementing State
class ConcreteState2 extends State {
    handle(context) {
        console.log("ConcreteState2 handle");
        context.changeState(new ConcreteState1());
    }
}

// Client code
const state1 = new ConcreteState1();
const context = new Context(state1);
context.request();
context.request();
```

Output:

```
ConcreteState1 handle
ConcreteState2 handle
```

Explanation:

1. In this pattern, an object's behaviour is determined by its state, which can change dynamically based on certain conditions. The pattern separates the behaviour of the object from its state, so that different behaviours can be easily implemented by changing the object's state.

2. In this specific implementation, we have a **Context** class that holds a **State** object representing the current state of the context. The **State** abstract class defines the interface for the concrete state classes to

implement. In this case, we have two concrete state classes: **ConcreteState1** and **ConcreteState2**.

3. The **Context** class has a method to change its state to a new state, and a method to request that the current state handle a certain action. When the **request()** method is called, it calls the **handle()** method of the current state, which then updates the context's state as necessary.

4. In the code provided, the initial state of the context is **ConcreteState1**. The first call to the **request()** method will cause ConcreteState1's **handle()** method to be called, which will print "ConcreteState1 handle" and change the context's state to **ConcreteState2**. The second call to the **request()** method will cause ConcreteState2's **handle()** method to be called, which will print "ConcreteState2 handle" and change the context's state back to **ConcreteState1**. The cycle can continue as long as necessary.

Problem: Implements a simple BulbControl system using the State Design Pattern. The problem is to create a mechanism that allows the bulb to change its state between "On" and "Off" and to manage the state transitions smoothly. The state of the bulb should be controlled through the BulbControl class, and the specific states (On and Off) should be represented by separate classes using the State Pattern.

Solution:

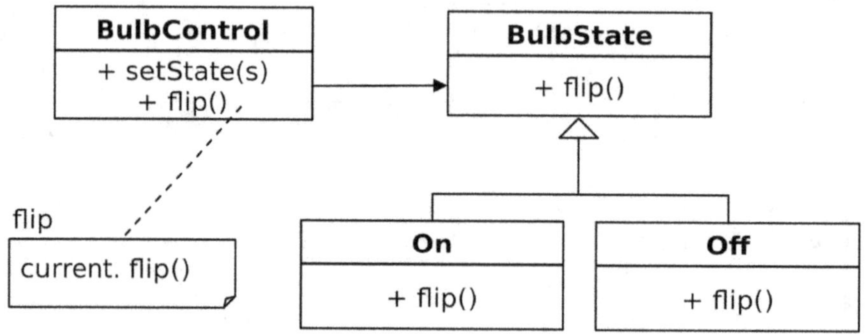

State pattern code demonstrate bulb states.

```
// Define BulbState interface
class BulbState {
    flip(bc) {
        throw new Error("flip method must be implemented");
    }
```

```javascript
    toString() {
        throw new Error("toString method must be implemented");
    }
}

// Define BulbControl class
class BulbControl {
    constructor() {
        this.current = new Off();
    }

    setState(state) {
        this.current = state;
    }

    flip() {
        this.current.flip(this);
    }

    toStringState() {
        return this.current.toString();
    }
}

// Define On class implementing BulbState
class On extends BulbState {
    flip(bc) {
        bc.setState(new Off());
    }

    toString() {
        return "On";
    }
}

// Define Off class implementing BulbState
class Off extends BulbState {
    flip(bc) {
        bc.setState(new On());
    }

    toString() {
        return "Off";
    }
}
```

```
// Client code
const c = new BulbControl();
c.flip();
console.log(c.toStringState());
c.flip();
console.log(c.toStringState());
```

Output:

```
On
Off
```

Explanation:

1. This code that implements the state pattern using a **BulbControl** class to control the state of a bulb. The **BulbState** abstract class defines the interface for bulb states, and the **On** and **Off** concrete classes implement the two possible states of the bulb.

2. The **BulbControl** class keeps track of the current state of the bulb and allows it to be flipped from **On** to **Off** or vice versa. The **toString()** method returns a string representation of the current state of the bulb.

3. The code demonstrates how the state pattern can be used to encapsulate the behaviour of an object in different states, making it easier to add or modify behaviour without affecting other parts of the system.

Consequences

1. **Modularity and Flexibility:** The State Pattern promotes modularity by representing each state as a separate class, making it easy to add or modify states without affecting other states or the context class. This leads to a more flexible and extensible design.

2. **Maintainability:** With the State Pattern, code maintenance becomes easier as each state class is responsible for its behaviour. Changes to a specific state can be done independently, reducing the risk of introducing bugs in other parts of the codebase.

3. **Readability and Understandability:** The pattern enhances the code's readability and understandability as it explicitly defines states and their transitions, making the code more intuitive and easier to follow.

4. **Complexity Management:** The State Pattern manages the complexity that arises from large, state-dependent switch or conditional statements.

By encapsulating each state's behaviour, the pattern avoids lengthy switch/case or if/else structures.

5. **Potential Overhead:** Introducing additional classes for each state can increase the number of classes in the system, potentially leading to a slight increase in memory overhead.

6. **Increased Number of Classes:** Depending on the complexity of the state machine, the State Pattern may introduce a higher number of classes, which can be more challenging to maintain and understand for small-scale systems.

7. **Appropriate Use Cases:** The State Pattern is most beneficial when dealing with objects that have multiple states and exhibit different behaviours based on those states. For simpler objects, implementing the State Pattern might be an unnecessary overhead.

SOLID principle applied

Here's how each SOLID principle can be applied to the State pattern:

1. **Single Responsibility Principle (SRP)**: The State pattern follows the SRP by separating the behaviour of an object into separate state classes. Each state class is responsible for handling a specific behaviour of the object, which ensures that each class has only one responsibility.

2. **Open-Closed Principle (OCP)**: The State pattern follows the OCP by allowing new states to be added without modifying the existing code. Each state class implements the same interface, which means that the existing code can work with new state classes without needing any modifications.

3. **Liskov Substitution Principle (LSP)**: The State pattern follows the LSP by ensuring that each state class implements the same interface and can be used interchangeably without affecting the correctness of the program.

4. **Interface Segregation Principle (ISP)**: The State pattern follows the ISP by defining a separate interface for each state class that defines the behaviour of the object. This ensures that each state class only has the methods it needs to implement, and the client only needs to know about the methods relevant to its current state.

5. **Dependency Inversion Principle (DIP)**: The State pattern follows the DIP by allowing the client to depend on the abstraction (the state interface) rather than the implementation (the specific state class). This means that the client can easily switch between different states without affecting the rest of the code.

Strategy Pattern

The **Strategy Design Pattern** is a Behavioural design pattern that allows objects to vary their behaviour at runtime by encapsulating a family of algorithms and selecting the algorithm to be used based on client requests or specific conditions.

Problem: In software development, you often encounter situations where different algorithms or strategies can be used to solve a problem. Without the Strategy pattern, you may end up implementing multiple versions of the same code with conditional statements to select the appropriate behaviour. This approach leads to code duplication, reduced maintainability, and increased complexity.

Solution: The Strategy pattern suggests decomposing the different algorithms into separate classes, implementing a common interface. Each strategy class represents a specific algorithm or behaviour. The client code interacts with an abstraction (interface or abstract class) that delegates the behaviour selection to a concrete strategy at runtime.

The pattern consists of three main components:

1. **Context**: This is the object that needs to change its behaviour based on the algorithm. It holds a reference to a Strategy object and delegates the work to it.

2. **Strategy**: This is the interface or abstract class that defines the algorithm to be used. It provides a method that the Context uses to call the algorithm.

3. **Concrete Strategy**: This is the implementation of the Strategy interface. It encapsulates the algorithm that is to be used by the Context.

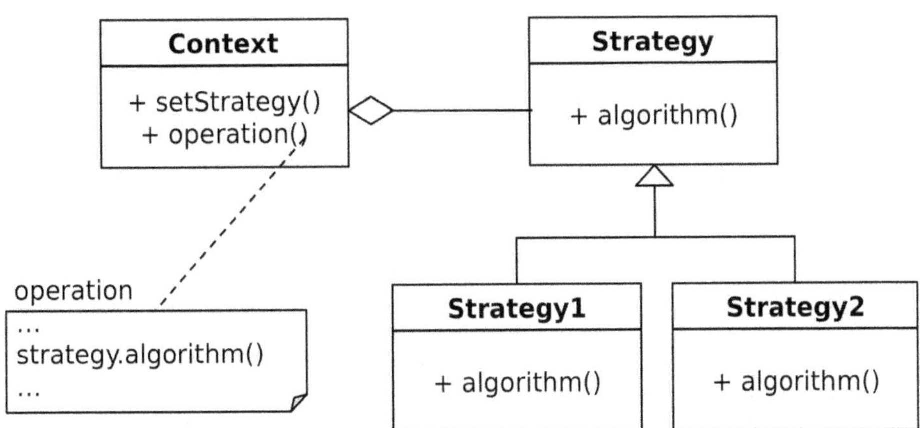

Here's an example implementation of the Strategy pattern :

```javascript
// Define Strategy interface
class Strategy {
    execute(data) {
        throw new Error("execute method must be implemented");
    }
}

// Define ConcreteStrategy1 class implementing Strategy
class ConcreteStrategy1 extends Strategy {
    execute(data) {
        console.log("ConcreteStrategy1 execute");
    }
}

// Define ConcreteStrategy2 class implementing Strategy
class ConcreteStrategy2 extends Strategy {
    execute(data) {
        console.log("ConcreteStrategy2 execute");
    }
}

// Define Context class
class Context {
    constructor(strategy) {
        this.strategy = strategy;
    }

    setStrategy(strategy) {
        this.strategy = strategy;
    }
```

```
    execute() {
        const data = 1;
        this.strategy.execute(data);
    }
}
```

```
// Client code
const context = new Context(new ConcreteStrategy1());
context.execute();

context.setStrategy(new ConcreteStrategy2());
context.execute();
```

Output:

```
ConcreteStrategy1 execute
ConcreteStrategy2 execute
```

Explanation:

The code provided implements the Strategy design pattern. Let's go through the classes and their roles:

1. **Strategy** (Interface):

   - This is the interface for the strategies. It declares a single method **execute**(data) that must be implemented by concrete strategy classes.

2. **ConcreteStrategy1** and **ConcreteStrategy2** (Concrete Classes):

   - These are two concrete implementations of the **Strategy** class. Each concrete strategy provides its own implementation of the **execute**(data) method. In this code, they simply print out a message indicating which strategy is being executed.

3. **Context** (Context Class):

   - The **Context** class represents the context in which the strategies are used. It has a reference to the current strategy (**self.strategy**) and provides methods to set a new strategy and execute the current strategy.

   - The constructor of the **Context** class initialises the **strategy** with **ConcreteStrategy1** by default, but you can also provide a different strategy during instantiation.

- The **setStrategy**(strategy) method allows you to change the strategy at runtime. It takes a strategy object as an argument and sets it as the new strategy.

- The **execute()** method executes the current strategy's **execute**(data) method. In this code, data is set to 1, but in a real-world scenario, it could be any data relevant to the specific algorithm being executed.

4. **Client Code**:

- The client code creates an instance of the **Context** class (c) without providing any strategy. By default, it uses **ConcreteStrategy1**.

- The **c.execute()** method is called, which prints "ConcreteStrategy1 execute" because the default strategy is **ConcreteStrategy1**.

- The client then changes the strategy to **ConcreteStrategy2** by calling **c.setStrategy(ConcreteStrategy2())**.

- The **c.execute()** method is called again, and this time, it prints "ConcreteStrategy2 execute" because the strategy has been changed to **ConcreteStrategy2**.

Problem: Implement two sorting algorithms, namely Bubble Sort and Selection Sort, using the Strategy Design Pattern. The client code should be able to switch between the sorting algorithms without modifying the existing code. The goal is to allow the client to choose which sorting algorithm to use dynamically.

Solution:

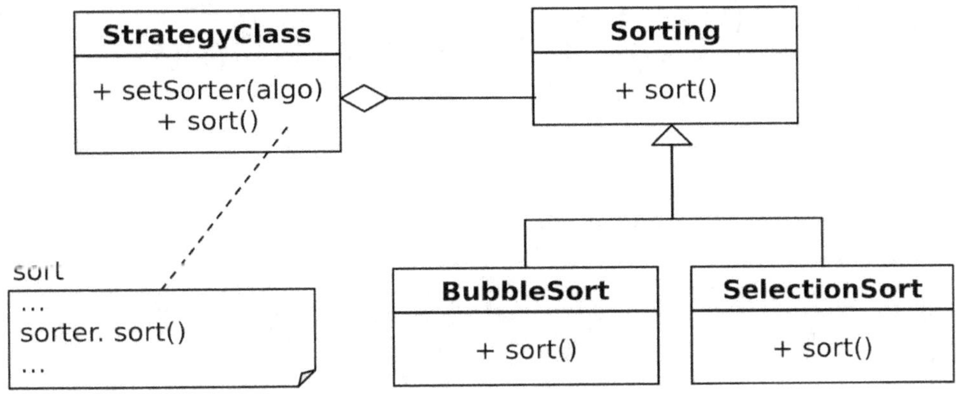

example implementation of the Strategy pattern :

```javascript
// Define Sorting interface
class Sorting {
    sort(numbers) {
        throw new Error("sort method must be implemented");
    }
}


// Define BubbleSort class implementing Sorting
class BubbleSort extends Sorting {
    sort(numbers) {
        // Bubble Sort Algorithm
        console.log("Bubble Sort Algorithm executed.");
        const size = numbers.length;
        for (let i = 0; i < size - 1; i++) {
            for (let j = 0; j < size - i - 1; j++) {
                if (numbers[j] > numbers[j + 1]) {
                    const temp = numbers[j];
                    numbers[j] = numbers[j + 1];
                    numbers[j + 1] = temp;
                }
            }
        }
    }
}


// Define SelectionSort class implementing Sorting
class SelectionSort extends Sorting {
    sort(numbers) {
        // Selection Sort Algorithm
        console.log("Selection Sort Algorithm executed.");
        const size = numbers.length;
        for (let i = 0; i < size - 1; i++) {
            let maxIndex = 0;
            for (let j = 1; j < size - i; j++) {
                if (numbers[j] > numbers[maxIndex]) {
                    maxIndex = j;
                }
            }
            const temp = numbers[size - 1 - i];
            numbers[size - 1 - i] = numbers[maxIndex];
            numbers[maxIndex] = temp;
        }
    }
}
```

```javascript
// Define StrategyClass
class StrategyClass {
    constructor(algo) {
        this.sorter = algo;
    }

    setSorter(algo) {
        this.sorter = algo;
    }

    sort(a) {
        this.sorter.sort(a);
    }
}

// Client code
const a = [4, 5, 3, 2, 6, 7, 1, 8, 9, 10];
const s = new StrategyClass(new BubbleSort());
s.sort(a);
console.log(a);

const b = [4, 5, 3, 2, 6, 7, 1, 8, 9, 10];
s.setSorter(new SelectionSort());
s.sort(b);
console.log(b);
```

Output:

```
Bubble Sort Algorithm executed.
[1, 2, 3, 4, 5, 6, 7, 8, 9, 10]
Selection Sort Algorithm executed.
[1, 2, 3, 4, 5, 6, 7, 8, 9, 10]
```

Explanation:

1. The code defines an abstract class **Sorting** with an abstract method **sort**(). This class serves as the base class for all sorting algorithms.

2. Two concrete classes, **BubbleSort** and **SelectionSort**, are defined that inherit from the **Sorting** class. Each class implements the **sort**() method with its respective sorting algorithm (Bubble Sort and Selection Sort).

3. The **StrategyClass** is a class that acts as a context for the Strategy Design Pattern. It has a sorter attribute, which holds an instance of the

Sorting class. The default sorting algorithm is set to **BubbleSort** in the constructor.

4. The **StrategyClass** has a method **setSorter()** that allows the client to set a different sorting algorithm dynamically.

5. The `sort` method in **StrategyClass** takes an array a and calls the **sort()** method of the current sorting algorithm (held in **sorter**). It then returns the sorted array.

6. The client code demonstrates how to use the Strategy Design Pattern for sorting arrays. It creates an instance of **StrategyClass** named s.

7. The client code then initialises an array a with unsorted numbers and calls **s.sort(a)** to sort the array using the default sorting algorithm (Bubble Sort). It prints the sorted array.

8. The client code initialises another array a with unsorted numbers again and sets the sorting algorithm to **SelectionSort** using the **setSorter()** method of **StrategyClass**. It then calls **s.sort(a)** again to sort the array using the new sorting algorithm (Selection Sort). It prints the sorted array.

Consequence

By employing the Strategy pattern, you achieve a more flexible and maintainable codebase. The main benefits include:

1. **Simplified Code Maintenance:** Each algorithm is isolated within its own class, making it easier to modify or add new strategies without impacting the client code.

2. **Improved Code Reusability:** Since each strategy is encapsulated, it can be reused across different parts of the application or even in different projects.

3. **Run-time Flexibility:** The client code can dynamically switch between different strategies at runtime, providing the ability to adapt to changing requirements or user preferences.

4. **Easy Extension:** It is straightforward to add new strategies by introducing new classes that adhere to the common interface.

5. **Better Testing:** Since each strategy is independent, it becomes simpler to write unit tests for each strategy in isolation.

SOLID principle applied

Here's how each SOLID principle can be applied to the Strategy pattern:

1. **Single Responsibility Principle (SRP)**: The Strategy pattern adheres to the SRP by separating the different algorithms into separate classes, each with a single responsibility. Each algorithm class has its own implementation of the strategy interface, with one specific method that performs the algorithm.

2. **Open-Closed Principle (OCP)**: The Strategy pattern follows the OCP by allowing new algorithms to be added as new classes that implement the same strategy interface. This way, the original code does not need to be modified, and the new algorithm can be added without breaking the existing code.

3. **Liskov Substitution Principle (LSP)**: The Strategy pattern follows the LSP by ensuring that each algorithm class implements the same strategy interface, with the same input and output parameters. This means that any algorithm class can be substituted for another algorithm class without affecting the correctness of the program.

4. **Interface Segregation Principle (ISP)**: The Strategy pattern follows the ISP by defining a separate interface for the algorithms, with a single method that performs the algorithm. This way, the client only needs to know about the strategy interface, and not the details of each individual algorithm.

5. **Dependency Inversion Principle (DIP)**: The Strategy pattern follows the DIP by allowing the client to depend on the abstraction (the strategy interface) rather than the implementation (the specific algorithm class). This way, the client can easily change the algorithm being used without modifying the code, by simply injecting a different algorithm class that implements the same strategy interface.

Template Method Pattern

The **Template Method Pattern** is a Behavioural design pattern that defines the structure of an algorithm in a superclass, but lets the subclasses override specific steps of the algorithm without changing its structure. In other words, the Template Method defines an abstract class that provides an outline of a method, with some steps implemented, and other steps to be implemented by the subclasses.

Problem: When dealing with algorithms or processes that have a common structure but varying implementation details, developers often face the challenge of finding a balance between code duplication and flexibility. Without a proper design, code duplication can lead to maintenance issues and inconsistency, while tightly coupling different parts of the algorithm can make the code difficult to extend and maintain.

Solution: The Template Method pattern addresses this problem by providing an abstract class (or interface) that defines the template method, representing the overall algorithm's structure. This template method calls several abstract or hook methods, which are implemented by concrete subclasses to customise specific steps of the algorithm.

The main idea of the Template Method Pattern is to separate the invariant parts of the algorithm from the variant ones, and to encapsulate them in separate methods. This pattern allows us to reuse the algorithm and change the implementation of the variant parts without affecting the structure of the algorithm.

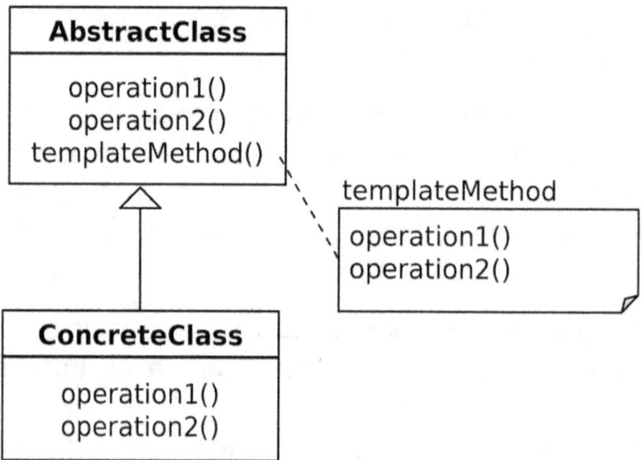

Here's an example implementation of the Template pattern :

```
// Define AbstractClass
class AbstractClass {
    templateMethod() {
        this.operation1();
        this.operation2();
    }

    operation1() {
        throw new Error("operation1 method must be implemented");
    }
```

```javascript
    operation2() {
        throw new Error("operation2 method must be implemented");
    }
}

// Define ConcreteClass1 extending AbstractClass
class ConcreteClass1 extends AbstractClass {
    operation1() {
        console.log("Concrete Class 1: Operation 1");
    }

    operation2() {
        console.log("Concrete Class 1: Operation 2");
    }
}

// Define ConcreteClass2 extending AbstractClass
class ConcreteClass2 extends AbstractClass {
    operation1() {
        console.log("Concrete Class 2: Operation 1");
    }

    operation2() {
        console.log("Concrete Class 2: Operation 2");
    }
}

// Client code
const concreteClass = new ConcreteClass1();
concreteClass.templateMethod();
```

Output:

```
Concrete Class 1 : Operation 1
Concrete Class 1 : Operation 2
```

Explanation:

1. In the code example provided, we have an abstract class **AbstractClass** that defines a template method **templateMethod()** which calls two abstract methods **operation1()** and **operation2()**. The concrete subclasses **ConcreteClass1** and **ConcreteClass2** implement the abstract methods and provide their own implementation.

2. When the client code creates an instance of the **ConcreteClass1** and calls the **templateMethod()**, it prints "Concrete Class 1 : Operation 1"

and "Concrete Class 1 : Operation 2" indicating that the algorithm defined in the base class is followed with the specific steps implemented in the concrete subclass.

Problem: Implement the Template Method design pattern for adding data to different destinations. The base class AddDataTemplate defines a template method addData(), along with three abstract methods open(), add(), and close(). The subclasses AddDataToFile and AddDataToDB implement these abstract methods to add data to a file and a database, respectively.

Solution:

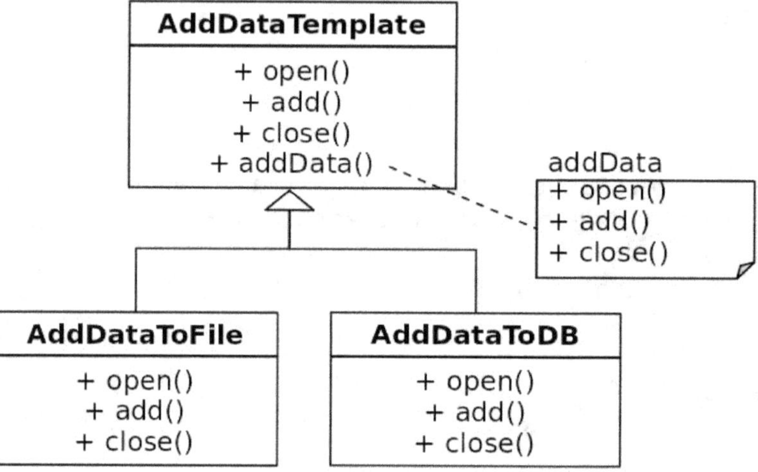

Here's an example implementation of the Template pattern :

```
// Define AddDataTemplate
class AddDataTemplate {
    addData() {
        this.open();
        this.add();
        this.close();
    }

    open() {
        throw new Error("open method must be implemented");
    }

    add() {
        throw new Error("add method must be implemented");
    }

    close() {
        throw new Error("close method must be implemented");
```

```javascript
        }
}

// Define AddDataToFile extending AddDataTemplate
class AddDataToFile extends AddDataTemplate {
    open() {
        console.log("Open file.");
    }

    add() {
        console.log("Add data to file.");
    }

    close() {
        console.log("Close file");
    }
}

// Define AddDataToDB extending AddDataTemplate
class AddDataToDB extends AddDataTemplate {
    open() {
        console.log("Open Database.");
    }

    add() {
        console.log("Add data to Database.");
    }

    close() {
        console.log("Close Database.");
    }
}

// Client code
const addDataToDB = new AddDataToDB();
addDataToDB.addData();
```

Output:

```
Open Database.
Add data to Database.
Close Database.
```

Explanation:

1. The code defines two concrete classes that implement the
   AddDataTemplate abstract class. The **AddDataToFile** and

 AddDataToDB classes implement the three template methods (**open()**, **add()**, and **close()**) in their own way.

2. The **AddDataTemplate** abstract class has a final method **addData()** which calls the three template methods in sequence. The **open()**, **add()**, and **close()** methods are abstract, so they must be implemented by the concrete classes.

3. The client code creates an instance of **AddDataToDB** and calls its **addData()** method. The method executes the **open()**, **add()**, and **close()** methods in sequence, producing the output `Open Database. Add data to Database. Close Database.`

Consequence

1. **Code Reusability:** The Template Method pattern promotes code reusability by encapsulating the common algorithm structure in the template method. Subclasses can focus on providing implementations for specific steps, which encourages reuse of the existing code.

2. **Flexibility:** By allowing subclasses to override specific steps, the pattern enables flexibility in algorithm customization without altering the overall structure. This makes it easier to adapt the algorithm to different scenarios.

3. **Reduction of Code Duplication:** By defining the common algorithm in one place, the Template Method pattern reduces code duplication. This leads to cleaner and more maintainable code.

4. **Clear Separation of Concerns:** The pattern separates the high-level algorithm from the details of its steps, promoting a clear separation of concerns. This enhances the code's readability and makes it easier to understand the overall flow of the algorithm.

5. **Inversion of Control:** The control flow is inverted in the Template Method pattern. Instead of subclasses controlling the algorithm's flow, the template method in the abstract class drives the process by calling specific methods in the subclasses.

6. **Lack of Runtime Flexibility:** One potential downside is that the template method defines the algorithm's structure at compile-time. It may lack runtime flexibility, making it challenging to change the algorithm's structure dynamically.

SOLID principle applied

Here's how each SOLID principle can be applied to the Template Method pattern:

1. **Single Responsibility Principle (SRP)**: The Template Method pattern follows the SRP by separating the overall algorithm into a base class that defines the overall structure and abstract methods that can be implemented by derived classes. This way, the base class is responsible for the overall algorithm, while the derived classes are responsible for implementing the specific steps.

2. **Open-Closed Principle (OCP)**: The Template Method pattern follows the OCP by allowing new derived classes to be added without modifying the existing code. The base class provides a skeleton of the algorithm, which can be overridden by the derived classes to implement specific steps.

3. **Liskov Substitution Principle (LSP)**: The Template Method pattern follows the LSP by ensuring that the derived classes adhere to the same interface or inheritance hierarchy. This means that the client can use the derived classes interchangeably, without affecting the correctness of the program.

4. **Interface Segregation Principle (ISP)**: The Template Method pattern follows the ISP by defining a clear interface for the base class, which provides a skeleton of the algorithm and abstract methods that can be implemented by the derived classes. This way, the client only needs to know about the base class interface, and not the details of each individual derived class.

5. **Dependency Inversion Principle (DIP)**: The Template Method pattern follows the DIP by allowing the client to depend on the abstraction (the base class interface) rather than the implementation (the specific derived class). This way, the client can easily switch between different derived classes without affecting the rest of the code.

Visitor Pattern

The **Visitor design pattern** is a Behavioural design pattern that allows you to add new behaviours or operations to a group of classes without modifying their code. It separates the algorithm from the object structure on which it operates, making it easier to extend the functionality of the classes.

Problem: In object-oriented programming, when dealing with a complex class hierarchy, adding new operations or functionalities to every class in the hierarchy becomes cumbersome and violates the Open/Closed Principle of SOLID design principles. Additionally, modifying existing classes may lead to potential side effects and break existing code.

Solution: The Visitor design pattern solves this problem by introducing a separate set of visitor classes that encapsulate the new operations or functionalities. Instead of modifying the classes themselves, the pattern allows you to define new operations by creating concrete visitor classes that can visit each class in the object structure.

The pattern involves two main components: the visitor and the element. The visitor is an interface or an abstract class that defines the operations that can be performed on the elements. The element is a class that defines an accept method that accepts the visitor and calls a method on it, passing itself as an argument.

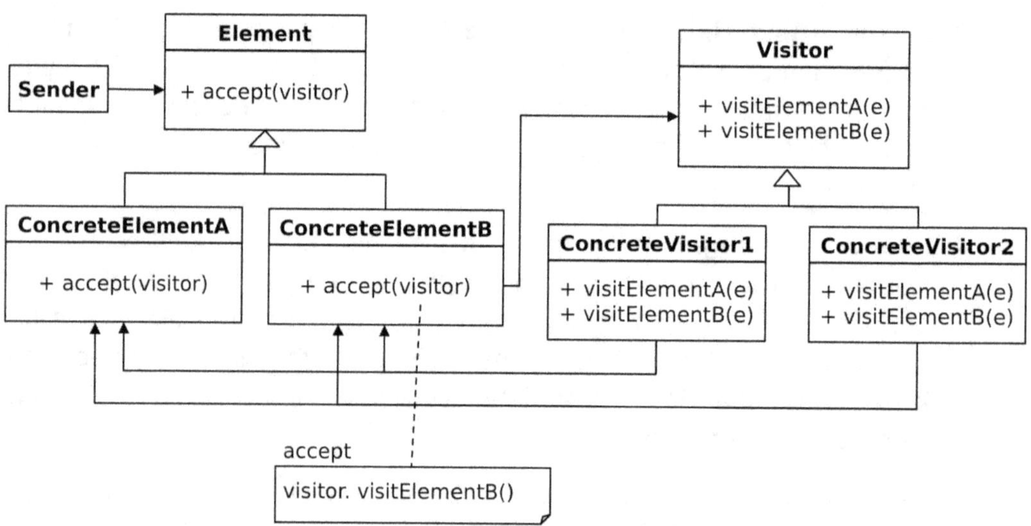

Here's an example implementation of the Visitor pattern :

```
// Define Element interface
class Element {
    accept(visitor) {
        throw new Error("accept method must be implemented");
    }
}


// Define ConcreteElementA implementing Element
class ConcreteElementA extends Element {
    accept(visitor) {
```

```javascript
        visitor.visitElementA(this);
    }
}

// Define ConcreteElementB implementing Element
class ConcreteElementB extends Element {
    accept(visitor) {
        visitor.visitElementB(this);
    }
}

// Define Visitor interface
class Visitor {
    visitElementA(elementA) {
        throw new Error("visitElementA method must be
implemented");
    }

    visitElementB(elementB) {
        throw new Error("visitElementB method must be
implemented");
    }
}

// Define ConcreteVisitor1 implementing Visitor
class ConcreteVisitor1 extends Visitor {
    visitElementA(elementA) {
        console.log("ConcreteVisitor1 visitElementA() method
called.");
    }

    visitElementB(elementB) {
        console.log("ConcreteVisitor1 visitElementB() method
called.");
    }
}

// Define ConcreteVisitor2 implementing Visitor
class ConcreteVisitor2 extends Visitor {
    visitElementA(elementA) {
        console.log("ConcreteVisitor2 visitElementA() method
called.");
    }

    visitElementB(elementB) {
        console.log("ConcreteVisitor2 visitElementB() method
called.");
```

```
    }
}

// Client code
const visitor1 = new ConcreteVisitor1();
const elementA = new ConcreteElementA();
elementA.accept(visitor1);
const elementB = new ConcreteElementB();
elementB.accept(visitor1);
```

Output:

```
ConcreteVisitor1 visitElementA() method called.
ConcreteVisitor1 visitElementB() method called.
```

Explanation:

1. It defines a set of classes and interfaces to represent elements and visitors. The **Element** interface defines the **accept()** method, which takes a visitor as an argument and calls the appropriate `visit` method on the visitor. The **ConcreteElementA** and **ConcreteElementB** classes inherit from **Element** and implement the **accept()** method to call the appropriate **visit()** method on the passed-in visitor.

2. The **Visitor** abstract class defines a set of `visit` methods for each concrete element class that it might encounter. The **ConcreteVisitor1** and **ConcreteVisitor2** classes inherit from `Visitor` and implement the `visit` methods to perform some action on the elements they visit.

3. Finally, in the client code, an instance of **ConcreteVisitor1** is created and used to visit a **ConcreteElementA** object and a **ConcreteElementB** object. The appropriate `visit` method is called on the visitor for each element, allowing the visitor to perform some action on the element.

Problem: Implements the Visitor design pattern to manage different shapes (Circle and Rectangle) in an "ObjectsStructure" class. The goal is to enable the addition of new operations (visitors) without modifying the shape classes themselves.

Solution: The code defines the following classes:

1. **Shape (abstract class):** It is an abstract class that represents a shape and defines an abstract method "accept" that should be implemented by subclasses.

2. **Circle (subclass of Shape):** Represents a circle with its coordinates (x, y) and radius.

3. **Rectangle (subclass of Shape):** Represents a rectangle with its coordinates (x, y), width, and height.

4. **Visitor (abstract class):** It is an abstract class that defines methods for visiting each shape class.

5. **XMLVisitor (subclass of Visitor):** Implements the visitor interface to generate XML representation for circles and rectangles.

6. **TextVisitor (subclass of Visitor):** Implements the visitor interface to generate text representation for circles and rectangles.

7. **ObjectsStructure:** Represents a collection of shapes and provides a method to add shapes, set the visitor, and accept visitors.

An example implementation of the Visitor pattern :

```
// Define Shape class
class Shape {
    accept(visitor) {
        throw new Error("accept method must be implemented");
    }
}


// Define Circle class extending Shape
class Circle extends Shape {
    constructor(x, y, radius) {
        super();
        this.x = x;
        this.y = y;
        this.radius = radius;
    }

    accept(visitor) {
        visitor.visitCircle(this);
    }

    getX() {
        return this.x;
    }

    getY() {
        return this.y;
    }
```

```javascript
    getRadius() {
        return this.radius;
    }
}


// Define Rectangle class extending Shape
class Rectangle extends Shape {
    constructor(x, y, width, height) {
        super();
        this.x = x;
        this.y = y;
        this.width = width;
        this.height = height;
    }

    accept(visitor) {
        visitor.visitRectangle(this);
    }

    getX() {
        return this.x;
    }

    getY() {
        return this.y;
    }

    getWidth() {
        return this.width;
    }

    getHeight() {
        return this.height;
    }
}

// Define Visitor class
class Visitor {
    visitCircle(circle) {
        throw new Error("visitCircle method must be
implemented");
    }

    visitRectangle(rectangle) {
        throw new Error("visitRectangle method must be
implemented");
```

```javascript
    }
}

// Define XMLVisitor class extending Visitor
class XMLVisitor extends Visitor {
    visitCircle(circle) {
        console.log(`<circle>\n  <x>${circle.getX()}</x>\n  <y>$
{circle.getY()}</y>\n  <radius>${circle.getRadius()}</radius>\
n</circle>`);
    }

    visitRectangle(rectangle) {
        console.log(`<rectangle>\n  <x>${rectangle.getX()}</x>\n
<y>${rectangle.getY()}</y>\n  <width>$
{rectangle.getWidth()}</width>\n  <height>$
{rectangle.getHeight()}</height>\n</rectangle>`);
    }
}

// Define TextVisitor class extending Visitor
class TextVisitor extends Visitor {
    visitCircle(circle) {
        console.log(`Circle ( (x : ${circle.getX()}, y : $
{circle.getY()}), radius : ${circle.getRadius()})`);
    }

    visitRectangle(rectangle) {
        console.log(`Rectangle ( (x : ${rectangle.getX()}, y : $
{rectangle.getY()}), width : ${rectangle.getWidth()}, height : $
{rectangle.getHeight()})`);
    }
}

// Define ObjectsStructure class
class ObjectsStructure {
    constructor() {
        this.shapes = [];
        this.visitor = null;
    }

    addShape(shape) {
        this.shapes.push(shape);
    }

    setVisitor(visitor) {
        this.visitor = visitor;
    }
```

```javascript
    accept() {
        for (const shape of this.shapes) {
            shape.accept(this.visitor);
        }
    }
}

// Client code
const os = new ObjectsStructure();
os.addShape(new Rectangle(6, 7, 8, 9));
os.addShape(new Circle(6, 7, 8));
os.setVisitor(new XMLVisitor());
os.accept();
os.setVisitor(new TextVisitor());
os.accept();
```

Output:

```
<rectangle>
  <x>6</x>
  <y>7</y>
  <width>8</width>
  <height>9</height>
</rectangle>
<circle>
  <x>6</x>
  <y>7</y>
  <radius>8</radius>
</circle>
<dot>
  <x>6</x>
  <y>7</y>
</dot>
Rectangle ( (x : 6, y : 7), width : 8, height : 9)
Circle ( (x : 6, y : 7), radius : 8)
Dot ( x : 6, y : 7)
```

Explanation:

1. The code defines an abstract **Shape** class and three concrete shapes - **Circle**, **Rectangle**, and **Dot** that implement the **Shape** interface. The **Shape** interface includes the **accept()** method that accepts a **Visitor** object as an argument. The **Visitor** is an abstract class with methods to visit each of the concrete shapes.

2. The **XMLVisitor** and **TextVisitor** classes implement the **Visitor** interface and provide different ways to visit each of the shapes. The **ObjectsStructure** class acts as the object structure that holds the shapes and can apply a **Visitor** to all the shapes in the structure.

3. When the **accept()** method of a **Shape** is called with a **Visitor** object, it calls the appropriate **Visitor** method based on the type of the **Shape**. The **Visitor** then performs some operation on the **Shape**, and the result is returned back to the **accept()** method of the Shape.

4. In the test code, the **ObjectsStructure** is created and shapes are added to it. Two Visitor objects are created - XMLVisitor and TextVisitor, and set on the **ObjectsStructure**. The **accept()** method of the **ObjectsStructure** is called twice with the two different **Visitor** objects, resulting in the two different representations of the shapes being printed.

Consequence

The Visitor pattern offers several benefits:

1. **Extensibility:** New operations can be added without altering the existing classes, promoting open-closed principle compliance.

2. **Separation of Concerns:** The pattern separates the algorithm (visitor) from the object structure, leading to better code organisation and maintainability.

3. **Single Responsibility Principle:** Each visitor encapsulates a single operation, keeping the responsibilities well-defined.

However, there are some trade-offs:

1. **Complexity:** Implementing the Visitor pattern might introduce additional complexity, especially if the object structure frequently changes or new operations are added.

2. **Dependency on Class Hierarchy:** The Visitor pattern often requires a stable class hierarchy since adding new classes to the hierarchy can be cumbersome.

3. **Performance Overhead:** The pattern may result in additional function call overhead due to the double dispatch mechanism used in some languages to achieve dynamic dispatch.

SOLID principle applied

Here's how each SOLID principle can be applied to the Visitor pattern:

1. **Single Responsibility Principle (SRP)**: The Visitor pattern follows the SRP by separating the operations that are performed on the visited objects into separate visitor classes. Each visitor has a single responsibility, which is to perform a specific operation on the visited object.

2. **Open-Closed Principle (OCP)**: The Visitor pattern follows the OCP by allowing new operations to be added as new visitor classes, without modifying the existing code. The visitor interface defines a method for each operation that can be performed on the visited objects, and new visitor classes can be added to implement these methods.

3. **Liskov Substitution Principle (LSP)**: The Visitor pattern follows the LSP by allowing the visitor classes to operate on any object that implements the visited interface. This means that any visited object can be substituted with another object that implements the same visited interface, without affecting the correctness of the program.

4. **Interface Segregation Principle (ISP)**: The Visitor pattern follows the ISP by defining a separate interface for the visitors, with a single method for each operation that can be performed on the visited objects. This way, the client only needs to know about the visitor interface, and not the details of each individual visitor.

5. **Dependency Inversion Principle (DIP)**: The Visitor pattern follows the DIP by allowing the client to depend on the abstraction (the visited interface) rather than the implementation (the specific visited object class). This way, the client can easily switch between different visited object implementations without affecting the rest of the code.

ARCHITECTURAL PATTERNS

Model-View-Controller Pattern

The **Model-View-Controller (MVC) pattern** is a design pattern commonly used in software development to separate the concerns of an application into three interconnected components: the Model, the View, and the Controller. The MVC pattern helps in achieving a clear separation of responsibilities, promotes code reusability, and enhances the maintainability of the application.

Here's an overview of the three components in the MVC pattern:

1. **Model**: The model represents the application's data and business logic. It encapsulates the data and provides methods for accessing and manipulating that data. It defines the structure and behaviour of the application's data, including validation, calculations, and interactions with the database or external services. The model notifies the view of any changes in the data, ensuring synchronisation between the model and the view.

2. **View**: The view is responsible for the presentation and visualisation of the data to the user. It defines the user interface and how the data is displayed. The view observes the model for any changes and updates its presentation accordingly. The view should not contain any business logic or directly modify the data; its main purpose is to present the data and handle user interactions, forwarding them to the controller.

3. **Controller**: The controller acts as an intermediary between the model and the view. It receives and processes user input from the view, interacts with the model to update the data. The controller contains the application's logic and orchestrates the flow of data and events between the model and the view. It separates the user interactions from the underlying data and delegates responsibilities to the appropriate components.

The MVC pattern promotes loose coupling between the components, allowing them to be developed and maintained independently. It enhances code modularity, reusability, and testability, as each component has a specific responsibility. Changes in one component can be made without affecting the others, facilitating application maintenance and evolution.

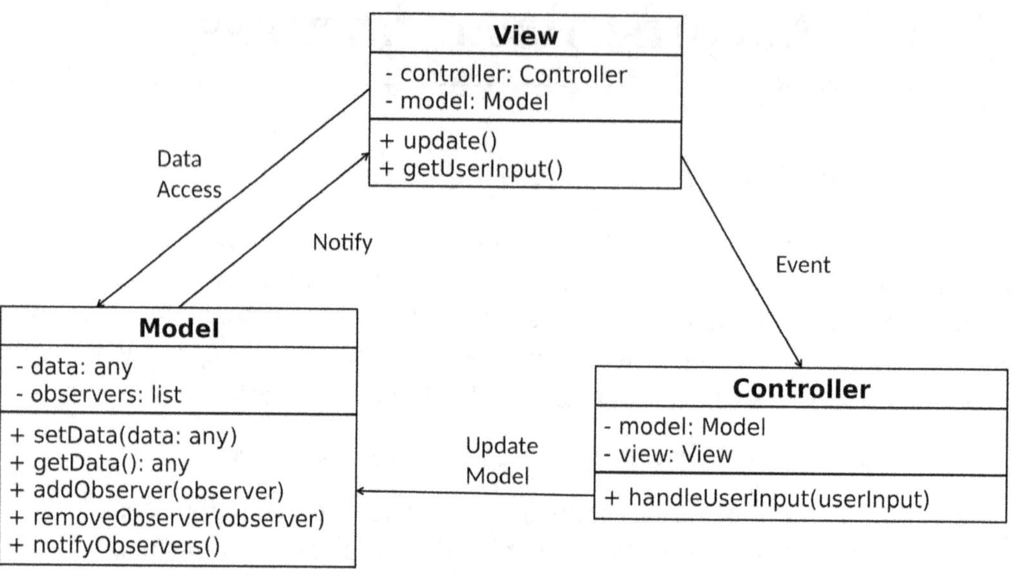

The interactions among the components in the MVC pattern are as follows:

1. The user interacts with the view, such as entering data or triggering actions.

2. The view forwards the user input to the controller.

3. The controller receives the input, performs the necessary operations, and updates the model accordingly.

4. The model notifies the view of any changes in the data. The Model maintains a list of observers (View). The Model notifies its observers when the data changes. Observer pattern is used here.

5. The view retrieves the updated data from the model and updates its presentation.

6. The user sees the updated view and can continue interacting with the application.

Here is an example implementation of the MVC pattern :

```javascript
// Model
class Model {
    constructor() {
        this.data = '';
        this.observers = [];
    }
```

```javascript
    setData(data) {
        console.log("Model : Set data.");
        this.data = data;
        this.notifyObservers();
    }

    getData() {
        console.log("Model : Get data.");
        return this.data;
    }

    addObserver(observer) {
        this.observers.push(observer);
    }

    removeObserver(observer) {
        this.observers = this.observers.filter(obs => obs !==
observer);
    }

    notifyObservers() {
        console.log("Model : Notify observers.");
        this.observers.forEach(observer => observer.update());
    }
}

// View
class View {
    constructor(model, controller) {
        this.model = model;
        this.controller = controller;
        this.model.addObserver(this);
    }

    update() {
        console.log("View : Update.");
        const data = this.model.getData();
        console.log("Data: " + data);
    }

    getUserInput() {
        const readline = require('readline').createInterface({
            input: process.stdin,
            output: process.stdout
        });
```

```javascript
        readline.question('View : Enter user input: ', userInput
=> {
            this.controller.handleUserInput(userInput);
            readline.close();
        });
    }
}

// Controller
class Controller {
    constructor(model) {
        this.model = model;
    }

    handleUserInput(userInput) {
        console.log("Controller : Handle user input.");
        this.model.setData(userInput);
    }

    setView(view) {
        this.view = view;
    }
}

// Client code
const model = new Model();
const controller = new Controller(model);
const view = new View(model, controller);
controller.setView(view);
view.getUserInput();
```

Output:

```
View : Enter user input: hello, world!
Controller : Handle user input.
Model : Set data.
Model : Notify observers.
View : Update.
Model : Get data.
Data: hello, world!
```

Explanation: This program follows these steps:

1. The **View** gets the user input and passes it to the **Controller**.

2. The **Controller** handles the user input and sets it in the **Model**.

3. The **Model** updates its data and notifies all registered observers (in this case, the **View**).

4. The **View** gets notified of the change and updates itself to display the new data from the **Model**.

It's important to note that there are variations and adaptations of the MVC pattern, such as Model-View-Presenter (MVP) and Model-View-ViewModel (MVVM), which introduce slight differences in the responsibilities and interactions of the components. However, the core idea of separating concerns remains consistent across these variations.

Drawbacks of MVC and Advantages of MVP

Drawbacks of MVC:

1. **Massive View Controllers:** In MVC, the Controller tends to become bloated with responsibilities, leading to what is commonly referred to as "Massive View Controllers." As the application grows in complexity, the Controller can become difficult to maintain and understand.
2. **Tightly Coupled Views and Controllers:** In MVC, the View and the Controller are often tightly coupled. The Controller must know the details of the View and vice versa, making it challenging to replace or modify one without affecting the other.
3. **Testing Challenges:** Properly unit testing MVC applications can be difficult, mainly due to the tight coupling between Views and Controllers. It can be challenging to test the interactions between the View and Controller independently.

Reasons for MVP:

1. **Better Separation of Concerns**: MVP improves the separation of concerns compared to MVC. In MVP, the Presenter acts as a mediator between the View and the Model, reducing direct interactions between them and promoting better isolation of responsibilities.
2. **Clearer Roles**: In MVP, each component (Model, View, Presenter) has a distinct role, making the codebase easier to understand and maintain. The Presenter handles user interactions and updates the Model, while the View handles rendering and user input.
3. **Easier Testing**: MVP makes unit testing more straightforward. The Presenter can be easily tested with mock implementations of the View and Model, allowing for more independent and focused testing.

4. **Enhanced Reusability**: Because the Presenter acts as an intermediary between the View and Model, the View can be implemented with minimal logic, making it easier to reuse across different platforms or UI frameworks.

5. **Support for Interfaces and Dependency Injection**: MVP encourages the use of interfaces and dependency injection, which enhances flexibility and decouples components. This enables easier swapping of implementations and better overall maintainability.

6. **Flexibility for UI Frameworks**: MVP is considered more flexible for working with various UI frameworks, as the Presenter can abstract the business logic from the specifics of the UI implementation.

Model-View-Presenter Pattern

The **MVP (Model-View-Presenter) pattern** is a software architectural pattern that separates the concerns of data presentation, user interaction, and business logic in an application. It aims to improve the maintainability, testability, and reusability of the code by promoting a clear separation of responsibilities.

Here's a description of each component in the MVP pattern:

1. **Model**:

   - The Model represents the data and business logic of the application.

   - It encapsulates the data structures, algorithms, and operations relevant to the application's functionality.

   - The Model does not have any direct dependencies on the View or Presenter.

2. **View**:

   - The View is responsible for the presentation of data to the user and capturing user interactions.

   - It is passive and does not contain any business logic.

   - The View is typically implemented using GUI elements, such as forms, dialogs, or web pages.

   - It provides interfaces or callbacks that the Presenter can use to communicate with the user.

3. **Presenter**:

   - The Presenter acts as an intermediary between the Model and the View.

- It retrieves data from the Model, processes it, and prepares it for presentation in the View.

- The Presenter handles user interactions from the View, interprets them, and invokes the corresponding actions on the Model.

- It decouples the View and the Model by abstracting their interactions through interfaces or contracts.

- The Presenter does not have any direct knowledge of the concrete implementation details of the View and the Model.

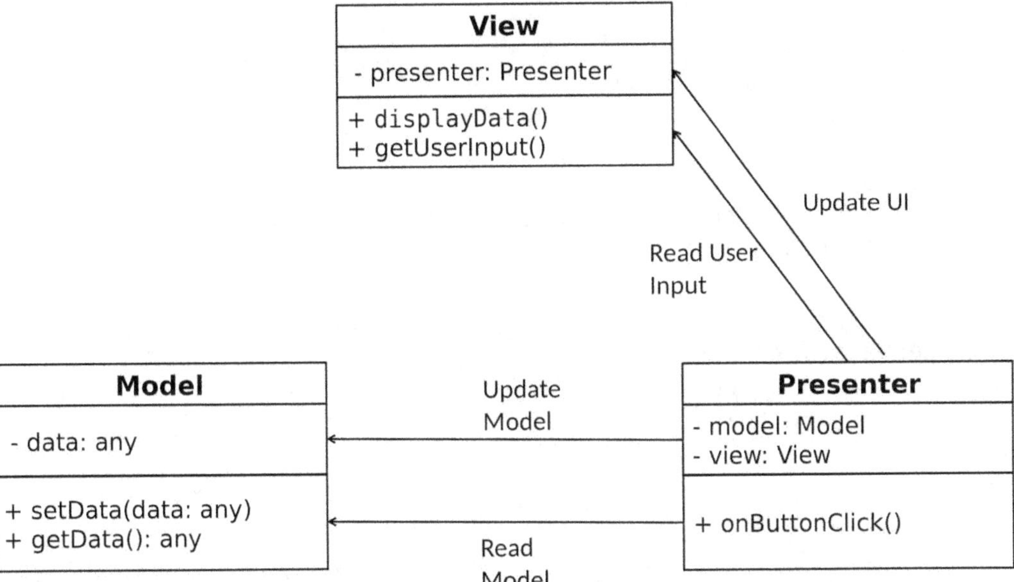

The flow of interaction in MVP follows these general steps:

1. The user interacts with the View, triggering an event or action.

2. The View notifies the Presenter about the user interaction.

3. The Presenter reads the user data from the View and processes it.

4. The Presenter updates the Model.

5. The Presenter reads the data from the Model and updates the View.

6. The View reflects the updated data to the user.

The MVP pattern promotes separation of concerns and improves the testability of the code. The Model can be tested independently, as it does not rely on the View or the Presenter. The View can be designed and modified without affecting the business logic encapsulated in the Model. The Presenter can be unit tested by mocking the View and the Model, ensuring that the business logic is correctly implemented and the interactions with the View are handled appropriately.

By keeping the responsibilities of each component clear and separate, MVP enables easier code maintenance, extensibility, and reusability. It is commonly used in GUI-based applications but can be applied to other types of applications as well.

Here's an example implementation of the MVP pattern :

```javascript
// Model
class Model {
    constructor() {
        this.data = "Hello";
    }

    setData(data) {
        console.log("Model: Set data: " + data);
        this.data = data;
    }

    getData() {
        console.log("Model: Get data: " + this.data);
        return this.data;
    }
}

// View
class View {
    getUserInput() {
        console.log("View: getUserInput");
        console.log("View: Enter user input: ");
        const userInput = "Hello, World!";
        console.log(userInput);

        return userInput;
    }

    getUserInput2() {
        console.log("View: getUserInput");
        const readline = require('readline').createInterface({
            input: process.stdin,
            output: process.stdout
        });
```

```javascript
            readline.question('View : Enter user input: ', userInput
=> {
                this.controller.handleUserInput(userInput);
                readline.close();
        });
    }

    displayData(data) {
        console.log("View: Display Result: " + data);
    }
}

// Presenter
class Presenter {
    constructor(model, view) {
        this.model = model;
        this.view = view;
    }

    onButtonClick() {
        console.log("Presenter: onButtonClick.");
        const data = this.view.getUserInput();
        this.model.setData(data);
        const newData = this.model.getData();
        this.view.displayData(newData);
    }
}

// Client code
const model = new Model();
const view = new View();
const presenter = new Presenter(model, view);
presenter.onButtonClick();
```

Output:

```
Presenter: onButtonClick.
View: getUserInput
View: Enter user input: Hello, World!
Model: Set data: Hello, World!
Model: Get data: Hello, World!
View: Display Result: Hello, World!
```

Explanation: Here's a step-by-step explanation of what the code does:

1. The Model class represents the data and has methods to set and get the data.

2. The View class interacts with the user to get input using the input function and displays the data.
3. The Presenter class acts as a middleman between the Model and the View. It receives user input from the View, updates the data in the Model, retrieves the data from the Model, and sends the data back to the View.
4. The client code creates instances of Model, View, and Presenter.
5. The Presenter handles the button click event (onButtonClick method), which represents a user action in the MVP pattern.
6. The Presenter interacts with the View to get user input, then updates the Model with the new data, and finally retrieves the updated data from the Model and sends it back to the View for display.

Drawbacks of MVP and Advantages of MVVM

Drawbacks of MVP:

1. **Boilerplate Code:** In MVP, there can be a significant amount of boilerplate code due to the need for explicit interfaces between the View, Presenter, and Model. This can make the codebase larger and more complex.
2. **Manual View-Update Synchronisation:** In MVP, the Presenter is responsible for updating the View with changes from the Model. This manual synchronisation can lead to potential bugs if not handled correctly.
3. **Presenter Overhead:** In MVP, the Presenter acts as an intermediary between the View and Model, which can lead to an increased number of classes and methods. This can make the architecture more complex and harder to understand.

Reasons for MVVM:

1. **Data Binding:** One of the significant advantages of MVVM over MVP is the concept of data binding. In MVVM, the ViewModel exposes properties that the View binds directly to. When data changes in the ViewModel, it automatically updates the View, reducing the need for manual synchronisation.

2. **Simplified View:** In MVVM, the View is simplified compared to MVP. It is primarily responsible for rendering the UI elements and binding to ViewModel properties. This leads to cleaner and more concise View code.

3. **Testability:** MVVM improves testability, similar to MVP. The ViewModel can be easily unit tested independently of the View, making it easier to write comprehensive and focused tests.

4. **Loose Coupling:** MVVM promotes loose coupling between the View and ViewModel, as the ViewModel doesn't know about the specific View implementation. This allows for better separation of concerns and greater flexibility in UI design.

5. **Platform Agnostic:** MVVM is widely used in frameworks that support data binding, such as WPF in .NET, Android Data Binding, or Knockout.js in JavaScript. This makes it a popular choice for cross-platform development, as the ViewModel can remain largely the same while adapting different Views.

6. **State Management:** MVVM often incorporates the concept of observable properties in the ViewModel, which simplifies state management and handling of user interactions.

Model-View-ViewModel Pattern

The **Model-View-ViewModel (MVVM) pattern** is a software architecture pattern used primarily in building user interfaces (UIs). The pattern is designed to separate the concerns of an application's user interface from the application's business logic and data models. It was first introduced by Microsoft in 2005 as a variation of the Model-View-Controller (MVC) pattern.

MVVM consists of three main components:

1. **Model**: This component represents the data and business logic of the application. It could be a database, a web service, or any other data source.

2. **View**: This component represents the user interface of the application. It includes everything that the user can see and interact with, such as buttons, text boxes, and images.

3. **ViewModel**: This component acts as a bridge between the View and the Model. It contains the presentation logic of the application, such as data formatting and validation, and communicates with the Model to retrieve or update data. The ViewModel also exposes data and commands that the View can bind to, which allows for a clean separation of concerns between the View and the ViewModel.

The key advantage of using the MVVM pattern is that it promotes separation of concerns, which makes it easier to maintain and test the application. It also allows for better code reusability, as the ViewModel can be reused across multiple Views.

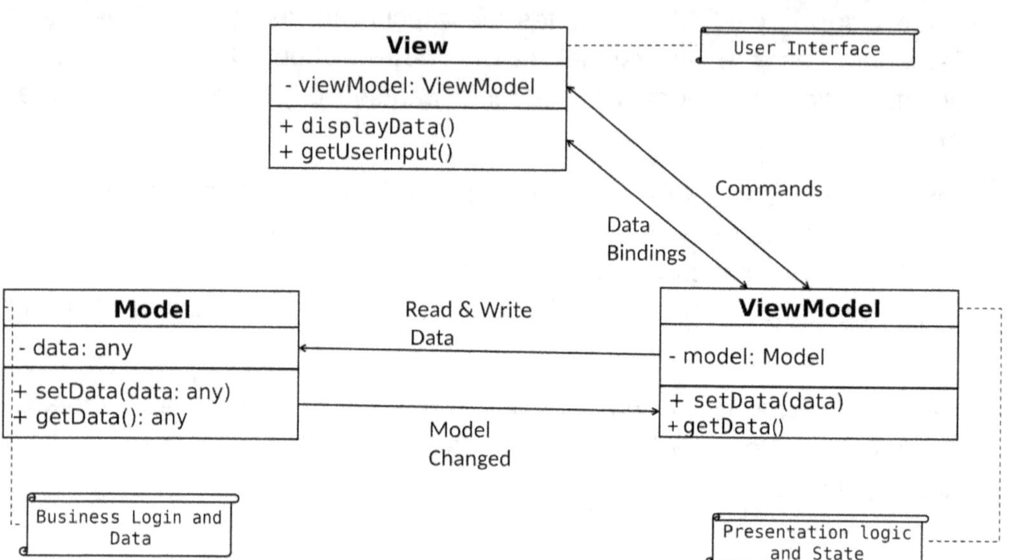

Here is a simplified implementation of the MVVM pattern :

```
// Model
class Model {
    constructor() {
        this.data = "Default.";
    }

    setData(data) {
        console.log("Model: Set data.");
        this.data = data;
    }

    getData() {
        console.log("Model: Get data.");
        return this.data;
    }
}

// ViewModel
class ViewModel {
    constructor(model) {
        this.model = model;
    }

    setData(data) {
        console.log("ViewModel: Set data.");
        this.model.setData(data);
    }
}
```

```javascript
    getData() {
        console.log("ViewModel: Get data.");
        return this.model.getData();
    }
}

// View
class View {
    constructor(viewModel) {
        this.viewModel = viewModel;
    }

    displayData() {
        console.log("Display Data: " + this.viewModel.getData());
    }

    getUserInput() {
        const readline = require('readline').createInterface({
            input: process.stdin,
            output: process.stdout
        });

        readline.question('View : Enter user input: ', userInput
=> {
            this.viewModel.setData(userInput);
            readline.close();
        });
    }
}

// Client code
const model = new Model();
const viewModel = new ViewModel(model);
const view = new View(viewModel);

// Display initial data
view.displayData();

// Get user input and update data
view.getUserInput();

// Display updated data
view.displayData();
```

Output:

```
ViewModel: Get data.
Model: Get data.
Display Data: Default.
View: Enter user input: hello, world!
ViewModel: Set data.
Model: Set data.
ViewModel: Get data.
Model: Get data.
Display Data: hello, world!
```

Explanation: Here's a step-by-step explanation of what the code does:

1. The Model class represents the data and has methods to set and get the data.

2. The View class interacts with the user to get input and displays the data.

3. The ViewModel class acts as an intermediary between the Model and the View. It sets the data in the Model and retrieves data from the Model.

4. The client code creates instances of Model, ViewModel, and View.

5. The View gets user input and calls the ViewModel to set the data in the Model.

6. The View then displays the data by calling the ViewModel to get the data from the Model.

Layered Pattern

The **Layered Pattern** is a software design pattern that involves breaking an application into layers or groups of related functionalities, with each layer providing services to the layer above it. Each layer typically communicates only with the layer directly above or below it, and has a defined interface for interacting with other layers. This pattern can help to improve modularity, maintainability, and scalability of an application.

There are different types of layered patterns, but one of the most common is the n-tier architecture, which breaks an application into three main layers:

1. **Presentation layer**: This layer contains the user interface and handles user input and output.

2. **Business layer**: This layer contains the business logic and rules that govern how the application functions.

3. **Data layer**: This layer contains the data access components and handles interactions with the data store, such as a database or file system.

Here's a simplified example of how the n-tier architecture:

```javascript
// Data Access Layer
class DataAccessLayer {
    constructor() {
        this.products = [];
    }

    getData() {
        return this.products;
    }

    addData(product) {
        this.products.push(product);
    }
}

// Business Logic Layer
class BusinessLogicLayer {
    constructor(dataAccess) {
        this.dataAccess = dataAccess;
    }

    getAllProducts() {
        return this.dataAccess.getData();
    }

    addProduct(product) {
        this.dataAccess.addData(product);
    }
}

// Presentation Layer
class PresentationLayer {
    constructor(businessLogic) {
        this.businessLogic = businessLogic;
    }

    displayProducts() {
        const products = this.businessLogic.getAllProducts();
        products.forEach((product, index) => {
            console.log(`${index + 1}. ${product}`);
        });
```

```javascript
    }

    addProduct(product) {
        this.businessLogic.addProduct(product);
    }
}

// Client code
const dataAccess = new DataAccessLayer();
const businessLogic = new BusinessLogicLayer(dataAccess);
const presentationLayer = new PresentationLayer(businessLogic);

presentationLayer.addProduct("Apple");
presentationLayer.addProduct("Banana");
presentationLayer.addProduct("Mango");
presentationLayer.displayProducts();
```

Output:

1. Apple
2. Banana
3. Mango

Explanation: The code follows these key points:

1. The Data Access Layer (DataAccessLayer) manages the products list and provides methods to get data (getData) and add data (addData).

2. The Business Logic Layer (BusinessLogicLayer) interacts with the Data Access Layer, exposing methods to get all products (getAllProducts) and add a product (addProduct).

3. The Presentation Layer (PresentationLayer) handles user interactions, utilising the Business Logic Layer. It has methods to display products (displayProducts) and add a product (addProduct).

4. The client code instantiates the layers and demonstrates the addition and display of products.

SOLID principle applied

The Layered Pattern is a software design pattern that separates the components of a system into distinct layers. Each layer represents a specific level of abstraction, with higher layers building upon lower layers to provide more complex functionality. Here's how each SOLID principle can be applied to the Layered Pattern:

1. **Single Responsibility Principle (SRP)**: The Layered Pattern follows the SRP by separating the responsibilities of each layer into distinct components. Each layer has a specific responsibility and should only handle the functionality related to that responsibility. This separation of responsibilities helps to keep the system organised and easier to maintain.

2. **Open-Closed Principle (OCP)**: The Layered Pattern follows the OCP by allowing new layers to be added to the system without modifying the existing layers. Each layer is independent of the other layers and can be extended or replaced without affecting the functionality of the other layers.

3. **Liskov Substitution Principle (LSP)**: The Layered Pattern follows the LSP by ensuring that each layer adheres to a well-defined interface. This means that any layer can be replaced by another layer that adheres to the same interface, without affecting the correctness of the system.

4. **Interface Segregation Principle (ISP)**: The Layered Pattern follows the ISP by defining clear interfaces for each layer. Each layer provides an interface for the layer above it to interact with it. This means that each layer only exposes the functionality that is necessary for the layer above it to use, which allows for better decoupling and flexibility.

5. **Dependency Inversion Principle (DIP)**: The Layered Pattern follows the DIP by allowing each layer to depend on abstractions instead of concrete implementations. This means that each layer can interact with the layer below it through an interface, without being dependent on the specific implementation of that layer. This allows for better modularity and easier testing.

Pipe and Filter Pattern

The **Pipe and Filter Pattern** is a software design pattern that involves breaking an application into a series of independent processing stages or filters, connected by pipes that transmit data between them. Each filter performs a specific task or transformation on the data, and passes the result to the next filter through a pipe. This pattern can help to improve modularity, maintainability, and scalability of an application, by making it easier to add or modify processing stages without affecting the rest of the system.

Here's a simplified example of how the Pipe and Filter Pattern might be implemented :

```javascript
// Filter Base Class
class Filter {
    process(data) {
        throw new Error('You have to implement the method
process!');
    }
}

// Filters
class CapitalizeFilter extends Filter {
    process(data) {
        return data.toUpperCase();
    }
}

class ReplaceSpaceFilter extends Filter {
    process(data) {
        return data.replace(/ /g, '_');
    }
}

class RemoveSpecialCharactersFilter extends Filter {
    process(data) {
        const specialCharacters = ",@!";
        let result = '';
        for (let i = 0; i < data.length; i++) {
            if (specialCharacters.indexOf(data[i]) === -1) {
                result += data[i];
            }
        }
        return result;
    }
}

// Data Processing Pipeline
class DataProcessingPipeline {
    constructor() {
        this.filters = [];
    }

    addFilter(filter) {
        this.filters.push(filter);
    }
```

```javascript
    processData(data) {
        let processedData = data;
        this.filters.forEach(filter => {
            processedData = filter.process(processedData);
        });
        return processedData;
    }
}

// Client code
const pipeline = new DataProcessingPipeline();
pipeline.addFilter(new CapitalizeFilter());
pipeline.addFilter(new ReplaceSpaceFilter());
pipeline.addFilter(new RemoveSpecialCharactersFilter());

const data = "Hello, World!";
const result = pipeline.processData(data);
console.log("Result: " + result);
```

Output:

Result: HELLO_WORLD

Explanation:

1. The code demonstrates the Pipe and Filter pattern, which is a design pattern used for designing and implementing data processing systems.

2. We have a base class **Filter** with several subclasses (**CapitalizeFilter**, **ReplaceSpaceFilter**, and **RemoveSpecialCharactersFilter**) representing different filters. These filters process data in various ways, such as capitalizing, replacing spaces, and removing special characters.

3. The **DataProcessingPipeline** class manages a sequence of filters. It allows filters to be added dynamically and applies each filter sequentially to process the data.

4. In the client code, we create an instance of the **DataProcessingPipeline**, add the desired filters to it, and then apply the pipeline to process the data.

SOLID principle applied

Here's how each SOLID principle can be applied to the Pipe and Filter Pattern:

1. **Single Responsibility Principle (SRP)**: The Pipe and Filter Pattern follows the SRP by separating the responsibilities of each filter into distinct components. Each filter has a specific responsibility and should only perform one task. This separation of responsibilities helps to keep the system organised and easier to maintain.

2. **Open-Closed Principle (OCP)**: The Pipe and Filter Pattern follows the OCP by allowing new filters to be added to the system without modifying the existing filters. Each filter is independent of the other filters and can be extended or replaced without affecting the functionality of the other filters.

3. **Liskov Substitution Principle (LSP)**: The Pipe and Filter Pattern follows the LSP by ensuring that each filter adheres to a well-defined interface. This means that any filter can be replaced by another filter that adheres to the same interface, without affecting the correctness of the system.

4. **Interface Segregation Principle (ISP)**: The Pipe and Filter Pattern follows the ISP by defining clear interfaces for each filter. Each filter provides an interface for the filter above it to interact with it. This means that each filter only exposes the functionality that is necessary for the filter above it to use, which allows for better decoupling and flexibility.

5. **Dependency Inversion Principle (DIP)**: The Pipe and Filter Pattern follows the DIP by allowing each filter to depend on abstractions instead of concrete implementations. This means that each filter can interact with the filter below it through an interface, without being dependent on the specific implementation of that filter. This allows for better modularity and easier testing.

ANTI-PATTERNS

The Blob Anti-Pattern

The **Blob Anti-Pattern** is a software design anti-pattern that occurs when a class becomes too large and complex, making it difficult to maintain and modify. The class may become a "blob" of code that handles many different responsibilities and contains many different methods, making it difficult to understand and modify the code.

This anti-pattern typically arises when developers do not adhere to the principles of separation of concerns and single responsibility, leading to code that is tightly coupled and difficult to maintain. The result is often code that is difficult to test, difficult to reuse, and difficult to modify.

The Blob Anti-Pattern can be avoided by adhering to best practices for software design, including:

1. **Separating concerns**: Classes should have a clear and single responsibility, with well-defined interfaces between components.

2. **Abstraction**: Using interfaces, abstract classes, and inheritance can help to break down large classes into smaller, more manageable components.

3. **Refactoring**: Regularly reviewing code and refactoring can help to identify and remove code smells, including overly complex or monolithic classes.

4. **Design Patterns**: Applying appropriate design patterns can help to address specific design problems and improve the overall maintainability of the code.

Here's an example of how the Blob Anti-Pattern might look :

```
class Blob {
    constructor(data) {
        this.data = data;
    }

    processData() {
        // Process data
    }
```

```
    validateData() {
        // Validate data
    }

    saveData() {
        // Save data to database
    }

    sendNotification() {
        // Send notification
    }

    generateReport() {
        // Generate report
    }

    backupData() {
        // Backup data
    }

    archiveData() {
        // Archive data
    }

    purgeData() {
        // Purge data
    }

    // And so on...
}
```

Analysis:

In this example, we have a `Blob` class that handles many different responsibilities, including processing data, validating data, saving data to a database, sending notifications, generating reports, backing up data, archiving data, purging data, and so on. The class is large, complex, and difficult to understand and maintain.

To avoid the Blob Anti-Pattern, we could separate the concerns into smaller, more manageable components, such as creating separate classes to handle data processing, data validation, data storage, and so on. By adhering to best practices for software design and avoiding the Blob Anti-Pattern, we can create code that is easier to maintain, test, and modify over time.

The Blob Anti-Pattern, also known as the God Class anti-pattern, is a common anti-pattern in object-oriented programming. It refers to a class that knows too much or does too much, making it difficult to maintain and test.

The Blob Anti-Pattern violates the Single Responsibility Principle (SRP) and can lead to issues with coupling and cohesion. When a class handles too many responsibilities, it becomes tightly coupled to other classes, making it difficult to reuse and test. This can result in code that is difficult to maintain and change over time.

The Blob Anti-Pattern is characterised by a class that has a large number of fields and methods, many of which are not related to the class's primary responsibility. It can be challenging to refactor a Blob class because it is often tightly coupled to other classes in the system.

To avoid the Blob Anti-Pattern, developers should strive to adhere to the Single Responsibility Principle by ensuring that each class has only one responsibility. This will result in a more maintainable and testable codebase that is easier to change over time.

In summary, the Blob Anti-Pattern is a common issue in object-oriented programming that can result in code that is difficult to maintain and test. By adhering to the Single Responsibility Principle, developers can avoid this anti-pattern and create more maintainable and scalable codebases.

The God Object Anti-Pattern

The **God Object Anti-Pattern** is a software design anti-pattern in which a single class or module becomes responsible for all aspects of an application or system. This can lead to code that is tightly coupled, difficult to maintain, and difficult to test.

The God Object Anti-Pattern typically arises when developers do not adhere to principles of separation of concerns and single responsibility. Instead of breaking down functionality into smaller, more manageable components, developers may implement all functionality in a single class or module. This can lead to code that is difficult to understand, difficult to modify, and prone to errors.

The God Object Anti-Pattern can be avoided by adhering to best practices for software design, including:

1. **Separation of concerns**: Classes should have a clear and single responsibility, with well-defined interfaces between components.

2. **Loose coupling**: Components should interact with each other through well-defined interfaces, rather than relying on global state or direct method calls.

3. **Abstraction**: Using interfaces, abstract classes, and inheritance can help to break down large classes into smaller, more manageable components.

4. **Refactoring**: Regularly reviewing code and refactoring can help to identify and remove code smells, including overly complex or monolithic classes.

5. **Design Patterns**: Applying appropriate design patterns can help to address specific design problems and improve the overall maintainability of the code.

Here's an example of how the God Object Anti-Pattern might look :

```
class GodsObject {
    constructor() {
        this.data = [];
        this.user = new User();
        this.db = new Database();
        this.mailer = new Mailer();
    }

    processData() {
        // Process data
        this.db.connect();
        this.user.authenticate();
        this.data = this.db.query();
        this.db.disconnect();
    }

    validateData() {
        // Validate data
        this.user.authorize();
        this.db.connect();
        this.db.validate();
        this.db.disconnect();
    }

    sendNotification() {
        // Send notification
        this.user.authorize();
        this.db.connect();
        const data = this.db.query();
```

```
        this.mailer.sendEmail(data);
        this.db.disconnect();
    }

    // And so on...
}
```

Analysis:

In this example, we have a GodObject class that handles all aspects of an application, including data processing, validation, database connectivity, user authentication, sending email notifications, and so on. This class is tightly coupled, difficult to understand, and difficult to maintain.

To avoid the God Object Anti-Pattern, we could break down functionality into smaller, more manageable components, such as creating separate classes for data processing, data validation, database connectivity, user authentication, and email notification. By adhering to best practices for software design and avoiding the God Object Anti-Pattern, we can create code that is easier to maintain, test, and modify over time.

The God Object Anti-Pattern, also known as the monolithic class anti-pattern, is a common anti-pattern in object-oriented programming. It refers to a class that knows too much or does too much, making it difficult to maintain and test.

The God Object Anti-Pattern violates the Single Responsibility Principle (SRP) and can lead to issues with coupling and cohesion. When a class handles too many responsibilities, it becomes tightly coupled to other classes, making it difficult to reuse and test. This can result in code that is difficult to maintain and change over time.

The God Object Anti-Pattern is characterised by a class that has a large number of fields and methods, many of which are not related to the class's primary responsibility. It often contains business logic, persistence logic, user interface logic, and other unrelated responsibilities, making it difficult to test and maintain.

To avoid the God Object Anti-Pattern, developers should strive to adhere to the Single Responsibility Principle by ensuring that each class has only one responsibility. This will result in a more maintainable and testable codebase that is easier to change over time.

In summary, the God Object Anti-Pattern is a common issue in object-oriented programming that can result in code that is difficult to maintain and test. By adhering to the Single Responsibility Principle, developers can avoid this anti-pattern and create more maintainable and scalable codebases.

The Spaghetti Code Anti-Pattern

The **Spaghetti Code Anti-Pattern** is a software development anti-pattern that arises when code becomes overly complex and difficult to understand due to lack of structure or organisation. This term is derived from the tangled appearance of spaghetti noodles, which represents the tangled flow of control in such code.

Spaghetti code can result from a lack of planning, poor coding practices, or changes in requirements that result in the code becoming overly complex. The resulting code is often difficult to read, modify, or maintain, and can cause a number of problems including:

1. **Reduced productivity**: It can be difficult to work on spaghetti code, as it is often hard to understand and takes longer to modify.

2. **Bugs and errors**: Spaghetti code is often prone to bugs and errors, as it can be difficult to understand the flow of control and identify issues.

3. **Reduced reusability**: Spaghetti code is often not reusable, as it can be difficult to extract useful code from the mess.

4. **Increased costs**: It can be expensive to maintain spaghetti code, as it often requires significant effort to modify, test, and fix.

To avoid the Spaghetti Code Anti-Pattern, developers should follow best practices for software design and development, such as:

1. **Planning**: Developers should plan their code carefully, considering the requirements, use cases, and architecture.

2. **Separation of concerns**: Code should be organised into smaller, more manageable components that handle specific tasks, such as input validation or database access.

3. **Modularity**: Code should be modular, with well-defined interfaces between components.

4. **Code reviews**: Developers should regularly review each other's code to identify potential issues and ensure that code is well-structured and organised.

5. **Refactoring**: Developers should be prepared to refactor code, when necessary, in order to improve structure and organisation.

Here's an example of how spaghetti code might look :

```javascript
class Spaghetti {
    constructor() {
        // Define connection parameters
        this.url = 'jdbc:postgresql://localhost:5432/mydb';
        this.user = 'user';
        this.password = 'password';
    }

    async processData(data) {
        // Validate input
        if (!data || data.trim() === '') {
            console.log('Invalid data');
            return null;
        }

        // Initialize variables
        let client = null;
        let resultSet = null;

        try {
            // Connect to the database
            client = new Client({
                connectionString: this.url,
                user: this.user,
                password: this.password
            });
            await client.connect();

            // Process data
            const query ='SELECT * FROM mytable WHERE data = $1';
            const values = [data];
            resultSet = await client.query(query, values);
            return resultSet.rows;
        } catch (error) {
            console.error('Error executing query:', error);
            return null;
        } finally {
            // Close the client connection
            if (client) {
                await client.end();
            }
        }
    }
}
```

Explanation:

In this example, we have a function called `processData()` that handles all aspects of processing data, including input validation, database connectivity, and processing logic. The code is difficult to understand, as it mixes several different concerns in a single function. A better approach would be to separate the code into smaller, more manageable components that handle specific tasks, such as input validation, database access, and processing logic. This would make the code more modular, easier to understand, and easier to modify over time.

The Spaghetti Code Anti-Pattern refers to a situation where code becomes tangled and difficult to maintain, with multiple interdependencies and no clear structure. It is characterised by code that is poorly organised and has a high degree of coupling, making it difficult to modify or extend the system.

The Spaghetti Code Anti-Pattern is a result of poor design and a lack of planning. It often arises when developers do not follow best practices such as modularization, encapsulation, and abstraction. Instead, code is written as a single, monolithic entity, with no clear separation of concerns.

The result of Spaghetti Code is code that is difficult to understand and modify. Changes to one part of the code can have unintended consequences on other parts of the system. Debugging and testing can also be challenging, as it is difficult to isolate specific functionality.

To avoid the Spaghetti Code Anti-Pattern, developers should follow best practices for software design, such as modularization, encapsulation, and abstraction. They should also strive to keep their code organised and structured, with clear separation of concerns. This will result in a codebase that is easier to maintain, extend, and debug.

In summary, the Spaghetti Code Anti-Pattern is a common issue in software development that can result in code that is difficult to maintain and extend. By following best practices for software design and keeping code organised and structured, developers can avoid this anti-pattern and create more maintainable and scalable codebases.

The Swiss Army Knife Anti-Pattern

The **Swiss Army Knife Anti-Pattern** is a software development anti-pattern that occurs when a single component or class tries to do too much, resulting in excessive complexity, tight coupling, and low cohesion. This term is derived from the Swiss Army Knife, which is a versatile tool that can perform multiple functions, but is often bulky and difficult to use for any one task.

The Swiss Army Knife Anti-Pattern can occur when developers try to add too many features to a single component or class, rather than breaking the functionality into smaller, more specialised components. This can result in code that is difficult to understand, maintain, and modify, as well as being more prone to bugs and errors.

Some common problems associated with the Swiss Army Knife Anti-Pattern include:

1. **Complexity**: The code becomes overly complex and difficult to understand due to the many functions that are combined into a single component.

2. **Tight coupling**: The component becomes tightly coupled with other components, making it difficult to modify or replace without affecting other parts of the system.

3. **Low cohesion**: The component has low cohesion, as its functions are not closely related to each other and may be better implemented as separate components.

4. **Code bloat**: The component becomes bloated with unnecessary features and functionality, leading to increased memory usage and decreased performance.

To avoid the Swiss Army Knife Anti-Pattern, developers should follow best practices for software design and development, such as:

1. **Separation of concerns**: Components should be designed to handle specific tasks, and should not be responsible for unrelated functionality.

2. **Modularity**: Components should be modular, with well-defined interfaces between them.

3. **Cohesion**: Components should have high cohesion, with related functions grouped together.

4. **Single responsibility principle**: Components should have a single responsibility, and should not be responsible for multiple unrelated tasks.

5. **Code reviews**: Developers should regularly review each other's code to identify potential issues and ensure that code is well-structured and organised.

Here's an example of how the Swiss Army Knife Anti-Pattern might look :

```
class DataProcessor {
    constructor(data) {
        this.data = data;
    }

    processData() {
        this.validateData();
        this.cleanData();
        this.filterData();
        this.sortData();
        this.groupData();
        this.calculateStatistics();
        this.formatOutput();
    }

    validateData() {
        // Validation logic
    }

    cleanData() {
        // Data cleaning logic
    }

    filterData() {
        // Data filtering logic
    }

    sortData() {
        // Data sorting logic
    }

    groupData() {
        // Data grouping logic
    }

    calculateStatistics() {
        // Statistics calculation logic
    }

    formatOutput() {
        // Output formatting logic
    }
}
```

```
// Client code
const data = "exampleData";
const processor = new DataProcessor(data);
processor.processData();
```

Analysis:

In this example, we have a class called `DataProcessor` that is responsible for processing data, including validation, cleaning, filtering, sorting, grouping, calculating statistics, and formatting output. This class tries to do too much, and would be better implemented as several smaller, more specialised components. A better approach would be to break the functionality into smaller, more cohesive components, each with a single responsibility. This would make the code more modular, easier to understand, and easier to modify over time.

The Swiss Army Knife Anti-Pattern refers to a situation where a class or module tries to do too much, performing multiple unrelated tasks instead of focusing on a single responsibility. It is characterised by code that is complex and difficult to understand, leading to issues with maintainability, testability, and extensibility.

The Swiss Army Knife Anti-Pattern arises when developers try to create a class or module that can be used in a variety of different contexts or situations. Instead of creating separate classes or modules for each responsibility, they try to include all the functionality in a single, all-encompassing class or module.

The result of the Swiss Army Knife Anti-Pattern is code that is difficult to understand and maintain. It can be challenging to modify or extend the system without breaking existing functionality. It can also be difficult to test, as it may be unclear which parts of the code are responsible for which functionality.

To avoid the Swiss Army Knife Anti-Pattern, developers should adhere to the Single Responsibility Principle and strive to create classes or modules that focus on a single responsibility. This will result in code that is easier to understand, maintain, and extend. Developers should also avoid creating overly complex classes or modules, as this can lead to issues with testability and scalability.

In summary, the Swiss Army Knife Anti-Pattern is a common issue in software development that can result in code that is difficult to understand, maintain, and extend. By adhering to the Single Responsibility Principle and avoiding overly complex classes or modules, developers can avoid this anti-pattern and create more maintainable and scalable codebases.

REAL-WORLD EXAMPLES OF DESIGN PATTERNS

This chapter demonstrates how design patterns can be applied to solve specific problems and provides case studies of their practical usage. Here are the various example case studies typically included in this chapter:

Case Study 1: E-commerce System

Description: The case study focuses on the design and implementation of an e-commerce system, which allows users to browse and purchase products online. The system includes features such as product catalogue management, shopping cart functionality, order processing, and payment integration.

Design Patterns Used:

Several design patterns can be applied in the design and development of an e-commerce system:

1. **Model-View-Controller (MVC) Pattern**: The MVC pattern can be used to separate the user interface (View), application logic (Controller), and data representation (Model) in the e-commerce system. This separation promotes modularity, reusability, and maintainability.

2. **Singleton Pattern**: The Singleton pattern can be applied to manage the shopping cart instance. It ensures that only one instance of the shopping cart exists throughout the user's session and provides a centralised and consistent shopping experience.

3. **Factory Method Pattern**: The Factory Method pattern can be used for creating different types of products. It allows the system to define a common interface for product creation while enabling subclasses to implement their own specific product creation logic.

4. **Strategy Pattern**: The Strategy pattern can be utilised for handling various payment methods. It allows the system to define a family of interchangeable payment strategies, such as credit card, PayPal, or bank transfer, and dynamically selects the appropriate strategy based on user preferences or system configurations.

5. **Observer Pattern**: The Observer pattern can be applied to notify users about order status updates. When an order's status changes, the system can notify the interested parties (observers) such as customers or administrators, ensuring timely and relevant information dissemination.

Case Study 2: Social Networking Platform

Description: The case study revolves around the design and development of a social networking platform, where users can create profiles, connect with friends, post updates, and interact with each other. The platform aims to provide a user-friendly and engaging experience for social networking enthusiasts.

Design Patterns Used:

Several design patterns can be applied in the design and development of a social networking platform:

1. **Decorator Pattern**: The Decorator pattern can be used to add additional features or functionalities to user profiles. It allows for dynamic and flexible customization of user profiles by attaching additional responsibilities to the base profile object.

2. **Composite Pattern**: The Composite pattern can be employed to represent hierarchical relationships between users and their connections. It provides a unified interface to treat both individual users and groups of users as interchangeable entities, enabling efficient management of social connections.

3. **Observer Pattern**: The Observer pattern can be applied to notify users about new posts, friend requests, or other relevant updates. Users can subscribe to specific events or users, and the system can notify them whenever new activities occur, enhancing real-time interaction and engagement.

4. **Template Method Pattern**: The Template Method pattern can be utilised to define a common structure for different types of posts. It allows for variations in the content and presentation of posts while maintaining a consistent overall structure.

Case Study 3: Financial Trading System

Description: This case study deals with a financial trading system where users can buy and sell various financial instruments such as stocks, bonds, and derivatives.

Design Patterns Used

In the context of a Financial Trading System, various design patterns can be utilised to ensure a robust, flexible, and efficient architecture. Here are some design patterns that could be applicable:

1. **Observer Pattern**: The Observer Pattern is widely used in financial systems to handle real-time updates and notifications. In a trading system, the Observer Pattern can be employed to notify users and interested parties about changes in stock prices, market movements, or specific events that affect the financial instruments they are interested in.

2. **Strategy Pattern**: The Strategy Pattern is useful in a financial trading system to handle different trading algorithms and strategies. Traders might have various approaches to execute trades, such as algorithmic trading, high-frequency trading, or manual trading. By using the Strategy Pattern, the system can switch between these different trading strategies easily without modifying the core trading logic.

3. **Factory Method Pattern**: The Factory Method Pattern can be applied in a financial trading system to create different types of financial instruments (e.g., stocks, bonds, derivatives) while adhering to a common interface. This pattern helps in decoupling the creation of objects from their usage, making the code more maintainable and scalable.

4. **Composite Pattern**: The Composite Pattern is useful when dealing with hierarchical structures. In a financial trading system, you might have portfolios containing multiple financial instruments, and those instruments could be further composed of sub-instruments. The Composite Pattern allows you to treat individual instruments and portfolios uniformly, simplifying portfolio management.

5. **Command Pattern**: The Command Pattern can be employed to encapsulate requests as objects, allowing for the parametrization of clients with different requests. In a financial trading system, this pattern can be used to implement undo/redo functionality for trade orders, where each trade order is encapsulated as a command.

6. **Singleton Pattern**: The Singleton Pattern can be useful in certain components of the trading system that need to have a single instance, such as a connection manager to interact with external trading platforms or data providers.

7. **Template Method Pattern**: The Template Method Pattern is beneficial for defining the skeleton of an algorithm in a method but letting subclasses override specific steps of the algorithm without changing its structure. In a financial trading system, this pattern can be applied to define the overall trading process while allowing different types of financial instruments to customise their specific trading behaviours.

8. **Facade Pattern**: The Facade Pattern can simplify the complexity of the trading system by providing a unified interface that hides the underlying subsystems. For instance, it can offer a simplified interface for placing trades, handling order execution, and managing positions, abstracting away the complexities of interacting with different trading platforms and exchanges.

Case Study 4: Mobile Application Development

Description: Mobile Application Development involves creating software applications that run on mobile devices, such as smartphones and tablets. These applications serve various purposes, including entertainment, productivity, communication, and more. The development process for mobile applications typically includes designing the user interface, implementing the application's functionalities, and ensuring compatibility with different mobile platforms (e.g., Android, iOS).

Design Patterns Used

Various design patterns can be used in mobile application development to enhance code organisation, maintainability, and scalability. Here are some design patterns commonly used in this context:

1. **Model-View-Controller (MVC) Pattern**: MVC is a fundamental architectural pattern that separates the application into three interconnected components: Model, View, and Controller. In mobile app development, the Model represents the data and business logic, the View handles the user interface elements, and the Controller manages user input and updates the Model and View accordingly. MVC promotes code separation and makes it easier to update and maintain the application.

2. **Model-View-Presenter (MVP) Pattern**: MVP is a variation of the MVC pattern, where the Presenter acts as an intermediary between the Model and the View. The Presenter is responsible for handling user interactions, updating the Model, and updating the View accordingly. MVP helps in making the View more independent and testable by moving the UI logic to the Presenter.

3. **Model-View-ViewModel (MVVM) Pattern**: MVVM is another variation of the MVC pattern, commonly used in mobile app development with data-binding frameworks. The ViewModel acts as an intermediary between the Model and the View and exposes data and commands to the View through data-binding. MVVM enhances code maintainability and allows for more straightforward testing of the UI.

4. **Singleton Pattern**: The Singleton Pattern is used to ensure that a class has only one instance, providing global access to that instance. In mobile app development, the Singleton pattern can be used for managing global application state, creating shared resources (e.g., network managers, database helpers), or handling configurations.

5. **Factory Pattern**: The Factory Pattern is employed to create objects without specifying their exact class. In mobile app development, the Factory pattern can be used to create different platform-specific implementations of a class without having to change the code that uses it. For example, a factory can be used to provide platform-specific implementations of a camera interface.

6. **Observer Pattern**: The Observer Pattern facilitates communication between different components of the app by allowing objects (observers) to subscribe to changes in other objects (subjects). In mobile app development, the Observer pattern can be used to implement event handling, notifying UI components about changes in data, or responding to user interactions.

7. **Decorator Pattern**: The Decorator Pattern allows behaviour to be added to individual objects dynamically, without modifying their class. In mobile app development, this pattern can be used to extend the functionality of UI components or add optional features to the application without altering its core implementation.

8. **Command Pattern**: The Command Pattern is used to encapsulate a request as an object, allowing parametrization of clients with different requests. In mobile app development, the Command pattern can be employed to manage and execute user actions, such as undo/redo functionality or handling gestures.

9. **Adapter Pattern**: The Adapter Pattern is used to make incompatible interfaces work together. In mobile app development, this pattern can be useful for integrating with external libraries, services, or APIs that have different interfaces than the ones required by the app.

Case Study 5: Web Development

Description: Web Development is the process of creating and maintaining websites or web applications for the Internet. It involves a combination of frontend development (client-side) and backend development (server-side) to deliver a seamless user experience and perform various tasks, such as presenting content, handling user interactions, processing data, and communicating with databases and external services.

Design Patterns Used

Design patterns play a crucial role in web development, helping to solve common problems and improve code organisation, reusability, and maintainability. Here are some design patterns commonly used in web development:

1. **Model-View-Controller (MVC) Pattern**: The MVC pattern is widely used in web development to separate the application's logic into three interconnected components:

- **Model**: Represents the data and business logic.

- **View**: Handles the presentation and user interface.

- **Controller**: Manages user input and orchestrates communication between the Model and View.

2. **Singleton Pattern**: The Singleton pattern ensures that a class has only one instance and provides a global access point to that instance. It is often used for components that need to be instantiated once and shared across different parts of the web application.

3. **Factory Pattern**: The Factory pattern is used to create objects without specifying the exact class of the object that will be created. In web development, it can be applied to create different types of objects, such as different types of database connections, based on configuration or runtime conditions.

4. **Observer Pattern**: The Observer pattern facilitates the one-to-many dependency between objects, where multiple observers (listeners) are notified automatically when the observed object (subject) undergoes a change. In web development, it is useful for handling real-time updates, notifications, and event-driven interactions.

5. **Decorator Pattern**: The Decorator pattern allows behaviour to be added to individual objects dynamically, without affecting other objects of the same class. In web development, this pattern can be useful for extending the functionality of web components, such as adding additional features or modifying rendering behaviour.

6. **Adapter Pattern**: The Adapter pattern is used to convert the interface of one class into another interface that clients expect. In web development, it can be applied to integrate different third-party libraries or APIs seamlessly into the application.

7. **Strategy Pattern**: The Strategy pattern allows for dynamic selection of algorithms or behaviour at runtime. In web development, it can be used for switching between different algorithms or implementations based on varying requirements.

8. **Facade Pattern**: The Facade pattern provides a simplified interface to a complex system, making it easier to use. In web development, it can be applied to create a unified interface to interact with various backend services or APIs, hiding their complexities from the frontend.

9. **Template Method Pattern**: The Template Method pattern defines the overall structure of an algorithm but lets the subclasses override specific steps. In web development, it can be used for defining the basic structure of a page or component and allowing customization through subclassing or template engines.

Case Study 6: Internet of Things (IoT) Systems

Description: Internet of Things (IoT) Systems are networks of interconnected physical devices, vehicles, appliances, and other objects embedded with sensors, software, and network connectivity that enable them to collect and exchange data. These devices can interact with each other and with central systems to perform various tasks, make intelligent decisions, and provide valuable insights. IoT systems have a wide range of applications, including smart homes, industrial automation, healthcare monitoring, smart cities, and more.

Design Patterns Used

Various Design Patterns used in IoT Systems:

1. **Publish/Subscribe Pattern**: The Publish/Subscribe Pattern is widely used in IoT systems to enable efficient communication and data sharing among devices and services. Devices can publish data to specific topics or channels, and other devices or services that are interested in that data can subscribe to those topics. This pattern allows for scalable and asynchronous communication in IoT systems.

2. **Command Pattern**: The Command Pattern is commonly used in IoT systems to control and manage remote devices from a centralised location. It involves sending commands from a central controller to IoT devices to trigger specific actions or changes in their behaviour. This pattern is essential for applications like smart home automation and industrial control systems.

3. **Observer Pattern**: The Observer Pattern is used in IoT systems to implement real-time monitoring and event handling. Observers (clients) subscribe to observable objects (sensors, data streams), and they receive notifications whenever there are changes or events of interest. This pattern is crucial for applications that require real-time data updates, such as environmental monitoring or security systems.

4. **State Pattern**: The State Pattern is useful in IoT systems when devices have different states and behaviours based on their current conditions or context. For example, a smart thermostat might have different states like "heating," "cooling," and "standby," each with specific rules and actions associated with it.

5. **Proxy Pattern**: The Proxy Pattern can be employed in IoT systems to represent and control access to remote devices or resources. Proxies act as intermediaries, handling communication, authentication, and security between the central system and IoT devices.

6. **Chain of Responsibility Pattern**: The Chain of Responsibility Pattern can be used in IoT systems to process data streams or events through a series of handlers or filters. Each handler in the chain can process the data and pass it along to the next handler, allowing for flexible data processing pipelines.

7. **Adapter Pattern**: The Adapter Pattern is useful when integrating existing or legacy IoT devices into a new system. Adapters convert the interface of one device or protocol to match the requirements of the new system, allowing seamless integration of diverse devices.

Case Study 7: Game Development

Description: Game development involves the creation of interactive experiences for players, typically implemented as video games. These games can be developed for various platforms, such as PC, consoles, mobile devices, or web browsers. Game development requires careful consideration of graphics, audio, user input, physics, game mechanics, and various other elements to create an engaging and enjoyable experience for players.

Design Patterns Used

Various Design Patterns Used in Game Development:

1. **State Pattern**: The State Pattern is widely used in game development to manage different states of game objects, characters, or scenes. For example, a game character might have different states like idle, running, jumping, attacking, etc., and using the State Pattern helps to handle the transitions between these states efficiently.

2. **Observer Pattern**: The Observer Pattern is commonly employed in game development to handle event-driven systems. Game events like collisions, input changes, or character actions can be observed by various game elements, such as AI controllers, UI elements, or audio systems.

3. **Factory Method Pattern**: The Factory Method Pattern is helpful in game development for creating objects based on certain conditions or configurations. It can be used to create game levels, enemy waves, or different types of game assets dynamically.

4. **Singleton Pattern**: The Singleton Pattern is often used in game development for creating globally accessible and unique instances of certain game components, such as game managers, audio managers, or resource managers.

5. **Flyweight Pattern**: The Flyweight Pattern is useful for optimizing memory usage in games. In scenarios where there are a large number of similar objects with shared properties (e.g., particles, trees, bullets), the Flyweight Pattern can reduce memory overhead by reusing shared data.

6. **Command Pattern**: The Command Pattern can be used to implement input handling and game controls. In game development, user input (e.g., keyboard, mouse, gamepad) can be captured and encapsulated as commands that can be executed or undone, allowing for more flexible input handling.

7. **Strategy Pattern**: The Strategy Pattern is beneficial for implementing different AI behaviours or game mechanics. For example, in a strategy game, different AI strategies can be encapsulated using the Strategy Pattern, allowing easy swapping of AI behaviours during runtime.

8. **Prototype Pattern**: The Prototype Pattern can be used for efficient object cloning and instantiation in game development. It allows for creating new instances of complex objects by copying existing ones, which is useful for spawning new game entities or generating procedural content.

Case Study 8: Data Processing and Analytics

Description: Data Processing and Analytics involves the collection, transformation, analysis, and interpretation of large volumes of data to derive meaningful insights and make data-driven decisions. This field encompasses a wide range of tasks, including data ingestion, data storage, data cleansing, data transformation, data mining, machine learning, and reporting.

Design Patterns Used

Design patterns play a crucial role in building scalable, maintainable, and efficient data processing and analytics systems. Here are some design patterns commonly used in this domain:

1. **MapReduce Pattern**: MapReduce is a programming model used for processing large-scale data sets in a parallel and distributed manner. It involves two main steps: "Map," where data is transformed into key-value pairs, and "Reduce," where the data is aggregated and processed. The MapReduce pattern is widely used in distributed data processing frameworks like Apache Hadoop for batch processing of massive datasets.

2. **Batch Processing Pattern**: Batch processing involves processing data in fixed-size chunks or batches. This pattern is suitable for scenarios where data latency is not critical, and computations can be done offline. Batch processing frameworks like Apache Spark and Apache Flink are often used to implement this pattern efficiently.

3. **Stream Processing Pattern**: Stream processing deals with processing data in real-time as it arrives. This pattern is suitable for applications requiring low-latency and real-time data analytics. Stream processing frameworks like Apache

Kafka Streams, Apache Storm, and Apache Beam are commonly used to implement stream processing pipelines.

4. **Lambda Architecture**: The Lambda Architecture combines both batch and stream processing to handle large-scale data processing and analytics. It provides a robust way to manage both real-time and batch data processing to ensure accuracy and low-latency results.

5. **Data Pipeline Pattern**: The Data Pipeline Pattern is used to design workflows for data processing and analytics. It involves a series of data processing steps, where the output of one step becomes the input to the next step. Apache Airflow is a popular tool for orchestrating and managing data pipelines.

6. **Observer Pattern**: The Observer Pattern is beneficial in the context of data analytics when you need to monitor changes in data sources, databases, or streams. For example, you can use this pattern to trigger data processing tasks when new data arrives in a data source.

7. **Adapter Pattern**: The Adapter Pattern can be used to integrate data from various sources into a unified format suitable for analysis. It allows you to adapt and transform data from different systems or databases into a common schema, making it easier to process and analyse.

8. **Facade Pattern**: The Facade Pattern can simplify complex data processing and analytics systems by providing a simplified interface to access and interact with various data sources, storage systems, and processing components.

9. **Composite Pattern**: The Composite Pattern can be utilised to organize and aggregate data from different sources into a hierarchical structure. It is especially useful when dealing with complex data models and aggregating data from multiple entities.

Case Study 9: Enterprise Software Systems

Description: Enterprise Software Systems are large-scale, complex software applications developed to address the needs of large organisations. They often involve multiple modules, integrate with various systems, and handle vast amounts of data. These systems support critical business processes, such as customer relationship management (CRM), enterprise resource planning (ERP), supply chain management (SCM), and human resources management (HRM).

Design Patterns Used

Here are some common design patterns used in Enterprise Software Systems:

1. **Layered Architecture Pattern**: The Layered Architecture Pattern divides the system into multiple layers, each responsible for specific tasks. Typically, there are presentation, business logic, and data layers. This pattern provides a clear separation of concerns and promotes maintainability and scalability.

2. **Service-Oriented Architecture (SOA)**: SOA is an architectural pattern that involves designing software components as services that are loosely coupled, independent, and interoperable. These services communicate with each other using standard protocols, enabling flexibility, reusability, and easy integration with other systems.

3. **Microservices Architecture**: Microservices is an architectural style where the application is decomposed into small, independently deployable services that communicate through APIs. Each microservice focuses on a specific business capability, allowing teams to work independently and scale different services based on demand.

4. **Singleton Pattern**: The Singleton Pattern is useful in enterprise systems when you need a single, global instance of a class. Common use cases include creating a centralised configuration manager or a connection pool to manage database connections.

5. **Factory Pattern**: The Factory Pattern is employed to create objects without specifying the exact class of the object that will be created. In enterprise systems, it can be used to create instances of different database connectors, data access objects, or other components.

6. **Observer Pattern**: The Observer Pattern is beneficial in enterprise systems to establish communication between components in a loosely coupled manner. For example, it can be used to notify various modules or services about changes in shared data or events.

7. **Data Access Object (DAO) Pattern**: The DAO Pattern abstracts the data access logic from the rest of the application. It provides a data access layer that encapsulates the underlying data storage (e.g., databases). This pattern helps in decoupling data access code from business logic and promotes maintainability.

8. **Command Pattern**: The Command Pattern is used to encapsulate a request as an object, allowing you to parameterize clients with different requests and

support undo/redo functionality. In enterprise systems, it can be utilised for various tasks, such as queuing and processing asynchronous tasks.

9. **Adapter Pattern**: The Adapter Pattern enables the integration of legacy systems or third-party components into the enterprise system by converting their interfaces to a common interface used by the system. This pattern allows seamless interaction with existing systems without changing their code.

10. **Composite Pattern**: The Composite Pattern helps in representing hierarchical structures of objects. In an enterprise system, it can be used to manage complex structures like organisational hierarchies, product categories, or workflow processes.

Case Study 10: Machine Learning and Artificial Intelligence

Description: Machine Learning (ML) and Artificial Intelligence (AI) are closely related fields that focus on the development of algorithms and systems capable of learning from data and making intelligent decisions. AI is a broader concept that encompasses any technique or system that exhibits human-like intelligence, whereas Machine Learning is a subset of AI that specifically deals with algorithms that learn patterns and make predictions from data without explicit programming.

In Machine Learning, models are trained on large datasets, and they use statistical techniques to identify patterns and relationships within the data. These models can then be used to make predictions or decisions on new, unseen data. AI, on the other hand, includes not only ML but also other techniques like rule-based systems, natural language processing (NLP), computer vision, robotics, and more.

Design Patterns Used

Various Design Patterns Used in Machine Learning and Artificial Intelligence:

1. **Model-View-Controller (MVC) Pattern** for AI Systems: The MVC pattern can be applied in AI systems where there is a clear separation of the model (data processing and ML model), the view (user interface or presentation layer), and the controller (business logic and decision-making). This pattern ensures a modular and scalable design for AI applications.

2. **Factory Pattern** for Model Creation: The Factory Pattern can be used to create ML models based on different parameters or configurations. It encapsulates the object creation logic, making it easier to switch between different model architectures or hyperparameters.

3. **Observer Pattern** for Real-Time Updates: The Observer Pattern is helpful when building AI systems that require real-time updates or notifications. For instance, in a real-time anomaly detection system, observers can be notified when anomalies are detected in the data.

4. **Strategy Pattern** for Algorithm Selection: In cases where multiple ML algorithms or techniques can be used for a task (e.g., classification, regression), the Strategy Pattern can be employed to choose the appropriate algorithm based on the problem context or data characteristics.

5. **Singleton Pattern** for Resource Management: The Singleton Pattern can be applied to manage shared resources, such as data pipelines, connection objects, or caching mechanisms, ensuring that there is only one instance of these resources throughout the AI system.

6. **Template Method Pattern** for Feature Engineering: The Template Method Pattern can be used in feature engineering, where different features are extracted from the raw data. A template method defines the overall feature extraction process, while subclasses can provide specific implementations for extracting particular features.

7. **Chain of Responsibility Pattern** for AI Processing Pipelines: The Chain of Responsibility Pattern can be used in AI systems that involve complex processing pipelines, such as natural language processing tasks. Each component in the chain handles a specific task, and the output of one component becomes the input for the next.

8. **Adapter Pattern** for Data Integration: The Adapter Pattern can be employed to integrate data from various sources or formats into a unified format that ML models can consume. It allows different data sources to be converted into a common interface for model training and prediction.

9. **Proxy Pattern** for Lazy Loading: The Proxy Pattern can be used to implement lazy loading of AI models or expensive computations. When the AI model is not in use, a proxy object can be used to defer its instantiation until it's actually needed.

Case Study 11: Internet Applications and Services

Description: Internet applications and services refer to software systems and platforms that are accessible over the internet, allowing users to perform various tasks, access information, and communicate with others. These applications and services run on remote servers and are accessed through web browsers or specialised client software. They cover a wide range of functionalities, including social media platforms, email services, online shopping websites, search engines, cloud storage services, and more.

Design Patterns Used

Various Design Patterns used in Internet Applications and Services:

1. **Model-View-Controller (MVC) Pattern**: The MVC pattern is commonly used in internet applications and services to separate the user interface (View) from the business logic and data processing (Model) and the control and coordination of interactions (Controller). This separation of concerns improves code maintainability, reusability, and testability.

2. **Singleton Pattern**: The Singleton pattern is utilised to ensure that certain critical components in internet applications and services have only one instance throughout their lifetime. For example, database connections, configuration managers, or authentication modules may be implemented as singletons to avoid unnecessary overhead and ensure consistency.

3. **Observer Pattern**: The Observer pattern is widely used in internet applications to handle real-time updates and notifications. For instance, in social media platforms, users can follow or subscribe to other users or topics, and the Observer pattern can be used to notify them about new posts or updates.

4. **Factory Method Pattern**: The Factory Method pattern is employed to create objects in a flexible and consistent way, abstracting the object instantiation process from the client code. In internet applications and services, this pattern can be used for creating various types of objects like user accounts, product instances, or API clients.

5. **Decorator Pattern**: The Decorator pattern allows behaviour to be added to individual objects dynamically. In internet applications, decorators can be used to add functionalities to services or components without modifying their core implementation. For example, in email services, decorators can add additional features like spam filtering, encryption, or read receipts.

6. **Strategy Pattern**: The Strategy pattern is utilised in internet applications to handle multiple algorithms or behaviour variations for specific tasks. For instance, in search engines, different ranking algorithms can be implemented using the Strategy pattern, and the search engine can dynamically switch between these algorithms based on user preferences and system requirements.

7. **Adapter Pattern**: The Adapter pattern is used to enable the collaboration of incompatible interfaces. In internet applications and services, this pattern can be helpful when integrating with external APIs or services that have different data formats or communication protocols.

8. **Facade Pattern**: The Facade pattern simplifies the complex interactions of internet applications by providing a unified interface that hides the underlying subsystems. For example, in cloud storage services, the Facade pattern can abstract away the complexities of interacting with various storage providers and offer a consistent API for file management.

9. **Command Pattern**: The Command pattern is employed to encapsulate requests as objects, allowing for parametrization and decoupling the sender and receiver of requests. In internet applications, this pattern can be used to implement undo/redo functionality or to handle user commands in a command-line interface.

Case Study 12: Embedded Systems and Firmware Development

Description: Embedded systems refer to computing systems that are designed to perform specific functions within a larger system, often with real-time constraints and limited resources. These systems are typically found in various applications, such as consumer electronics, automotive, industrial automation, medical devices, and more. Firmware development involves creating software that runs directly on the hardware of embedded systems, controlling their behaviour and functionality.

In embedded systems and firmware development, the focus is on efficient use of resources, reliable performance, low power consumption, and meeting real-time requirements. It often involves working with microcontrollers, sensors, actuators, and other hardware components.

Design Patterns Used

Design Patterns used in Embedded Systems and Firmware Development:

1. **State Pattern**: The State Pattern can be used to manage the different states of an embedded system and control its behaviour accordingly. For example, in a state machine representing a communication protocol, the system's behaviour might change based on the current state, such as initialising, waiting for data, or processing data.

2. **Singleton Pattern**: The Singleton Pattern can be used in firmware development to ensure that certain hardware access or configuration objects have only one instance. This can help avoid resource conflicts and promote efficient resource management.

3. **Observer Pattern**: The Observer Pattern is valuable for implementing event-driven communication between different parts of an embedded system. For instance, sensors can act as subjects, and various components can be observers, reacting to changes in sensor data.

4. **Factory Method Pattern**: The Factory Method Pattern can help abstract the creation of different components in an embedded system. For example, when dealing with various types of sensors or actuators, a factory method can create the appropriate instances based on specific requirements or configurations.

5. **Command Pattern**: The Command Pattern is useful for encapsulating requests or operations as objects. In embedded systems, this pattern can be employed to implement command objects that represent specific actions or tasks to be executed by the system.

6. **Template Method Pattern**: The Template Method Pattern can be applied to define a high-level algorithm in a firmware module while allowing subclasses or configuration settings to implement specific steps or behaviour.

7. **Adapter Pattern**: The Adapter Pattern can help integrate existing software libraries or drivers with new firmware or hardware interfaces. It allows the firmware to work with different components seamlessly, even if their interfaces are different.

8. **Composite Pattern**: The Composite Pattern can be useful when dealing with hierarchical structures of embedded components. For example, in a system with multiple sensors and actuators, the Composite Pattern can help manage them as a unified entity.

9. **Memento Pattern**: The Memento Pattern can be used to capture the internal state of an embedded system or firmware component and restore it later if needed. This is useful when dealing with state transitions and error recovery.

10. **Proxy Pattern**: The Proxy Pattern can be used to control access to hardware resources or provide an interface to interact with remote components efficiently.

Case Study 13: Robotics and Automation Systems

Description: Robotics and Automation Systems involve the design, development, and implementation of machines, robots, and software to automate tasks and processes. These systems can range from simple automated machines in manufacturing to complex robotic systems used in various industries, including healthcare, logistics, and exploration. The goal is to increase efficiency, precision, and safety while reducing human intervention.

Design Patterns Used

Various Design Patterns Used in Robotics and Automation Systems:

1. **State Pattern**: In Robotics and Automation Systems, robots often have different states, such as idle, moving, executing a task, or in an error state. The State Pattern can be used to model and manage these states efficiently. Each state is represented as an object, and the robot's behaviour changes based on its current state. Transitions between states are well-defined, making the system more manageable and extensible.

2. **Command Pattern**: The Command Pattern is useful in Robotics and Automation Systems to encapsulate commands as objects. Robots can receive various commands, such as moving to a specific location, picking up an object, or executing a particular action. By encapsulating these commands, the system can manage and execute them more flexibly and decouple the sender (e.g., a control system) from the receiver (e.g., the robot).

3. **Strategy Pattern**: The Strategy Pattern is commonly used in Robotics and Automation Systems to handle different algorithms or strategies for robot behaviour. For instance, robots might have different ways to navigate and avoid obstacles, pick up objects, or plan trajectories. By using the Strategy Pattern, the system can easily switch between different algorithms without modifying the robot's core functionality.

4. **Observer Pattern**: The Observer Pattern is employed in Robotics and Automation Systems to enable communication between various components and sensors. Robots often have sensors (e.g., cameras, proximity sensors, force sensors) that observe the environment. The Observer Pattern allows other components to be notified of changes in sensor data, enabling appropriate responses and actions.

5. **Decorator Pattern**: The Decorator Pattern can be used to extend the functionality of robotic components dynamically. In automation systems, robots might need to be equipped with different tools or sensors for specific tasks. The Decorator Pattern allows adding these functionalities to the robot at runtime without affecting its core behaviour.

6. **Factory Method Pattern**: The Factory Method Pattern can be employed to create different types of robots or automation modules while adhering to a common interface. This pattern allows the system to decouple the creation of robot instances from their usage and makes it easier to introduce new robot types.

7. **Composite Pattern**: In some Robotics and Automation Systems, there might be a need to work with groups of robots or robot modules as a single entity. The Composite Pattern can be used to treat individual robots and robot groups uniformly, simplifying the management and coordination of multiple robots working together.

8. **Template Method Pattern**: The Template Method Pattern can be useful when defining the overall structure of robot behaviour, allowing subclasses (specific robot types) to implement specific actions or algorithms. This pattern helps promote code reuse and standardisation across different robot implementations.

Case Study 14: Natural Language Processing and Text Processing

Description: Natural Language Processing (NLP) is a field of artificial intelligence that focuses on enabling computers to understand, interpret, and process human language in a way that is meaningful and useful. NLP involves a range of tasks such as text processing, language translation, sentiment analysis, speech recognition, information retrieval, and more. The goal is to bridge the gap between human language and machine understanding, allowing computers to interact with humans in a more natural and intuitive manner.

Text processing is a subset of NLP that specifically deals with the manipulation, analysis, and transformation of textual data. It involves various operations such as tokenization, stemming, lemmatization, part-of-speech tagging, named entity recognition, text classification, sentiment analysis, and text generation. Text processing is fundamental to many NLP applications, as it helps in extracting meaningful information from unstructured text data.

Design Patterns Used

Design Patterns Used in NLP and Text Processing:

1. **Pipeline Pattern**: The Pipeline Pattern is commonly used in NLP and text processing workflows. It involves chaining together multiple processing steps into a sequence to transform raw text into a structured and processed format. Each step in the pipeline performs a specific NLP task (e.g., tokenization, POS tagging, sentiment analysis), and the output of one step becomes the input for the next step.

2. **Decorator Pattern**: The Decorator Pattern can be used to add additional functionalities or features to text processing components without modifying their core behaviour. For instance, in sentiment analysis, you may use decorators to include sentiment intensifiers or negation handling, enhancing the accuracy and context of the analysis.

3. **Factory Method Pattern**: The Factory Method Pattern can be used to create different NLP models or text processing algorithms while adhering to a common interface. This pattern helps decouple the creation of NLP components from their usage, making it easier to switch between different implementations.

4. **Observer Pattern**: The Observer Pattern can be applied in NLP and text processing to handle real-time updates and notifications. For example, in a chatbot application, the observer pattern can be used to notify the bot of user inputs, triggering appropriate responses.

5. **Interpreter Pattern**: The Interpreter Pattern is used for designing domain-specific languages or grammars. In NLP, this pattern is valuable for creating custom rule-based language processing systems or designing query languages for information retrieval.

6. **Adapter Pattern**: The Adapter Pattern can be employed to integrate different NLP libraries or APIs into the system that might have incompatible interfaces. By using adapters, the system can interact with multiple NLP tools seamlessly.

7. **Singleton Pattern**: In some cases, components in NLP and text processing might be resource-intensive or have shared states. The Singleton Pattern ensures that only one instance of such components exists in the system, avoiding redundant processing and resource wastage.

8. **Strategy Pattern**: The Strategy Pattern can be useful when dealing with multiple algorithms or models for a specific NLP task (e.g., sentiment analysis). The pattern allows the system to switch between different strategies dynamically, depending on the context or requirements.

Case Study 15: User Interface Design

Description: User Interface Design (UI Design) is the process of creating interfaces that enable users to interact with a digital product or system. It focuses on the visual layout, user interactions, and overall user experience. The goal of UI design is to make the interface intuitive, user-friendly, and aesthetically pleasing, ensuring that users can easily achieve their tasks and goals.

Design Patterns Used

Various Design Patterns Used in User Interface Design:

1. **Model-View-Controller (MVC)**: MVC is an architectural pattern that separates an application into three components: Model, View, and Controller. In UI design, the MVC pattern can be applied to divide the user interface into distinct layers. The Model represents the data and business logic, the View deals with the visual presentation, and the Controller manages user interactions and updates the Model and View accordingly.

2. **Observer Pattern**: The Observer Pattern is used to maintain a one-to-many dependency between objects. In UI design, this pattern allows UI elements to subscribe to changes in the underlying data or state. When the data changes, the UI elements are automatically notified and updated, ensuring that the user interface remains synchronised with the application's data.

3. **Decorator Pattern**: The Decorator Pattern is used to dynamically add new features or behaviours to objects. In UI design, this pattern can be used to enhance UI elements without modifying their original class. For example, decorators can add borders, shadows, or animations to buttons or other visual elements.

4. **Adapter Pattern**: The Adapter Pattern is employed to allow incompatible interfaces to work together. In UI design, this pattern can be used when integrating external components or libraries that have different interfaces into the application. The adapter acts as a bridge, making the integration seamless.

5. **Singleton Pattern**: The Singleton Pattern ensures that a class has only one instance and provides a global access point to that instance. In UI design, this pattern can be used when there should be only one instance of a particular UI component, such as a global configuration manager or a theme manager.

6. **Factory Method Pattern**: The Factory Method Pattern provides an interface for creating objects but allows subclasses to decide which class to instantiate. In UI design, this pattern can be used to create various UI components (e.g., buttons, text fields, dropdowns) while adhering to a common interface. It allows for flexible component creation and customization.

7. **State Pattern**: The State Pattern allows an object to change its behaviour when its internal state changes. In UI design, this pattern can be used to manage different states of UI elements based on user interactions or system events. For instance, a button may have different behaviours based on whether it's enabled, disabled, or in a loading state.

8. **Command Pattern**: The Command Pattern is used to encapsulate a request as an object, allowing for parametrization of clients with different requests. In UI design, this pattern can be used to handle user actions as commands, allowing for undo/redo functionality or queuing user interactions.

Case Study 16: Internet Security and Cryptography

Description: Internet security and cryptography are essential components of modern computing, ensuring the confidentiality, integrity, and authenticity of data transmitted and stored over the internet. Internet security encompasses a wide range of measures and protocols aimed at protecting information and systems from unauthorised access, data breaches, and cyberattacks. Cryptography, on the other hand, is a fundamental aspect of internet security that involves the use of mathematical algorithms and techniques to encode data, making it unintelligible to unauthorised parties.

Design Patterns Used

Various Design Patterns Used:

1. **Singleton Pattern**: The Singleton Pattern can be used to create a single, globally accessible instance of cryptographic services or security configurations. For example, a singleton encryption manager or a cryptographic key store can be utilised to ensure consistent and secure access to encryption/decryption services throughout the application.

2. **Factory Method Pattern**: The Factory Method Pattern can be used to create cryptographic objects, such as encryption algorithms or hash functions, while abstracting the specific implementations from the client code. This helps maintain code flexibility and allows for easy switching between different cryptographic algorithms.

3. **Chain of Responsibility Pattern**: The Chain of Responsibility Pattern can be applied to create a chain of cryptographic handlers, each responsible for a specific security task, such as signature verification, encryption, or decryption. Incoming data can pass through this chain to undergo various security checks and transformations before being processed.

4. **Decorator Pattern**: The Decorator Pattern can be used to add additional layers of security to data or network communications. For example, encryption can be wrapped with a decorator to add authentication and data integrity verification on top of confidentiality.

5. **Observer Pattern**: The Observer Pattern can be utilised to implement logging and auditing mechanisms in security-related components. Observers can monitor security events and log them for auditing and forensic purposes.

6. **Proxy Pattern**: The Proxy Pattern can be applied to create proxy objects that act as intermediaries between clients and actual cryptographic or security services. Proxies can provide additional security measures, such as access control, logging, and rate limiting.

7. **Template Method Pattern**: The Template Method Pattern can be used to define a common structure for security protocols or cryptographic operations, while allowing specific steps to be implemented by subclasses. This ensures consistency in implementing security procedures across the application.

8. **Adapter Pattern**: The Adapter Pattern can be employed to convert between different cryptographic interfaces or formats, allowing existing cryptographic libraries or algorithms to be integrated seamlessly into the application.

9. **Command Pattern**: The Command Pattern can be utilised to encapsulate cryptographic operations as commands. This allows for better management of security operations, such as queuing and undo/redo functionalities.

Index